The French Joyce

The French Joyce

Geert Lernout

Ann Arbor
THE UNIVERSITY OF MICHIGAN PRESS

1993 1992 1991 1990   4 3 2 1

Library of Congress Cataloging-in-Publication Data

Lernout, Geert Maria Jan, 1954–
    The French Joyce / Geert Lernout.
        p.   cm.
    Includes bibliographical references and index.
    ISBN 0-472-10195-1 (alk. paper)
    1. Joyce, James, 1882–1941—Criticism and interpretation—
History.   2. Joyce, James, 1882–1941—Appreciation—France.
3. Criticism—France—History—20th century.   I. Title.
PR6019.09Z696   1990
823'.912—dc20   90-39435
                                                            CIP

Preface

No book is ever a purely personal venture, and this is all the more true for a study like this that derives most of its insights from the work of innumerable critics, theorists, and reviewers. Although I have tried to acknowledge my most immediate sources in the text and in the bibliography, it would have been more honest if I had listed everything I have read in the last fifteen years.

This is why I want to express my gratitude here to everybody who has helped or encouraged me in any way: the teachers and fellow students at the University of Toronto who were willing to read my work and talk about it, especially Linda Hutcheon, Peter Nesselroth, Cyrus Hamlin, Michael Sidnell, Mario Valdés, Joe Adamson, Sylvia Soderlund, Barbara Havercroft, Ruth Ronen, David Parkinson, Ann Rigney, Kevin and Elena Corrigan, and David Wright; the colleagues and students at the universities of Brussels, Amsterdam, Antwerp, and Athens, Georgia, especially Luc Herman, Wim Neetens, Joris Duytschaeuer, Kris Humbeeck, Françoise Parmentier, and Mihai Spariosu, and all the Joyceans who helped me by sending published and unpublished material or by commenting on earlier versions of this material at various Joyce conferences. I also thank the staff at the libraries of the University of Toronto, the University of Georgia, and the University of Antwerp for their invaluable help in locating journals no one had ever heard of. I am also greatly indebted to the staff at the University of Michigan Press, and to LeAnn Fields and the two anonymous readers for their helpful suggestions.

The greatest debt of all I owe the person to whom this book is dedicated, Linde Dedrie.

Contents

Introduction

The literary critics in the early seventies who pre-dicted the imminent demise of literary theory have been proven wrong: theory and especially the poststructuralist and deconstruc-tionist variety is alive and well, even after the controversy over Paul de Man's wartime writings. A cursory glance at professional journals or publishers' lists, a look at conference titles or symposium programs is enough to indicate the success of a movement that originated in France and that is associated mainly with the names of Jacques Lacan and Jacques Derrida. For reasons that need to be studied more closely, the adoption of this new paradigm has been more controversial and dramatic in the field of English studies than in those of comparative literature or French.

That the theoretical developments have reached the study of James Joyce and have, at least since the mid-eighties, acquired a consider-able following, should be clear to anybody who has recently attended a Joyce conference or who has read recent books or articles on Joyce. In 1986, Harold Bloom distinguished in the introduction to a book that "gathers together a representative selection of the best criticism available on the writings of James Joyce" two American schools of Joyce criticism: the school of Ellmann and that of Kenner. But most of the essays in Bloom's collection represent "a new movement in Joyce studies, much influenced by current modes of criticism," and one essay, by Daniel Ferrer, is even poststructuralist and deconstructionist (ix–x). In the proceedings of two Joyce conferences (Frankfurt 1984 and Philadelphia 1985) that were published in 1988 the poststructuralist Joyce is everywhere. In his introduction to *James Joyce: The Augmented Ninth*, Bernard Benstock writes: "In short, the Frankfurt symposium was marked by the dominance of new critical approaches to Joyce's texts in an area where more conventional readings had long dominated" (1988, 4), and this is quite clear in the rest of the volume. The same is true for *New Alliances in Joyce Studies*: in her introduction Bonnie Kime Scott concludes that "clearly, applications of recent theory dominate" (1988a, 15). In order to understand the impact of the "new" Joyce, we must first understand Joyce's exact role in the literary domain.

Few authors have been so important for modern literature and recent criticism as James Joyce. Hailed by contemporaries such as Ezra Pound, T. S. Eliot and William Butler Yeats as the most important novelist of his day—Joyce himself seems to have agreed with that judgment—he was venerated by a younger generation of writers who flocked to Paris to catch a glimpse of the author of *Ulysses*, among them Scott Fitzgerald, who offered to jump out of the window as proof of his devotion (*JJ II*, 581). After World War II, *Ulysses* became a classroom classic and a paradigm for several new generations of novelists, among them Vladimir Nabokov, Thomas Pynchon, John Barth, Gilbert Sorrentino, and many others.

Theoreticians of literature have also remained interested in Joyce; when Robert Scholes, Northrop Frye, or Wayne C. Booth has a theoretical point to make, he turns to Joyce as a supreme example. This is the case not only in the United States, where so much of Joyce criticism originates, but also in Germany, where Max Bense and Wolfgang Iser have used Joyce's texts in the exposition of their theories of literature. Joyce also figures prominently in the German debates about postmodernism: in a recent book on the dialectics of the modern and the postmodern, Albrecht Wellmer describes *Finnegans Wake* as a work in which an aesthetic totality of meaning cannot be attained anymore, it is a postmodern work (1985, 67). In Italy, Umberto Eco has continued to refer to Joyce from *Opera aperta* (1962a) onward; and even England, which had until the mid-seventies managed to keep itself aloof from continental theoretical fashions and from a too enthusiastic appraisal of Joyce's accomplishments as a writer, was confronted with a regular scandal over Colin MacCabe's doctoral dissertation which managed to combine both sins (1978). Maybe as a reaction, Terry Eagleton, not really an enthusiastic supporter of too much theorizing, has described *Finnegans Wake* as a touchstone for any literary theory (Eagleton 1983, 82).

France, where almost every recent theory of literature seems to have originated, has accomplished this modern theoretical reception of Joyce's works relatively late, but it has quickly made up for time lost. In just a few years *Finnegans Wake* became the most central piece of radical *écriture*, and in this book I will attempt to show where this sudden success comes from and how it developed out of the early reception of Joyce's work and out of the theoretical assumptions elaborated in the sixties and seventies. I am therefore more interested in influences than in the numerous similarities among elements in Joyce's later works and characteristics of recent critical writing that were studied by Stephen Tanner (1984). Central in this analysis will be the fact that Joyce's influence is not, as in most other countries, a purely academic matter; on the contrary, a lot of French academics have been reluctant to confront Joyce's work. The reception has been literary in the first place, from the support Joyce received from fellow-writers in Paris to the efforts by Michel Butor and Raymond Queneau to disseminate Joyce's works in the fifties and sixties and, finally, to his presence by means of allusions and quotations in the novels and poetry of the seventies and eighties. But the emphasis in this book is on the critical reception, not on the creative appropriation that accompanied it, and I only discuss Joyce's presence in novels or poems by authors who have also written on his work critically.

That Joyce has been adopted by the French as one of their own is not too difficult to demonstrate: Gallimard's prestigious series *La Pléiade* published one volume with translations of Joyce's early works and has announced a second volume with a new translation of *Ulysses*. This series publishes complete standard editions of more than a hundred "classic" writers and philosophers, five of them German and only nine English or American: we find Joyce in the company of William Shakespeare, Daniel Defoe, Henry Fielding, Charles Dickens, E.A. Poe, Joseph Conrad, William Faulkner, and Ernest Hemingway. Apart from this, nearly every word Joyce wrote has been translated and published, in most cases by Gallimard. France can boast the only complete version of *Finnegans Wake* in a foreign language, as the last event in a series of translations that also includes *The Cat and the Devil, Giacomo Joyce,* the *Letters, Critical Writings,* and Stanislaus Joyce's *Dublin Diary* and *My Brother's Keeper.*

My original intention in writing this study was a direct result of a culture clash. As an undergraduate my training was predominantly theoretical: Belgium, as a small country wedged between France, Germany, and England, has traditionally been very open to intellectual influences from abroad, and in the seventies this meant heavy doses of Roland Barthes, Julia Kristeva, Jacques Lacan, and Jacques Derrida (the first book-length study on Derrida and the first dissertation on Lacan were written by Belgians). When I began to read Joyce, I found in *Ulysses* and *Finnegans Wake* examples of the radical *écriture* the poststructuralist theoreticians were writing about. The problem was that I could find nothing in the American and English criticism on Joyce that came close to what I had read on Joyce in *Tel Quel,* and a one-year stay in Dublin at University College in Dublin did not help matters much. So I decided to do for Joyceans what Jonathan Culler in *Structuralist Poetics* (1975) had done for American theoreticians of literature. It was clear to me that I belonged to a different paradigm from that of most Joyce scholars, and I started to read works on the philosophy of science in order to understand the exact nature of the difference between the American and the French Joyce because a nonpartisan perspective seemed to be necessary for what I wanted to achieve. Thomas S. Kuhn's *The Structure of Scientific Revolutions* taught me that in order to describe a school, one can use extrinsic and sociological evidence when one introduces the notion of paradigm, which is "what the members of a scientific community share, *and,* conversely, a scientific community consists of men who share a paradigm" (Kuhn 1970, 176). Since 1962, when Kuhn's book was first published, this definition still stands, and the term seems to have acquired a universal applicability. In any case, Kuhn did prove that the empirical and extrinsic ways of defining a scientific community are nontrivial, and it seems appropriate to try to apply these principles to a study of the history and evolution of literary criticism, and more specifically to a description of a critical school or method.

Kuhn distinguishes different ways of identifying a paradigm; first there is the geographical location. Scientists who share the same paradigm will work at the same institute, university, or laboratory as the inventor(s) or strongest supporter(s) of the paradigm. In literary criticism we could think of the Yale critics, the Chicago school, or the school of Constance. The name of a city is used only when it is not the intellectual capital of a country, in which case a group or tendency may be identified by the name of the school or its location (e.g., the Rue d'Ulm). A second distinctive feature may be the means of publication: often like-minded critics and theorists will start a journal or take over an existing one in order to disseminate their ideas: examples could be *Poétique, Glyph, Boundary 2*, or collections and series such as "Tel Quel," "Champ freudien" and "Poetik und Hermeneutik." A third criterion may be the presence at colloquia, the membership in professional organizations, and the subscription to journals. Lastly there is the network of quotations: members of the same group will quote and acknowledge one another's work and ignore or criticize that of others who do not belong to the group. Critics who belong to the same group, who share a paradigm, conform to the code of that group, which may even include a denial that there is such a group. This is less important for established members of established paradigms than for outsiders or newcomers who want to prove the seriousness of their allegiance to the new group or for the pioneers of a novel paradigm who have to establish its right to exist. In this, the introduction of a new critical approach resembles the efforts of an artistic generation to make a mark on their time, and sometimes the two even cooperate or coincide: one could think of the relationship between Russian formalism and futurism (Medvedev 1976, 74) or of the co-presence of literature and criticism in *Tel Quel*.

What the members of such a community have in common, according to Kuhn, is a way of perceiving and/or describing the world, *world-versions* to use Nelson Goodman's term, *language-game* in Ludwig Wittgenstein's, gestalts, codes, languages. In a postscript that Kuhn added to a later edition of his book, he distinguished between the notion of paradigm as "shared example" and what he used to call paradigm, that which members of a scientific community have in common and which he now calls a "disciplinary matrix" (1970, 182). The latter can consist of four different components that function in different ways: the first are "symbolic generalizations," formal or formalizable definitions that can function either as laws of nature or as redefinitions of existing symbols. In the first case Kuhn expects a different kind of commitment from scholars since laws can be corrected piecemeal, and definitions, as tautologies, cannot (183). Theories of literature or criticism have few symbolic generalizations, and when they do have them, they generally belong to the second, most contested kind: an example could be Derrida's notions of *écriture* or *text*, which include a lot of phenomena that are not generally considered to be writing or texts. The functions of these symbolic generalizations can range from radical redefinitions of literature, poetry, or specific areas of inquiry to simple observations about a single writer, movement, work, or image. An example of such a "minimal generalization" is Paul de Man's observation that "figure" in "The Triumph of Life" can also have the meaning of the French word *figure* (1979), an idea that has been applied by other critics to other texts. A second component of the disciplinary matrix consists of what Kuhn calls "metaphysical paradigms" or models. The scholars' commitment to them may vary according to whether they are ontological or merely heuristic models, but they all serve the same purpose: "they supply the group with preferred or permissible analogies and metaphors" (Kuhn 1970, 184). A good example of this type of paradigm is Derrida's habit of punning on an author's name as he does in *Glas* (1974), where he points to the fact that Hegel mispronounced in French sounds like *aigle*, eagle. The German poststructuralist philosopher Werner Hamacher does a similar thing in his introduction to an edition of *Der Geist des Christentums* (1978) when he runs Hegel's name through a series of more or less homophonous words; *Ekel, Igel, häkeln*, etc. Examples in literary theory could be the metaphor of *Horizontverschmelzung* (the merging of horizons) in post-Gadamerian hermeneutics, the comparison of text to tissue in Kristeva, or Jakobson's concept of literature as a code.

The third component of a disciplinary matrix is the paradigm as shared example, which seems particularly suitable in a study of the history of literary criticism and theory. Groups of scholars generally do not refer to purely theoretical statements about the aims and methods of their approach but seem to base their allegiance to a certain model on an individual reading of a single work. This also seems the case for the innovator himself: it is much easier to apply a new model to a specific text than to describe it in theoretical and programmatic terms. Obvious examples are the reading of Baudelaire's "Les chats" by Roman Jakobson and Claude Lévi-Strauss (1962), Jacques Lacan's reading of Poe's "The Purloined Letter" in *Écrits* (1966), and Derrida's interpretation of Plato's *Phaedrus* (1968a; 1968b). Thomas Kuhn argues that these concrete problem solutions supply the empirical content of the abstract laws and theories and that their prime importance lies in their role in the training of young scholars, who are first confronted with these concrete problem solutions and are then trained to recognize similar problems in reality and to apply the model by solving them in an analogical manner. This phenomenon may be linked to an insight into the nature of the reading process that has been applied to the reading of literature but strangely enough not to our reading of criticism itself. Wolfgang Iser writes in *Der Akt des Lesens* (1976) that reading is a selective process based on the horizon of expectations of each reader. One does not perceive and retain every segment of a communicated message, but one selects elements of the message that either conform to or differ from what one expected to find. We do not simply absorb Lacan's *Écrits* completely; we will read different sections with more or less attention depending on our previous knowledge of psychoanalysis, on our opinion of Freud's work, on the stories we have heard about Lacan, etc. Our reading of theoretical writings and, more precisely in this context, of critical analyses of a text as shared examples, can be motivated in different ways, depending on the focus of our interest. If we read an analysis in order to learn more about Baudelaire's poem, Plato's dialogue, or Joyce's novel, we will read differently from the way we read when we want to find out more about Jakobson, Derrida, or Iser and differently again from how we read when we intend to apply their findings to our own reading of other literary texts. In the first case we will have the text to be analyzed constantly in mind, and we will compare the findings in the critical analysis to our own; in the other cases, we will have to conclude our reading with a digest of what we perceive as the critic's creed, a shorthand version of his ideas about literature in general and about strategies of reading texts in particular. When members of a community of scholars accept the same paradigm, the matrix has to be at least potentially concretizable: the members should be able to describe their agreement. This digest is by definition limited and may well resemble an entry in an encyclopedia or in a student's handbook. The same is true in religion: all Christians base their faith on the same book, yet their allegiance goes to a group of people who share a particular interpretation of the Bible, a perspective that can be concretized in articles of faith, catechisms, or other forms of digest.

This is precisely one of the difficulties in the case of poststructuralism, which is notoriously difficult to define and which owes some of its polemic power to that simple fact. Poststructuralist theory casts doubt on the very possibility of definition and stresses the violence involved in the process of naming. When they describe their own work, poststructuralist writers usually talk of an activity, a practice, and a rhetoric, rather than of a set of beliefs or doctrines. Panelists on the deconstruction panel at the Joyce symposium in Frankfurt carefully avoided the question of what their different papers had in common, either because they were too much impressed by Derrida's presence in the room or because there simply was no such unity of purpose. But it is clear that most readers of recent criticism will be able to recognize poststructuralist writing when they are confronted with it, and I will propose here a number of different possible definitions. First a diachronic one: as its name implies, poststructuralism follows structuralism. In 1966 and 1967, Jacques Derrida, Jacques Lacan, Michel Foucault, Roland Barthes, and the members of the *Tel Quel* collective published a number of key texts in which they criticized the scientific and positivist tendencies in formalist structuralism. These critics and philosophers saw the scientific pretensions of formalism as part of the Western metaphysics from which they wanted to escape, and their new analysis often involved a critique of the earlier generation of structuralists, using their rhetoric against themselves: Derrida's reading of Lévi-Strauss is paradigmatic here (1967c). This diachronic definition finds confirmation in the German term *Neostrukturalismus* popularized by Manfred Frank (1984); and in the career of single critics one can observe this break in the shift, for example, between Barthes's *Le Plaisir du texte* (1973), where he explicitly situates his present project outside of the science of literature as he had defined it in *Critique et Vérité* (1966).

Another definition could point to precursors, which is a strategy employed by Vincent Descombes when in his survey of French philosophy he claims that the postwar thinkers have remained under the influence of German philosophers—until 1960 of Hegel, Husserl, and Heidegger; after that date of Marx, Nietzsche, and Freud (1979, 13). But Descombes immediately adds that the influence should not be thought of as absolute since, strangely enough, the major texts of these master thinkers have not been translated. This lack of availability of the primary texts has resulted in a "productive transformation" of their thought: "Let us not think that a work becomes authoritative because it is read, studied and finally found convincing. The opposite is true: one reads it because one is already convinced" (14). The absence in the list of Ferdinand de Saussure, the founding father of a structuralist linguistics and therefore of semiotics, is striking and would have been unimaginable if Descombes had been writing a couple of years earlier. This represents a mistake that is not uncommon in writers on recent French intellectual history. The impact of poststructuralism has managed to obscure the formalist phase of structuralism, and it sometimes seems as if poststructuralism simply reacted against the dominant phenomenological and hermeneutic approaches. One of the themes that will emerge from this study is the dominance of Heideggerian themes in French antirationalist thinking, at least since Kojève's lectures on Hegel's *Phänomenologie des Geistes* in the thirties (Hegel 1971; Kojève 1979), and precisely bridging the gap that separates Sartrean existentialism and poststructuralism, but this should not blind us to the structuralist/formalist phase of structuralism before 1968.

Reference to precursors or models alone cannot be enough: another example is the strange fate of Freud's work in France. Psychoanalysis failed to make much of an impact on French intellectual life before 1940, dedicated as the French were to clear and distinct ideas. The only exception was the surrealist movement, which attempted to bring into practice some of Freud's concepts. Lacan was among the earliest French Freudians; yet it is precisely on the basis of his version of Freudianism that *Tel Quel* will completely dismiss surrealism and its references to Freud. The view that poststructuralism is an heir to German philosophy should be studied from the perspective of German-French intellectual relations, which have always included an important political factor.

Another attempt at definition is essentially negative, but it does correspond to a self-understanding of the critics involved. Poststructuralist thinking is explicitly avant-garde and ambitious. It posits itself as a radical and revolutionary rejection of traditional criticism and the assumptions it is based on, and it sees itself as not just another methodology but the only way in which texts can meaningfully be read. Derrida, Foucault, and Lacan look for the kind of discourse that escapes the domination of metaphysics and logocentrism. With Heidegger, they all accept the end of philosophy as the basis for the elaboration of something entirely new. These *antagonistic* and *agonistic* tendencies, to use terms that have been developed by Renato Poggioli to describe the essential characteristics of the historical avant-garde (1981), force it to define itself not so much by what it is opposed to but by the oppositional activity itself. This is clear if we look at what it is that poststructuralism reacts against: whether it is metaphysics, or onto-theology, logocentrism, formalism, phallocentrism, or simply the university as an institution does not really affect the arguments. This is most obvious in Roland Barthes, who wrote in his last book about his resistance against any system whatsoever: whenever he felt that his language would harden into a sociological, semiological, or psychoanalytical system, he "would gently leave and seek elsewhere" (1980, 21). Similarly, Lacan always managed to change his theory whenever it threatened to freeze into a doctrine, and the same goes for Philippe Sollers, who has even published a book called *Théorie des exceptions* (1986a), which seems to cover the same ground as what Roland Barthes called the *mathesis singularis*, the impossible science of the unique being.

The resistance to an intrinsic definition that we have observed mirrors the lack of agreement among critics and theoreticians about a definition of the very object of their study, and it is one of the most serious symptoms of the current malaise in the discipline. A definition of literature cannot use terms that belong to one kind of discourse because that would define the results of the study even before it has started. If it is my ambition to present work in one tradition to readers who belong to another, I must avoid using terms of either discourse. In other words, my definition of literature must be extrinsic, relative, and descriptive because if it were intrinsic, essential, and prescriptive, I would lose the possibility of comparing it with alternative definitions. Literature will therefore be defined here as the body of texts that are considered to be literature by the community of its recipients, a definition that is essentially sociological, since it is based on the observable behavior of a group of individuals. Most theorists of literature in the past chose the prescriptive path and have only mentioned the descriptive definition as a horrible example to be avoided at all costs. Friedrich Schlegel, for example, writes: "A definition of poetry can only claim what it should be, not what it in reality was and is; otherwise it might just as well read like this: Poetry is that which somewhere sometime has been called by that name" (Schlegel and Schlegel 1970, 204). To return to the example of religion: the Bible exists independently of its Christian interpretations; if we want to describe the system of beliefs of one particular group of Christians, Methodists, for example, it would seriously hamper our attempts to be objective if we adopted a strictly Catholic point of view. We do not even need to know what the Bible means by and in itself: a careful observation of the behavior of the groups of people who claim they do is enough.

The early years of a paradigm constitute its most interesting phase, and it is especially fascinating to observe how a paradigm is introduced into another national or linguistic context. The success of poststructuralism in North America is a good example, especially since Americans have consistently relied on French culture to provide them with exemplary figures (Booth 1978, 327). Language is one of the important factors in the French connection: French departments are generally the largest foreign language departments at American universities, and professors of French and comparative literature have been crucial to the reception of structuralist and poststructuralist thinking.

The evolution from the first introduction of a new paradigm to its acceptance can be demonstrated in reference to the American translations of Derrida's books. *La Voix et le phénomène* was translated by David B. Allison and published by Northwestern University Press in 1973. In the preface, Newton Garner carefully articulates the differences between Derrida's approach and philosophy as it is practiced in Britain and in the United States. This edition still fits into the reception of philosophical hermeneutics: the translation is subtitled *and Other Essays on Husserl's Theory of Signs*. Northwestern University Press had already published translations and books by Heidegger and Ricoeur. The covers of two other books by Derrida, published by the university presses of Johns Hopkins (1976) and Chicago (1978), respectively, boast a quotation of a professor from Yale: *Of Grammatology* from J. Hillis Miller and *Writing and Difference* from Geoffrey Hartman. The rest of the text on the cover of *Of Grammatology* stresses Derrida's importance in France and the "lively controversy" his work occasioned in "the vanguard of European and American criticism." Although *La Dissémination* was translated by a young Ivy League professor of English literature and published by the University of Chicago Press (1981), the cover is different; apart from a brief biographical note on Derrida, it contains only a difficult passage from "Hors livre." Apparently by 1981 the prospective buyer of a book by Derrida did not have to be told what he would find or why he should buy the book. The prefaces to these translations also change from an introduction to Derrida's thought from the perspective of an American philosophical or critical tradition to a writing that increasingly adopts the Derridean style.

What I originally intended to do was to translate the new Joyce into the language of traditional criticism, much as Kuhn described the process in *The Structure of Scientific Revolutions*:

> Briefly put, what the participants in a communication breakdown can do is recognize each other as members of different language communities and then become translators. Taking the differences between their own intra- and inter-group discourse as itself a subject for study, they can first attempt to discover the terms and locutions that, used unproblematically within each community, are nevertheless foci of trouble for inter-group discussions. (1970, 202)

It seemed to me that the lack of communication between the French and the traditional critics was not just due to an innate Anglo-Saxon rejection of difference and dissemination. In the proceedings of the Paris Joyce Symposium, I read between the lines that there was a genuine willingness on the part of American Joyceans to find out what the French were so excited about and an equally genuine unwillingness on the part of the French to offer that explanation. So I would be an interpreter.

But when I started to reread the French criticism of the sixties and seventies and to study the work that had been published in the meantime, I discovered first that the critics I was reading did not often mention other French critics' work and that when they did, they attacked each other vigorously. How could they be part of the same paradigm? The role of *Tel Quel* seemed crucial, and it became evident that I could not simply describe the contours of a single poststructuralist Joyce. I would also have to write the history of a very turbulent phase in French intellectual life. The problem with this type of work is that, partly as a direct result of poststructuralism, *Ideengeschichte* or the history of ideas has been extremely unfashionable until very recently. This meant that I had very little secondary material to base my analysis on; there are no thorough studies of the reception of Heidegger's ideas in France or of Hegel's influence, although general statements about these topics and about real or imagined filiations between writers and philosophers abound. When I started the project, there were almost no biographies of the major participants in this story and next to no histories of structuralism, poststructuralism, or psychoanalysis in France. Since I did not have any informants within the French context, it also meant that I had to work purely on the basis of the texts published by the protagonists of the story so that Derrida's dictum "il n'y a pas de hors-texte" took on its own peculiar meaning for me. Although I was able, after a while, to see how the different lines in the battlefield had been drawn—who was quarreling when, with whom, and why—I discovered to my surprise that these enmities and conversions did not matter all that much for the practical criticism. The picture of James Joyce and his work that emerged from the writings of Hélène Cixous, Jacques Lacan, Jacques Derrida, Philippe Sollers, and their followers was remarkably consistent, and there definitely seemed to be a paradigm after all.

My second discovery was, for my own point of view, more dramatic. Sometime in my first year in graduate school, I stopped thinking of myself as a part of the poststructuralist paradigm, and I have since found it much easier to analyze other people's conversions than to analyze my own. Since I cannot pretend that I believe my own position is entirely irrelevant to my handling of these texts, I cannot keep my own particular gestalt switch out of the discussion. One of the reasons was certainly overexposure: like all graduate students in comparative literature departments in North America, I read far too much theory, and I heard too many theoretical papers. It did not take long to recognize recurrent patterns in the rhetoric, to read all the relevant books, and then to "do the deconstruction" as we used to say. Another factor had to do with the act of reading: in Dublin, in the absence of theoretical books, I had concentrated on Joyce's own works and on other novels of the period; since then *Ulysses* and *Finnegans Wake* still seem more interesting than anything written about them. When I read French and American poststructuralists, I found it increasingly difficult to link their texts to Joyce's; when I could, Joyce very often came out saying something that however much I tried I could not find in the original. A close reading of an essay by Philippe Lacoue-Labarthe on the German poet Friedrich Hölderlin (1978) revealed the rhetorical ploys and the shallowness of some of this criticism, and in a course on Joyce I wrote a paper on Joyce's use of Dutch-Flemish language lists in which I discovered the *Finnegans Wake* notebooks and the perverse delight of applying old philology to an avant-garde text.

The change in my own perspective has made it necessary to make my disagreements with the theory and practice of poststructuralism explicit, but I hope that it did not affect my ability to present poststructuralists' work fairly. In the Joycean context my position had become precarious: more and more to be young, dynamic, and ambitious became synonymous with following Lacan and Derrida. Joyceans who shared my distrust of poststructuralism could not see why I still bothered to read and study deconstruction. Another traditionalist objection was one of relevance: if literature is the prime object of criticism, studying studies about literature and studies about studies about literature becomes progressively more frivolous and irrelevant. This objection is not simply a corollary of a more general antitheoretical position; it also betrays a fundamental misunderstanding of the reading process and of the acquisition of knowledge in general. If Kuhn and the theoreticians of reader reception are right, perception is never an innocent activity: an individual perceives the world around him in ways that relate to a large number of factors, some social and some personal. The social factors can, according to Kuhn, be studied by the philosophy and sociology of science, and I believe they can also be isolated in literary criticism. If we find that the same phenomenon, in this case the work of James Joyce, is interpreted differently by two groups of scholars, a responsible student of Joyce cannot afford to ignore this fact. He or she will have to confront the alternative view; the other paradigm will have to be studied and decisions will have to be made whether it can be accepted or rejected. Before we can make such a decision, a full presentation of the French Joyce criticism is necessary, not only simply in order to understand the French paradigm, its sources and consequences, but also in order to comprehend one's own paradigm. It is only when we are confronted with a fully defined alternative perspective that we can really formulate and understand our own premises. This is precisely what could have happened when poststructuralism was introduced in Joyce studies. But it did not, and the reasons for this failure need to be addressed.

The Joyceans have had everything going for them. Most of them read French and quite a lot of them have taught in comparative literature departments where the impact of French theory registered ten years earlier than in most English departments. Every two years the James Joyce Foundation organizes a large-scale symposium in Europe, and most of the French poststructuralist thinkers have presented major addresses in Paris (1975), Zürich (1979), Dublin (1982), Frankfurt (1984), and Copenhagen (1986). Panels and workshops have been devoted to the new approaches and in Venice (1988) it was very difficult not to be confronted with a young man or woman who began his or her paper with the statement "What follows should be seen in the context of the epoch-making studies of J. Derrida (or J. Lacan)."

The first meaning of the word *symposium* in my *Webster's* is "any meeting or social gathering at which ideas are freely exchanged," but this type of *agora* or *forum* has in recent years degenerated into a marketplace, a Modern Language Association convention *extra muros*, the sole purpose of which seems to be to avoid an exchange of ideas at all costs. Against this notion of a free exchange of ideas, it could be argued that a symposium or an MLA convention really *is* a marketplace, a very deregulated exchange of professional prestige.

Untenured professors have to give papers at conferences, preferably abroad; the same is true for ambitious associate professors. Articles have to be written and published for professors to get tenure; books have to come out regularly if you want to become a full professor. The term *Joyce industry* really begins to mean something here. The number of publications on Joyce and the number of young academics at Joyce conferences suggest that Joyce still is a hot academic property. If we look at the kinds of panels that attract a large audience or the kind of paper that is likely to be published in the proceedings, the conclusion from a career-planning perspective is clear enough: at the moment, poststructuralism and feminism sell well. The choice involved is not trivial. On the contrary, it is of vital importance to the young academic, especially in the very competitive market of the eighties and early nineties: it can mean the difference between a good job and a lousy job or between a lousy job and unemployment. From this perspective the lack of reaction from traditional Joyceans to the poststructuralist challenge is equally understandable: a bad review from a senior professor can cost somebody a career. When one studies the evidence, the only conclusion can be that there seems to be a silent consensus on the part of both sides not to engage in a serious debate.

At the level of hiring practices, the field coverage model of departmental organization has made the adoption of new methodologies friction free (Graff 1987, 6–7). American universities answer the challenge of a disruptive new ideology by hiring one of its representatives, and the field coverage model ensures that the inevitable clash between conflicting methods or ideologies can be avoided:

> The division of fields according to the least controversial principles made the department easy to administer but masked its most interesting conflicts and connections. To put it another way, the field-coverage principle enabled administrative organization to take the place of principled thought and discussion. (8)

The result for the students of these departments is dramatic since they are the ones who, individually, have to work out the discrepancies between the different paradigms they are confronted with during the course of their undergraduate and graduate training; this is something that radically distinguishes students of the sciences from students of the humanities and that seriously qualifies the usefulness of the concept of paradigm in a study such as this. Few science students will ever be confronted with more than one paradigm whereas most graduate schools in the humanities will make a point of offering at least a survey course on the different methodologies. The whole purpose of graduate school seems to be that the student, at the end of his study, should be able to make up his mind and to choose one particular paradigm.

The presentation and critique of poststructuralist Joyce criticism that are offered in this book cannot but be contextual. Just as I do not think that it is useful to abstract Joyce's texts from the context in which they originated, neither can one read poststructuralist criticism simply as texts; it plays a specific role in specific sociohistorical conditions. A study of the American poststructuralist reception of Joyce still remains to be written, and my comments here and in chapter 5 are only introductory notes to an inquiry along the lines of the institutional critique of the academic study of literature that has repeatedly been promised by poststructuralist critics but that has been delivered by nondeconstructionists such as Gerald Graff and Michael Fischer.

It cannot be an accident that the only critic who has published a serious close reading and textual analysis of Joyce criticism is somebody outside the American academic context. Paul Van Caspel's *Bloomers on the Liffey* (1986) offers the kind of uncompromising, detailed criticism of specific readings of *Ulysses* that one would like to see more often in reviews of new Joyce books. The book's own reviewers seem to be rather nonplussed at what they see as the ungenerous nature of such a work, but I would argue that we cannot afford not to have such books and reviews. My own work is different, although I will at times show where misreadings or bad translations occur. But what interests me more is what the critics do with their (mis)readings and how different readings cohere. At the other end of the spectrum, this book also differs from books such as Suresh Raval's

Metacriticism (1981), which are concerned more with critical theory than with practical criticism.

In order to establish the context of poststructuralist criticism on Joyce, I offer in chapter 1 a survey of the early criticism in France and in the United States, Britain, and Ireland. The three most influential poststructuralist critics are undoubtedly Hélène Cixous, Jacques Lacan, and Jacques Derrida and in chapter 2 I look in detail at their writings on Joyce. Although these three thinkers have at least an ambiguous relationship with the French university system, their influence in the academy is incontestable, and in chapter 3, the major contributions of the academic poststructuralist critics are discussed. Chapter 4 is entirely devoted to the influence on Joyce studies of the members of the *Tel Quel* collective: Philippe Sollers, Julia Kristeva, and Marcelin Pleynet. In the mid-sixties this Parisian journal became the center of a radically avant-garde literary and critical practice, and Sollers became the leader of an unacademic and often antiacademic criticism that lived through and often anticipated the shifts and changes in the French cultural scene. In chapter 5 I discuss briefly the work of the American and British poststructuralist critics and in the conclusion I attempt to explain where poststructuralism comes from and why it could flourish in France.

ONE

Joyce Criticism:
The Early Years

Slowly but steadily the pile of studies on James Joyce has grown to a size rarely seen in the history of literary criticism. Joyce's reputation has reached a level no other twentieth-century writer can aspire to, and the sheer number of critical studies devoted to his work every year can be compared only to those on Shakespeare. The astonishing thing is that Joyce has not yet had to suffer a setback; if anything, his reputation keeps growing, and every new generation of readers and critics finds new reasons for admiring and studying his work. The result is an absolutely daunting number of books, articles, and reviews that was at the last count reaching the ten thousand mark. In the last fifteen years very few critics have dared to offer surveys of Joyce criticism, and I can base my own only on the studies of Tom Staley (1976), Bernard Benstock (1976), and Sidney Feshbach and William Herman (1984).

The history of Joyce criticism starts with the author himself. Few modern writers have been so aware as Joyce was of the importance of criticism for the reception of his later and more difficult novels, and he personally inspired and supervised almost all of the major studies on his work that were published during his lifetime. These efforts were of course mainly directed at *Ulysses*: Joyce gave schemes of the novel's structure and the Homeric correspondences to Herbert Gorman and Carlo Linati; he talked to Valery Larbaud and other French critics, and he personally supervised the writing of Gorman's biography (1924; 1939) and Stuart Gilbert's *James Joyce's "Ulysses"* (1930). He was not directly involved in Frank Budgen's *James Joyce and the Making of "Ulysses"* (1934), but he did supply details and the book is largely based on Budgen's conversations with Joyce during the writing of *Ulysses*. In the meantime he did not neglect his last novel; in 1929 he organized the publication of a collection of twelve essays on "Work in Progress," ten years before the book would be finished; originally there was even supposed to be a second volume with four essays (*JJ II*, 613).

A second period started in the year Joyce died with the publication of Harry Levin's *James Joyce: A Critical Introduction* (1941). In its independence of Joyce's personal involvement and in its positive evaluation of the work by situating it in a general modernist European framework, Levin's book was preceded by Edmund Wilson's *Axel's Castle* (1932), but Levin's study had the additional merit of making Joyce academically respectable. Both books also inaugurated the shift away from Paris to the United States, where the center of the Joyce industry has remained ever since. Not only did the rapid expansion of American universities in the forties and fifties result in the creation of graduate programs and the hiring of thousands of young teachers; it also made available large funds for the establishment of important library holdings. In the first two decades after World War II all of the Joyce manuscripts that became available were bought by American universities and moved to Buffalo, Cornell, Yale, and, somewhat later, the University of Texas at Austin.

The first doctoral dissertation on Joyce was written in 1944 by Joseph Prescott, and in the same year Joseph Campbell and Henry Morton Robinson published their pioneering study, *A Skeleton Key to "Finnegans Wake."* Under the influence of psychoanalysis, and especially of Jung's mythological and archetypal approach, the two authors showed that the *Wake* could be read as a novel and that it was based on a limited number of schematic patterns, thereby doing more or less for *Finnegans Wake* what Stuart Gilbert had done for *Ulysses*. In the late forties and fifties this type of study became very popular among Joyce critics; symbol hunting was the prevalent mode in *James Joyce: His Way of Interpreting the Modern World* by William York Tindall (1950) and in his later books *A Reader's Guide to James Joyce* (1959) and *A Reader's Guide to "Finnegans Wake"* (1969); in Marvin Magalaner's *Time of Apprenticeship* (1959) and of course in Northrop Frye's "Quest and Cycle in *Finnegans Wake*" (1957). The period was more or less closed off with the publication by Richard M. Kain and Marvin Magalaner of *Joyce: The Man, the Work, the Reputation* in 1956.

The next period saw a move away from symbols to hard facts, and it was announced by William M. Schutte in his survey of the criticism in *Joyce and Shakespeare: A Study in the Meaning of "Ulysses"* (1957) but marked decisively by the 1959 publication of *James Joyce*, Richard Ellmann's biography (*JJ I*). The Ellmann book has been the alpha and omega of all Joyce criticism since its publication, and it remains, next to the texts themselves, an indispensable tool. The exceptional status of the book was sanctioned by the Joyceans when the *James Joyce Quarterly* decided to include it in its list of standard editions. Its importance cannot be exaggerated (Staley 1976, 378), and although Ellmann's critical works on Joyce have not been equally influential, his presentations of the early works and the letters remain the standard editions. Ellmann's insistence on the relevance of biographical material in Joyce's work may have impeded the influence of New Criticism, which was responsible for another shift toward a more novelistic and scholarly approach. In the next decade most of the important Joyce critics published their first studies: Hugh Kenner his *Dublin's Joyce* (1956), Robert M. Adams's *Surface and Symbol: The Consistency of James Joyce's "Ulysses"* (1962) and *James Joyce: Common Sense and Beyond* (1967), S. L. Goldberg's *The Classical Temper* (1961), all detailed and rigorous analyses of the texts. Around 1965 explication gave way to more extended interpretations, which resulted in a lot of controversies and discussions. Critics started to use philosophical and psychological systems in their study and evaluation of Joyce's work: Kierkegaard in Arnold Goldman's *The Joyce Paradox* (1966) and Freud in Darcy O'Brien's *The Conscience of James Joyce* (1968). Another important development was the institutionalization of Joyce studies, marked by the start of the *James Joyce Quarterly* in 1963 and of the international James Joyce Symposia in 1967.

These two events, and the establishment of the James Joyce Foundation, have resulted in a solidification of Joyce criticism. Although *Ulysses* and *Finnegans Wake* have stopped being esoteric books for an initiated happy few, their difficulty did produce one of the important reasons why Joyce studies differ so much from the criticism of other authors. Since the mid-fifties an enormous number of reference books—glossaries, concordances, gazetteers, and lexicons—have been published; the most important are *Song in the Works of James Joyce* by Matthew J. C. Hodgart and Mabel P. Worthington (1959); Weldon Thornton's *Allusions in "Ulysses": An Annotated List* (1968); Don Gifford and Robert Seidman's *Notes for Joyce: "Dubliners" and "A Portrait of the Artist as a Young Man"* (1967) and *Notes for Joyce: An Annotation of Joyce's "Ulysses"* (1974); Zack Bowen's *Musical Allusions in the Works of James Joyce: Early Works Through "Ulysses"* (1974); Clive Hart and Leo Knuth's *A Topographical Guide to James Joyce's "Ulysses"* (1975); and Bernard and Shari Benstock's *Who's He When He's At Home: A James Joyce Directory* (1980). For *Finnegans Wake* we have Adaline Glasheen's *A Census of "Finnegans Wake"* (1956, 1963, 1977), James Atherton's *The Books at the Wake* (1959), D. B. Christiani's Scandinavian (1965), Helmut Bonheim's German (1967) and Brendan O'Hehir's Gaelic (1967) and Classical Lexicons (1977); Louis O. Mink's *A "Finnegans Wake" Gazetteer* (1978) and Roland McHugh's *Annotations to "Finnegans Wake"* (1980).

A second difference from the criticism of other modern authors is the exceptionally high percentage of amateurs among Joyceans. Some of the major figures in Joyce criticism are not academics. This is extremely interesting for both parties because these critics will be less under the influence of academic paradigms. Roland McHugh, an entomologist, has even described in detail how he consciously avoided any contact with the academic Joyce scholars (McHugh 1981). This may well be another reason why New Critical doctrines such as the intentional fallacy have had little influence, and it does demonstrate the appeal of Joyce's oeuvre beyond the normal modernist and post-modernist audience as described by one of Gilbert Sorrentino's writer characters: "One wishes to create characters who will speak directly to the minds of comparative literature professors and intelligent book reviewers" (1979, 38).

A third difference is again destined to hurt New Critical sensibilities: the still growing importance of genetic studies of Joyce's texts. This emphasis on the process of creation instead of on the finished product also dates from the sixties. Important studies are Fred H. Higginson's *Anna Livia Plurabelle: The Making of a Chapter* (1960) and A. Walton Litz's *The Art of James Joyce* (1961). Most of the manuscripts and drafts were also published: Thomas Connolly edited *Scribbledehobble* in 1961; David Hayman *A First-Draft Version of "Finnegans Wake"* in 1963; Robert Scholes and Richard M. Kain edited *The Workshop of Daedalus* (1965); Phillip F. Herring *Joyce's "Ulysses" Notesheets in the British Museum* in 1972; and one year later Clive Driver edited *James Joyce's "Ulysses." A Facsimile of the Manuscript.* In 1978 Danis Rose edited *Finnegans Wake* notebook VI.B.46, and in the same year all the existing Joyce manuscripts, drafts, and notebooks were published by Garland Press. Genetic and textual studies continue to flourish, partly fueled by Hans Walter Gabler's edition of a synoptic text of *Ulysses* in 1984 and the controversy created by the accompanying definitive edition and partly the result of the work of a small but dedicated group of enthusiasts centered around *A Wake Newslitter* first and *A Finnegans Wake Circular* later. The latest contribution to date is Danis Rose and John O'Hanlon's edition of a lost notebook for *Ulysses* (1989).

Joyce's status as the most complex of modern authors has also attracted the attention of two groups of readers and critics: the writers of theories of literature and the prophets of a new era in the history of humankind. Many important writers on the theory of literature have used Joyce as a supreme example: Umberto Eco, Wolfgang Iser, and Robert Scholes have referred to Joyce's work in the elaboration of their critical theories, and Terry Eagleton recently wrote, "It is always worth testing out any literary theory by asking: How would it work with Joyce's *Finnegans Wake?*" (1983, 82). Two of the most important American prophets of the new *episteme*, Marshall McLuhan and Norman O. Brown, have attempted to turn Joyce into a prophet and *Finnegans Wake* into the Gospel of the Age of Aquarius. McLuhan, who was after all a professor of English literature, published on Joyce from the early fifties onward, and he mentions Joyce with Stéphane Mallarmé as forerunners of a new sensibility (McLuhan 1969); Norman O. Brown introduced Joycean themes and phrases from the *Wake* into the Freudo-Marxist collage of *Closing Time* (1973).

While McLuhan and Brown refer to Joyce in a general manner and remain by and large faithful to the text, Frances Mott Boldereff has chosen the alternative approach. In the last three decades she has published five books on Joyce in which she attempts to explicate a presumed esoteric content of *Ulysses* and *Finnegans Wake*. *Reading "Finnegans Wake"* (1959) concentrated on the Irish allusions in the *Wake*, but the book already betrayed a strong interest in the arcane and esoteric that was to come to full fruition in *Hermes to his Son Thoth* (1968), ostensibly about Joyce's use of Bruno in *Finnegans Wake* and in *Verbi-Voco-Visual*, published under the pseudonym Thomasine Rose. Boldereff's interest in Blake found its impact in two studies: *A Blakean Translation of Joyce's "Circe"* (1965) and *Let Me Be Los* (1987), published under the pseudonym Frances Phipps. Boldereff's work can be characterized by the critic's assumption that there is a master key that can once and for all crack the hidden code of these two very difficult books. A similarly Gnostic approach can be found in Rolf R. Loehrich's *The Secret of "Ulysses"* (1953), although in this book Freud seems to have taken over from Blake.

Since the twenties and thirties Irish and British critics have been much less thrilled with Joyce than their American colleagues have been. They are for the most part very suspicious of American symbol hunting, an attitude that is obvious in most British or Irish reviews of American Joyce books until the mid-seventies, when it became rare, though not extinct: Anthony Burgess is a typical example (1973, 82–87). Irish and British critics tend to be rather parochial in their readings, choosing Dublin detail over symbols or Homeric parallels, and historical facts over literary or philosophical influences. This results in the notion that *Ulysses* and *Finnegans Wake* are basically simple books that should be taken away from the professors and given back to the people or in the much more common stance of dismissing Joyce altogether. Examples are Anthony Burgess's *Here Comes Everybody* (1965), John Garvin's *The Disunited Kingdom* (1976), and the Irish biography *James Joyce: A Portrait of the Artist* (1975) by Stan Gébler Davies. The negative side of this attitude is the failure to credit American scholars with any real discoveries; e.g., in Roland McHugh's *Annotations to "Finnegans Wake"* (1976) and in *Understanding "Finnegans Wake"* (1982) by Danis Rose and John O'Hanlon.

Not surprisingly with over 9,000 titles, Joyce criticism in the English-speaking world has been rich and varied. During the author's lifetime its center was the international avant-garde based in Paris; in the war it shifted to the States, where it has remained. In Ireland and the United Kingdom the few critics who are interested in Joyce's achievement prefer the naturalist Dublin details over literary and philosophical aspects in an outspoken rejection of what is seen as the American colonization of Joyce country. In the United States Joyce's work to an important extent escaped the impact of New Criticism; maybe because of the influence of nonacademic readers, because of the availability of an abundance of draft and manuscript material, or because of the presence of an authoritative biography. Joyce's status as the most important modernist writer has attracted the attention of the theoreticians of literature, of the prophets of a new time, of avant-garde artists such as John Cage, and of the eccentric.

When Joyce and his family left France in 1940, never to return, the relativity of his success quickly became apparent. Without Joyce himself, the group of people who had supported him fell apart and although some of them did write on Joyce after World War II, France seemed to have lost interest in the Irishman. In the fall of 1968 the French review *L'Arc* devoted a whole issue to the works of Joyce. In his introduction, suitably entitled "Retour à Joyce," Henri Ronse complained of the lack of French interest in Joyce: "In France, where the lack of knowledge about foreign literatures has become a sign of culture, one only bothers about Joyce in order to turn him into something precious and adulatory and to make of him, at best, a pedigree for the modern novel" (1968, 1). This lacuna, which L'Arc was trying to fill, seems difficult to imagine now, especially after Joyce's centenary year. As in so many aspects of French intellectual and cultural life, 1968 was a turning point; the ascendancy of this new Joycean era is announced two pages later when Ronse mentions the publication of Hélène Cixous's monumental doctoral dissertation on Joyce, the first such thesis in France. In the rest of this chapter, I will discuss the French interest in Joyce before Cixous, from Joyce's early champions, collaborators, and translators, to the introductory studies by university anglicistes in the sixties and the publication of Ulysses in "Livre de Poche" in 1965.

Joyce lived with his family in Paris between 1920 and 1940. He wrote and published his most important works there; he was very much part of the English and American émigré scene in the French capital, but it remains to be ascertained whether Joyce played any significant role in the French literature of the period. Opinions are divided on this issue, as they are on the question of who did what for whom. Jean-Pierre Meylan states that "France made Joyce's fortune" (1969, 390); Pierre Joannon says that France discovered Joyce (1982), while in the same article Joannon stresses Joyce's lack of interest in the French literature of his time.

Every reader of Ellmann's biography must be struck by Joyce's well-documented genius for exploiting the resources of relatives, benefactors, and friends; Joyce effectively made use of the interest and talents of quite a number of French writers and critics. The first important French intellectual to support Joyce was Valery Larbaud, a prolific writer and a translator of English literature. He became interested in England and its culture in 1901, and at the time of his death his library contained 3,500 titles in English (Kuntz 1978, 99). Sylvia Beach lent Larbaud the Little Review sections of Ulysses, and in December 1920 she introduced him to Joyce. At this time Larbaud was a highly respected critic, "recognized as a tastemaker among the French literary elite and his seal of approval was eagerly sought by young authors and by publishers" (Brown 1982, 31). By the middle of February Larbaud wrote to Sylvia Beach: "I am raving mad over *Ulysses*. Since I read Whitman I have not been so enthusiastic over any book" (quoted in Brown 1982, 32). The two writers met and corresponded regularly, and in the summer of 1921 the Joyce family moved into Larbaud's apartment on the rue Cardinal Lemoine. On 7 December Larbaud read a lecture on Joyce's work in Adrienne Monnier's *La maison des Amis des Livres*, and he published the paper in the April issue of the prestigious *Nouvelle Revue Française*. After the success of this evening, it became clear that *Ulysses* should become available to the French reading public. Larbaud, determined to get on with his own writing, refused to commit himself and suggested the name of Auguste Morel, who consented to translate *Ulysses* under Larbaud's supervision. The article in the *Nouvelle Revue Française*, later reprinted as the preface to *Gens de Dublin* and in *Ce vice impuni, la lecture*, is an excellent early introduction to Joyce's life and work. For the section on *Ulysses* Larbaud had been amply provided with notes and charts, so he was able to elaborate confidently about the Homeric pattern, but he stressed the basic humanity of the characters and of the book itself. Larbaud wrote on Joyce only once more when again in the *Nouvelle Revue Française* he replied to an article by Ernest Boyd (Larbaud 1925). Boyd was one of the first representatives of the view that Joyce was essentially an Irish writer, a direct heir to the Irish Literary Renaissance (the title of a study in which Boyd had first attacked Larbaud), while Joyce's continental supporters such as Larbaud saw the Irish revival as merely the prologue to Joyce's oeuvre.

In the meantime Auguste Morel had started to work on the *Ulysses* translation in the spring of 1924, but Larbaud's frequent trips abroad and Morel's increasing uneasiness about Larbaud's supervision slowed things down considerably. Stuart Gilbert's arrival in Paris with a list of errors in the translation of "Calypso" was "providential" as Adrienne Monnier put it (Brown 1982, 40), but it complicated matters even more. By the early fall of 1927 there was such animosity between the translators and the publishers and among the translators themselves that Joyce had to negotiate a treaty, which gave Larbaud the final authority.

When the French *Ulysses* finally did get published in February 1929, the supervisor with veto rights refused to have anything to do with it; the relationship between Larbaud and Joyce had considerably cooled in the later twenties. Larbaud's interest in Joyce may have had different reasons: both were exiled artists from narrow-minded and provincial cities; Larbaud was only one year older than Joyce, and he had converted to Catholicism in 1910. As a "rich amateur" he seems to have been impressed by Joyce's erudition and more specifically by the Irish writer's ambition to recreate the *Odyssey*.

The importance of Larbaud's support cannot be denied (Anne Chevalier even writes that Joyce was "un petit inconnu" before Larbaud started to talk about him [1981, 62]), but there is another critic who was equally important in promoting Joyce, Louis Gillet. Whereas Larbaud published in the *Nouvelle Revue Française*, Gillet was responsible for foreign literature in the more conservative *Revue des deux mondes*. The *Nouvelle Revue Française* was the more obvious place to publish on Joyce: it was interested in innovative, young writers and it published new work by Gide, Proust, and Valéry. The *Revue des deux mondes* was so conservative that the very names of Proust and Gide were taboo (Gillet 1941, 13). Gillet's first essay on *Ulysses* was unfavorable, and it may be read as an implicit response to Larbaud's admiration: Joyce is the world champion of long books (1925, 686), Joyce's *monologue intérieure* ("ce tac tac d'appareil morse") does not resemble what Gillet himself hears when he listens to his interior voices (694), and Joyce's work shows neither the pity nor the "modernity" that Larbaud found in it (697). Gillet's article, "Du Côté de chez Joyce," also suggested in its title a similarity with Proust, a popular opinion among French opponents that Joyce seems to have been particularly sensitive to (Saurat 1924; *Letters III*, 69). The essay elicited different reactions: Joyce saw it as an attack, though a mild one (*JJ II*, 634n), but Georges Duplaix satirized Gillet for his "deification" of the Irishman (1925, 23). In a new essay published in 1931 after Gillet had met Joyce, he compared *Work in Progress* to the *Divine Comedy*. Gillet anticipated

Roland Barthes's description of the literary text as an onion (Gillet 1941, 60; and Barthes quoted in Culler 1975, 259), and he stressed the metaphysical implications of the book. Gillet continued to publish on the *Wake* and even joined the group of close friends and collaborators Joyce had gathered around him.

It is this group of people that Marcel Brion, the only French contributor to *Our Exagmination Round his Factification for Incamination of Work in Progress* (Beckett 1972), had described in 1927 as "a true cult, ardent, exclusive, not without fanaticism." Brion is the only apostle who described the Joyce entourage in these terms; the coterie aspect of the admiration for his work was usually reserved to detractors, and it played a central role in the polemic between Boyd and Larbaud. The former resented the coalition of French surrealists and American expatriate aesthetes that conspired to give Joyce a prematurely cosmopolitan renown; the latter replied that he had only wanted to present to the elite of French letters a writer who had not even been discovered in Ireland at the time. Larbaud denied that he had acted as a spokesperson of the Joyce *entourage* and claimed that Joyce had not even read his paper in advance (1925, 14).

Boyd's association of the Joyce group with the surrealists is understandable at the time but quite wrong: there were almost no links between the two groups. The Joyce coterie was engaged, in the late twenties and the thirties, in the writing and rewriting of *Finnegans Wake*, the translation of *Ulysses* and, even more chaotically, the translation of "Anna Livia Plurabelle." One of these translators was Philippe Soupault, an exsurrealist since November 1926 when André Breton, Louis Aragon, and Paul Eluard broke with Antonin Artaud, Roger Vitrac, Robert Desnos, and Philippe Soupault over the political issue (Nadeau 1964, 104). Soupault met Joyce through Ezra Pound (Soupault 1980, 40), became closely associated with the Joyce menage and collaborated with Samuel Beckett, Alfred Péron, Paul Léon, Eugene Jolas, and Ivan Goll on the translation of "Anna Livia Plurabelle" (see Costanzo 1971). Although Artaud's linguistic games are often compared to the language games in *Finnegans Wake*, there is no evidence that Artaud and Joyce were aware of each other's existence.

Georges Bataille, on the other hand, did mention the *Wake* in an essay published in *Deucalion* (1955, 39), and he wrote one year later that he admired Joyce's work but that it did not have an influence on his own writing (1976, 615).

The official surrealists did not appreciate Joyce's work: Aragon read *Ulysses* in English in *The Little Review* serialization, but he dismissed the Joyce fashion in 1931 (Chénieux-Gendron 1983, 122). The differences between Joyce's endeavor and that of the surrealists are clear enough: Breton admits in 1953 that the "écriture automatique" and the interior monologue have in common a hatred of the tyranny of a degraded language, but he stresses that they start from radically different assumptions. Whereas Joyce uses the free association of ideas for literary purposes, surrealism has discovered the presence in the human mind of the *materia prima* (in its alchemical meaning) of language. Instead of moving from the signified to the sign, surrealism goes straight to the birth of the signifier (Breton 1972, 312–13).

After the break with Breton and Aragon, Soupault started to write for *transition*, explicitly hailed as the only journal in English that was interested in surrealism. It was edited by Eugene Jolas, who was introduced to Joyce in December 1926 and who gave pride of place to *Work in Progress* in the first issue of *transition* in April 1927 and continued to publish chapters until 1938. Jolas, too, had had a Catholic education, and his revolution of the word had a clearly religious character. In his book on *transition*, Dougald McMillan writes that Jolas's later work and theory "reflect his almost medieval belief that poetry is a means of experiencing a transcendental state which is essentially religious" (1975, 10). Jolas found confirmation of his beliefs in Heraclitus, in the Eleusian mysteries, the Christian Gnostics, the mystics, the German romantics, and in all types of visionary writing. In New York during World War II, Jolas edited *Vertical: A Yearbook for Romantic Mystical Ascensions*, and his essays on Joyce in *transition* reflect these concerns: Joyce has revolutionized literary expression. He has shaken the static world of phenomena to its foundation (Jolas 1932, 250); *Work in Progress* is the "first mantic myth written in our age. A cosmography in hierophantic terms" (Jolas 1933, 101), and

Joyce himself is a "mythmaker" (Jolas 1938). But although it was based in Paris, *transition* was not a French journal, and Joyce himself characteristically refused to associate himself fully with it (*JJ II*, 587; McMillan 1975, 220), only preferring *transition* over other magazines because of its apolitical stance (McMillan, 183).

University criticism could not avoid Joyce either. The *Revue Anglo-Américaine* was a bastion of the establishment; it had in its *comité de patronage* the British and American ambassadors to Paris, the French ambassadors to London and Washington, four members of the Académie Française, the principals of the University of Paris and of the École normale supérieure. Its editorial board consisted of three Sorbonne professors; and one of them, Louis Cazamian, opened the December issue of 1924 with an essay on Joyce. The reason for the essay is obvious: *Ulysses* is the most sensational book, and it has been impossible to ignore Joyce. After a short biographical note and a brief account of the earlier works, Cazamian attempts to situate *Ulysses* in the context of European literature: it is a modern epic like *Joseph Andrews* but it lacks its structure; it is a romantic drama like *Faust* but without the philosophical depth. The book's only direct precursor is *Tristram Shandy*, and its real importance lies in its rigorous development of a psychological realism that takes into account the unconscious. At the same time *Ulysses* lacks structure, it does not have the "strong framework of ideas" that could have supported it. In addition, Cazamian reiterates the charge that *Ulysses* lacks human generosity. In all, it is difficult to disagree with R. M. Albérès (1972), who writes that Joyce did not have an immediate influence in France in the twenties and thirties, dominated as it was by the aestheticisms of Jean Cocteau and Jean Giraudoux. In a country where the metaphysical and tragic novels of the *condition humaine* were being written by François Mauriac, Georges Bernanos, André Malraux, and Julien Green, there was little room for a writer like Joyce.

But Albérès sees an important contribution Joyce did make to the history of the modern novel in the technical innovations of the interior monologue and in the use of a classical model. The controversial discovery of the interior monologue was satirized by Giraudoux in his

Juliet au Pays des Hommes: "At that moment Paris was intrigued, not by death, but by the interior Monologue" (quoted in Raimond 1966, 257n). The debate was opened by Larbaud in his lecture on Joyce. In the next decade the discussion credited Joyce with the invention although he himself claimed he had been inspired by Edouard Dujardin's *Les Lauriers sont coupés* (1924), a book for which he organized a rediscovery and an English translation (*JJ II*, 520). Larbaud himself used the technique in his *Amants, Heureux Amants* (1923), and André Gide claimed that the credit was due to Edgar Allan Poe, Robert Browning, and Fyodor Dostoyevski (quoted in Raimond 1966, 262). The publication of the French *Ulysses* in 1929 rekindled the controversy, and old Dujardin himself published a history of the interior monologue in 1931, presumably to set the record straight once and for all.

Before and just after World War II the French critics saw Joyce as the writer of *Ulysses* and as the inventor of the interior monologue; they stressed the discontinuity and the randomness of the book, and few seem to have read it in its original language, if at all: Albérès even turns Bloom into a small stockbroker (1972, 119). Even fewer critics mention *Finnegans Wake*, but slowly at first it is the novelists and not the university critics who begin to discover Joyce's last book. Two writers stand out. The first is Raymond Queneau, according to Vivian Mercier, "perhaps the greatest French writer to be profoundly influenced by Joyce in his creative work, from his first novel *Le Chiendent* (1933) to the farcical *Les Oeuvres Complètes de Sally Mara* (1962)" (1965, 64). Queneau read *Ulysses* when it was first published in French and borrowed the idea of an overall structure for his own first novel (Mercier 1974, 223); he has also translated the beginning of *Gueule de Pierre* into "Joycien," a French Wakese (Queneau 1950b). Gilbert Pestureau has studied Joyce's influence on Queneau both in his *Doctorat d'état*–thesis at the Sorbonne (1981) and in an essay published in 1983, in which he looks at Queneau's novels *Chiendent, Saint Glinglin, Contes et Propos, Zazie dans le métro*; and Jean-Michel Luccioni has done the same thing for *Les Oeuvres Complètes de Sally Mara* (1984). Both critics stress Queneau's reading of *Ulysses* in 1929 and again at the end of the forties, his borrowings of structures, themes, characters, and even words from *Ulysses* and *Finnegans Wake*.

The second writer is Michel Butor, who published his first essay on Joyce in 1948 in *La Vie Intellectuelle*, a review of the French Dominicans. It is a very general introduction to the whole of the Joycean oeuvre, and it relies heavily on Stuart Gilbert and Joseph Campbell and Henry Morton Robinson's *A Skeleton Key to "Finnegans Wake."* A second essay, published originally in 1957 and also reprinted in *Répertoire I* (1960), deals exclusively with the *Wake*. Butor describes the impossibility of reading the book word-by-word, at the same time stressing the joy of reading it anyway. He comments also on the dream language, its roots in Lewis Carroll, the generalization of parody, and the power of the book to activate self-analysis. The description of the characters and the survey of the plot clearly derive from the *Skeleton Key*. In 1975, Butor chaired a session on "Joyce and the Modern Adventure" at the International Joyce Symposium in Paris. He stressed the influence on his own work of *Ulysses* and, even more, of *Finnegans Wake*. Since the panel itself has its own importance in the later history of French Joyce interpretations, I will return to it later. More recently Butor has contributed to the Joyce centenary section in *Le Monde*, an essay reprinted in *Répertoire V* (1982). Some of his novels have been compared to Joyce's work, among them *L'Emploi du temps* (de Labriolle 1985).

Apart from these two eminent writers the interest in Joyce in France was minimal in the first two decades after the war and Joyce is only discussed as the inventor of the interior monologue by historians of the crisis of the novel (Raimond 1966; Albérès 1972). This topic had once more become an important issue since the appearance on the Parisian scene of the *nouveaux romanciers* (Butor was considered to be one of them). The Nouveau Roman writers claimed Joyce as one of their predecessors; and although some, mostly foreign scholars agreed (Mercier 1971, 23–42; Wehle 1972; Heath 1972a), their French critics seemed to think that Joyce's interior monologue was such a subtle technique that it had not been surpassed, "only imitated and coined in the French 'nouveau roman' from 1953 onwards" (Albérès

1972, 190). In 1968 Henri Ronse even wrote, as we have seen, that Joyce by 1968 had been reduced to nothing but a precursor of the modern novel.

Robbe-Grillet mentions Joyce a number of times in his theoretical writings (1975, 11, 26, 79, 115), but mostly in vague terms. In "Nouveau Roman, Homme Nouveau" (originally published in 1961), he evokes a novelistic evolution in the names of Gustave Flaubert, Marcel Proust, Franz Kafka, Joyce, William Faulkner, and Samuel Beckett and adds that his friends do not want to make a tabula rasa of the past, "it is about the names of our predecessors that we most easily agree" (Robbe-Grillet 1975, 115). But on the whole Joyce belongs to a generation that has to be surpassed and any direct influence seems to be absent. At a Cérisy-la-Salle conference on the *nouveau roman* in 1971, Jean Ricardou disagreed with Renato Barilli's statement that Joyce had little to do with the work of Roussel and the writers of the *nouveau roman*. Robbe-Grillet replied that he did read Roussel with more passion than either Joyce or Proust (Ricardou and Van Rossum-Guyon 1974, 122).

The same holds true for Claude Mauriac, Claude Simon, and Nathalie Sarraute. Mauriac quotes Joyce in his novels *La Marquise sortit à cinque heures* (1961) and *Agrandissement* (1963), and Joyce is very much present in his theoretical writings: in the introduction to a collection of essays, published in 1958, he defines *l'alittérature* as literature that has lost the pejorative connotations of the word. Most representatives of this new kind of writing share the same language, and the criticism of their work is often interchangeable: "Most critics keep writing the same article. Only the names change, but those of Joyce and Kafka appear again and again" (1958, 133). The real challenge for the new generation of writers will be "to reconcile in one novel the discoveries of Proust and those of Joyce. Proust will then be the last in the French novelistic tradition and Joyce the first of the modern writers" (247).

Claude Simon, who does not appear among the writers of Mauriac's *alittérature*, voiced his admiration for Joyce's achievement in interviews and in correspondence (Loubère 1975, 40n). Nathalie Sarraute wrote in *L'Ère du soupçon* of Joyce as a predecessor (1964) but with enough reservation to earn her the respect of Mauriac (Mauriac 1958, 244). René Micha writes in his study of Sarraute's work that he knows no other modern novel that is not an heir of *Ulysses* and that Sarraute has been open in acknowledging her debt (1966, 61). The *nouveaux romanciers* themselves acknowledge Joyce's influence first and foremost as the inventor of the interior monologue (other models were Virginia Woolf and Faulkner). Their critics also mention the use of an overall classical structure (Albérès 1972, 143; Wehle 1972, 223). In addition, Vivian Mercier (1971) mentions the limiting of the narrated time to a single day or even an hour, and other elements taken from *Ulysses*. *Finnegans Wake* is mentioned only rarely for its linguistic innovations: Claude Mauriac identifies a genealogy that runs from Rimbaud and Mallarmé to Artaud and Joyce (1958, 10), but France had had a local advocate in Raymond Roussel.

Another symptom of the lack of critical interest is the fact that when magazines publish special issues or sections of an issue on Joyce, they have to rely almost exclusively on biographical reminiscences of Joyce's European friends and on translations of English and American critical studies. In its May-August issue of 1950, the *Mercure de France* published reminiscences by Stuart Gilbert, Sylvia Beach, Maria Jolas, and Adrienne Monnier, and thirteen years later, in an issue devoted to Sylvia Beach, more memories, some translated from the English. The *Figaro Littéraire* did the same thing in 1966: brief memoirs by Gisèle Freund, Stuart Gilbert, André Chamson, Guillaume Gillet, and brief essays by André Maurois and Jules Romains. A number of Joyce's friends published their memoirs in French: Paul Léon (1942), Philippe Soupault (1945, 1963), Nino Frank (1949, 1967), Maria Jolas (1950, 1966), and Jacques Mercanton (1967).

Another important basis for the boom in Joyce studies after 1968 was the series of translations that succeeded in making almost all of Joyce's work available in French by the end of the sixties: *Exiles, Chamber Music,* and *Pomes Penyeach* in 1950; Stuart Gilbert's edition of the *Letters* in 1961; fragments of *Finnegans Wake* and Ellmann's biography in 1962; the first *Portrait* in 1965; *The Cat and the Devil, Critical Writings* and Stanislaus Joyce's *My Brother's Keeper* in 1966; and *Giacomo Joyce* in 1973. All these books sold well too: in 1959, Michel Mohrt at Gallimard claimed that the French *Ulysses* had sold more than 22,000 copies (Handler 1961, 283).

In the same period, three general introductions to Joyce's work were published. For the series *Écrivains de Toujours* Jean Paris wrote *Joyce par lui-même*, a conventional introduction that does not differ too much from similar works in other languages and that contains the same kind of generalizations and errors: he writes that "Penelope" does not have any punctuation or pause, which is not even true of the French translation (1957, 124); a picture on page 139 depicts a different Martello tower than Joyce's, and on page 151 Paris describes Bloom choosing among three different books: "*Sweets of Sin* (erotic), Aristotle's *Masterpiece* (philosophic) and *The Awful Disclosures of Maria Monk* (monastic)," while of course all three are pornographic. Joseph Majault's *Joyce* shares with Jean Paris's book a rather romantic idea of Ireland. Jean Paris writes: "Open by night towards the infinite, Ireland is not of this world, it is a mystical place" (9) and Majault: "this wild, mystical, ferocious and passionate Ireland" (1963, 5). The book is divided into two parts: one describes *L'Homme*, the other *L'Oeuvre*. In the section on *Dubliners*, Majault attributes Stephen's description of the artist to Jean Paris and he quotes *Joyce par lui-même* all through his analysis of *Ulysses* and *Finnegans Wake*. He concludes by noting briefly Joyce's influence on the *nouveau roman*. Jean-Jacques Mayoux' *Joyce* has the same organization of the material but adds a lot of information: witness accounts, extracts, and aphorisms from the works and letters, and brief judgments from other writers. In the section on *L'Oeuvre*, Mayoux stresses first of all the importance of autobiography in Joyce, and he isolates some major themes in the three novels: the characters, symbolism, parody, and the night language. Of these three books, *Joyce par lui-même* was most influential, although Mayoux' work does not suffer from the same inaccuracies and also seems to rely more on independent research.

These three introductory studies had had a predecessor in the catalog of the La Hune exhibition in the fall of 1949. The booklet is divided in three sections: "sa vie, son oeuvre, son rayonnement," and it describes a great number of photographs, manuscripts, and letters that were sold after the exhibition and that have been dispersed or even lost since. Especially interesting is the genealogical tree that identifies eight French writers as influences on Joyce—François Rabelais, Molière, Jules Michelet, Gustave Flaubert, Maurice Maeterlinck, Stéphane Mallarmé, Edouard Dujardin, and Paul Verlaine—and a liberal number of works as having been influenced by Joyce: Louis Aragon's *Les voyageurs de l'Impériale* (1943); Valery Larbaud's *Amants, heureux amants* (1923); *Les Épiphanies* by Henri Pichette (1952); Raymond Queneau's *Saint Glinglin* (1948), and *Petite cosmogonie portative* (1950b); *Le Voyage au bout de la nuit* by Louis-Ferdinand Céline (1932); René Crevel's *La Mort difficile* (1926); *Les Mendiants* by Louis-René des Forêts (1943); *Exil* (1942) and *Vents* (1946) by Saint John Perse, and Jean-Paul Sartre's *La Nausée* (1949a), *Le Sursis* (1949b), and *La Mort dans l'âme* (1949c).

Henri Ronse's complaint about the lack of interest in Joyce was certainly not entirely correct: the author of *Ulysses* was constantly being hailed as a precursor by the postwar novelists, but his work was also translated and widely distributed and seems to have been commercially attractive enough to publish three different general introductions in just a few years. What was still lacking at this point was an ambitious, thorough, and academic reading of Joyce's work, and that is exactly what Hélène Cixous had been working on in the sixties.

TWO

Cixous, Derrida, Lacan

In the summer of 1968 immediately after *les événe-
ments* in May, Jean-Jacques Mayoux directed a doctoral dissertation by
Hélène Cixous that was published as *L'Exil de James Joyce ou l'art du
remplacement* and that still is, with Richard Ellmann's biography, the
biggest book ever written on Joyce by a single author. Cixous, for-
merly Hélène Berger, heralds the beginning of a renewed interest in
Joyce in France. Parts of her thesis had been published before in
slightly different forms, and these were incorporated later in a rather
haphazard way (Berger 1964, 1965, 1966; Cixous 1967b). The thesis
itself is only loosely structured; although it clearly belongs to the
general genre of biographical criticism, it does not have a strict chronological order nor does it focus on the individual works. Instead it
looks at a number of different themes, usually autobiographical (the
family, heresy), that it studies in detail both in the work and in the life
of the author, who is usually referred to as "Jim" or "Jimmy." The
biographical bias is explained in the preface:

> The best way to get to know Joyce is to turn to the numerous and rich
> testimonies that are available today: the majority of studies, dissertations,
> guides or collections of essays, though often interesting, are nothing but
> additional glosses on biographical documents of an exceptional quality.
> (1968, 10)

And in the introduction Cixous writes that Stephen's analysis of
Shakespeare's life by means of his writings gives the key to "a critical

method suggested by the author" (17). For Cixous, Joyce's life and work are consubstantial; his work is a copy of his life, his life is a repetition of his work. In this, she seems to belong to two traditions at the same time: that of the French *doctorat* (and the Sorbonne thesis with its emphasis on "the man and the work" in particular) and that of the Sartrean biography. One of Cixous's first reviewers calls the book "a swan song of the Sorbonne thesis at its best: objectivity and personal resonance, confident criticism and light presentation in spite of its 850 pages" (Cote, 10). The book does have the footnotes and the bibliography of such a critical work, and it has a reference to the supervisor's work in the introduction, but this does not explain David Thorburn's outburst when he calls it "Hélène Cixous's pretentious doctoral thesis" (1973, 306). This kind of reaction can best be accounted for by what is to an American critic the unsettling influence of existentialist biography exemplified by studies such as *Baudelaire*, *Saint Genet*, and *L'Idiot de la famille* and of Bachelardian thematic criticism. Cixous took from Sartre the emphasis on the earliest years of a writer's life, on his family, and on the society he grows up in: "At twenty-two, one can say that Joyce has lived his life and accomplished the ruptures he deemed necessary" (Cixous 1969b, 6). There is also the insistence on *l'autrui*: "Stephen knows from childhood that he is caught in the gaze of the other" (1968, 357) and the use of a Sartrean terminology. The book suffers from the same weaknesses as Sartre's biographies: although it is based on extensive research, it tends to be more a reflection of the author's preoccupations than of those of his subject or, as Germaine Brée puts it: "Intrinsic to Sartre's ontology, these criteria of judgment were extrinsic to the literary works under review. What they lost in objectivity, they gained in consistency" (1983, 154). This is observed repeatedly by Cixous's critics (Villelaur 1969, 10; Rossman 1973, 362; Van Laere 1970, 266; Thorburn 1973, 306f), and it is especially true in the references to Ireland, of which Thorburn writes: "Cixous's resources of condescension seem nearly limitless, and she is capable of judgments so patronizing and reductive as to move one beyond mere disagreement to a kind of melancholy awe" (307).

Another critique centers on her use of sources: like Sartre (and most French critics), Cixous reads the author's life as a novel. She relies too exclusively on Stanislaus Joyce's two books and on Ellmann, and this bias affects her portrait of Joyce's parents and his wife, Nora. This results in very schematic and doubtful judgments about people that would be perfectly acceptable if she had been dealing with mere characters in a novel: "Nora was a simple woman with a misty and sensual mind, like Gretta Conroy, like Bertha, Richard Rowan's young wife. Uneducated, unassuming, without ideas, her soul could be molded at will by him who dominates her" (Cixous 1968, 578). Cixous's book is still pre-structuralist; and in this I disagree with Thorburn, who sees structuralism as "the dominant influence." Cixous does not use "analytic techniques devised by anthropologists and linguists" (Thorburn 1973, 307), at least not in the main body of the text, and she clearly describes the structuralist approach as something that remains to be done (Cixous 1968, 11f). I would suggest that there are three sections in Cixous's book that were added later, maybe even after the defense of the thesis. These passages are different in both style and content: the appendix "Thoth et l'écriture," which was published separately in *L'Arc*; footnote 1 on page 207, singled out by Van Laere as a particularly dense passage (1970, 263); and "L'effacement des noms" (Cixous 1968, 321–41).

The first text is based on a number of studies about Egyptian religion, on *The Golden Bough* and especially on

> the remarkable study by Jacques Derrida on the origin of writing. . . . This study is a critical analysis of Plato's *Phaedrus*, published as "La Pharmacie de Platon" in *Tel Quel*, No. 32, Winter 1967 (pp. 3 to 48), "this whole essay being itself nothing, as one will soon have understood, but a reading of *Finnegans Wake*" (note 17 on p. 22). (Cixous 1968, 841)

Cixous's "Thoth et l'écriture" is a hasty confrontation of Jacques Derrida and James Atherton, although its bibliography refers to quite a number of studies. But Cixous had already been accused of simply copying Jean-Jacques Mayoux' bibliography, including its mistakes (Villelaur 1969, 10). If we look closely at the list of studies Cixous bases her analysis on, we find that Festugière, Morenz, and Vandier (the numbers 5, 6 and 7 of the bibliography) are also used by Derrida; number 3 ("The Apparition of Thoth in *Portrait de l'Artiste*") is used as a motto in "La Pharmacie de Platon" (Derrida 1968a, 19–20; 1972a, 95–96), which leaves us with only the *Wake* itself, James S. Atherton and, to a lesser degree, Clive Hart's *Structure and Motif in "Finnegans Wake"* (1962), which Cixous uses for its theory of the cross structure of the book. If we read Cixous closely, we find that most of her text remains very close to Derrida and is almost entirely made up of literal quotations, although sometimes they are not even accurate. Cixous quotes Râ's words, via Derrida, who himself is quoting Adolphe Erman (not mentioned by Cixous), but she misrepresents the pun. She writes: "The emblem of the 'ibis' (*hib*) is also a result of a pun on 'those greater than you' (*hob*)" (Cixous, 834), but *hob* means "to send" (Derrida 1968a, 23; Derrida 1972a, 101; Erman 1934, 65). Cixous's statement in the following paragraph that Thoth's modifications and his "supplementarity" are "linked to, caused by puns," finds no support in Derrida's text. When Cixous later cites from Plato's *Timaeus*, she identifies her quotation as "(p. 89)," without mentioning the edition (Cixous 1968, 836). In reality she simply copies the beginning of a longer quote in "La Pharmacie de Platon" in which Derrida uses the Stephanus references "89 a-d" (Derrida 1968a, 32–33; 1972a, 114–15).

When Cixous attempts to show the relevance of Derrida's insights to the Joycean oeuvre, especially to *Finnegans Wake*, she is considerably more successful in reading Joyce's critics than his own texts. According to Cixous, everything Derrida writes about the relationship between Thoth and Horus can be applied to Shem-Shaun. The relevance of Egyptian mythology and *The Book of the Dead* had already been studied in considerable detail by Atherton in *The Books at the Wake* (1959) and the function of the Shem-Shaun enmity for the structure of the book (Cixous, 834–35) is borrowed straight from Clive Hart's *Structure and Motif in "Finnegans Wake"* (1962). When Cixous refers directly to Joyce's texts, she disregards their context and offers very partial translations: "The right is for Shaun the Same, taken as 'Undivided reawlity' (*F.W.*, p. 292), the 'crualité indivise' of the 'Same

Patholic' (*F.W.*, p. 611)" (836). The first quotation is not necessarily spoken by Shaun, and the translation suggests *cruauté*, which is absent in the original; the second quote is more than 300 pages away.

Cixous's conclusion is as clear as it is predictable: Joyce refers to Plato's analysis and has come to the same findings as Derrida. Joyce identifies fully with Stephen, Thoth, and Shem: "Here, Joyce, author of *Ulysses*, takes his distance from every form of paternity, theology, solarity [*solarité*] or truth associated with the word" (837). It is easy to prove that this section was written after the main body of the thesis: on page 520, Cixous refers to the notion of *pharmakos* but she mentions only one Norkhrop [*sic*] Frye's discussion of it in *Anatomy of Criticism*. Derrida himself had made the reference to Frye, but only in the second part of "La Pharmacie de Platon," (1968b, 27). This again proves that Cixous must have finished "Thoth et l'écriture" before the publication in *Tel Quel* of "La Pharmacie de Platon II."

The same goes for note 1 on page 207. In terms that resemble the Derrida of "Edmond Jabès et la question du livre" and "Ellipse" (1967a, 99–116, 429–36) or the Blanchot of *Le Livre à venir* (1959), Cixous defines the death of literature as the end of the idea of the Book as the continuity of the word and the development of something new in *Finnegans Wake* "in the interior space between the word that completes itself in its beginning (and that therefore eliminates its own history) and begins in its end." The section entitled "The Effacement of the Names," printed at the end of chapter 2, also deals with such poststructuralist concerns as the erasure of names, full writing, and the name of the father (Cixous 1968, 338–41).

This tentative presence of the new ideas in *L'Exil de James Joyce ou l'art du remplacement* is replaced by full-blown deconstruction in a short essay, "Joyce, la ruse de l'écriture," a reading of "The Sisters" later published as part of *Prénoms de personne* (1970c, 1974a). This essay is fully deconstructive: there are no more references to the biography or to the circumstances in which *Dubliners* was written. The biographical bias is replaced by a Lacanian interest in the *signifiant*, in the breach of the subject, and in metaphysics. This is reflected in Cixous's style:

Quest, odyssey, of which the hero is many people, question whose answer is never that which it could have been in the interrogation itself, question that does not offer an answer itself and that has as its answer the error of the answer and as its effect the eternal rebounding of the interrogation whose point of punctuation does not know anymore where to place itself, will not place itself anymore. (1970c, 420; partly in 1974a, 239)

Cixous also refers to a "subject that deconstitutes itself in the precise moment that it constitutes itself" (1970c, 420; 1974a, 239) and she claims that in "The Sisters" we witness simultaneously the appearance of limits between the conscious and the unconscious mind and the disappearance of these limits. Like other critics associated with *Tel Quel*, Cixous is fascinated by the materiality of language: "The discourse exhausts itself in its pursuit of a meaning and it butts against the occlusion of an Elsewhere situated there by an ancient tongue (g-k *EuKlid*, *KateKhism*, *gnomon*)" (1970c, 426–27; 1974a, 246). In reality of course the "g" in *gnomon* is silent, as Cixous knows because in a footnote she writes that the word can be read phonetically as *no man*. *Gnomon* is added to the list because "g" is, like "k", a velar plosive (*occlusif* in French).

When we look at the revisions this text underwent before it was incorporated into *Prénoms de personne*, we find omissions and additions. Apart from the correction of minor errors (but "Dedalus" inexplicably becomes "Dædalus"), we notice first of all the disappearance of the references to Kristeva and Barthes, which may well be a result of the break with *Tel Quel* in 1971. Secondly, the text becomes more doctrinaire: in *Poétique* there were still two different ways of reading Joyce, one bad, one good (1970c, 424). In 1974, the bad (reassuring) reading has disappeared (1974a, 244) and a brief analysis of the opposition *unheimlich/heimlich* is gone (1970c, 422). The additions also strengthen the deconstructive tendencies in the text: the introduction of the word *déconstruire* (1974a, 241), of the unclassifiable (245), that which escapes the *Aufhebung* (246), of a discussion of the propriety of proper names (252), etc. As a matter of fact, the whole "Ensemble Joyce" in *Prénoms de personne* could very well pass as the work on Joyce that Derrida himself never wrote. This is also evident in the terms with which Cixous describes the process of rewriting in an interview with Christiane Makward, which is illustrated with a drawing of an Egyptian god who is identified as "Thor, the scribe": "Anyway it ["Joyce, la ruse de l'écriture"] is a text which is already obsolete, I reworked all that in *Prénoms de personne*. There I was working almost on the level of the signifier" (Makward 1976, 29).

Like Derrida's *La Dissémination*, which opens with a text called "Hors livre," the "Ensemble Joyce" in *Prénoms de personne* begins with a "Texte du hors" (Derrida 1972a, 9–67; Cixous 1974a, 233–37) and ends in the kind of creative lyricism with which Derrida closes most of his essays in this period. In her introduction Cixous establishes the theoretical framework of her political deconstruction:

> *all of* Joyce's gestures, gestures of writing, of his biography, went in the direction of a world-wide challenging [*contestation*] of property-propriety in all its forms, imperialism, capitalism, the family, marriage, bureaucracy, formalism, psychoanalysis, paternalism and its counterpart maternalism, etc. (233–34)

She even sees Joyce as an analyst of phallocentric discourse, and she believes that his work is "the grand opera of deconstruction" (236).

"La ruse de l'écriture" is incorporated in a first larger unit called "The Heresistances of the Subject." It sets out to show how the logocentric order "is subverted on all fronts and on all levels of the hierarchy" (237). The section on "The Sisters" is followed by a brief discussion of the name of the artist in which Cixous draws heavily on Lacan's concept of the *nom du père*, which establishes "in the Irish system" a link between the mother and God, who is also Death. Young Stephen can break out of this vicious circle only by "a work on the *name* of God" (257) and in this way also on his own name.

A third section deals with "Proteus," a chapter in which sound is essential: "one may be tempted by its incitement; by its breath which sweeps this space always same different, moving unmoving, beach-text, empty space between consciousness and the unconscious, but a constitutive emptiness" (264). In this chapter Cixous discovers a feminine style, "Here, the text, female, menstruates: the menstrual flux which supplies the rhythm and which repeats it, and the reflux-repulsion of the male subject which that kind of blood assails" (265). Whereas Cixous does make a number of bold generalizations, her readings have been, until now, very detailed, and she has not misrepresented Joyce's words. She does make some mistakes: she writes that "'Circe' is undoubtedly the mark of Lucia Joyce in her father's text" (235 note 1), after having claimed in an interview that Lucia was introduced only late in her father's work: "It is only when she has become a troubled adolescent that she imposes her presence in *Finnegans Wake*. . . . The dates leave no doubt: Lucia's problems only appear after Joyce had finished 'Circe.'" Cixous then offers the theory that the chapter was written under the influence of hallucinatory drugs used to treat Joyce's eyes (1969b, 6–7). There is in *Prénoms de personne* no explanation for the adoption of a theory that she had explicitly dismissed five years before.

In the fourth section of "The Heresistances of the Subject," Cixous looks at Stephen's attitude toward his mother in the first chapter of *Ulysses*. He is simultaneously repulsed and attracted by his mother, who is also Dublin Bay (*la mer, la mère*), Dublin itself, and Death. It is the mother who makes the textual energies function: *Ulysses* is a "text of separation" (1974a, 271). The dying mother stands for "suffering, paralysis, the threat of castration, treason, History" (272) and is interiorized by the son and transformed into the textual corpus, while at the same time, as a castrating Penelope, she weaves and unweaves the body of her son. The fifth section pursues this psychoanalytical analysis with reference to "Circe," a schizo-text which involves "the power of the Other, of the Other Sow (*de l'Autrui, de l'Autre truie*)" (275). One of the major theoretical advances effected in this book is the turn to Freud, who had been wholly absent in *L'Exil de James Joyce*. In the interview just quoted Cixous had explained her reasons for this to a rather reluctant, incredulous interviewer:

> If psychoanalysis wants to approach a work of literature, it must concentrate on the dark part which has escaped the attention of the conscious control of the creator. But in Joyce's work this part is minimal. Joyce is the opposite of a poet, he is very careful to eliminate the power of chance,

inspiration or the unconscious. You will not find a single uncontrolled metaphor in his work. (1969b, 7)

Cixous's new debt to Freud may explain why she writes that *Nothung* is Sigmund's sword (1974a, 275).

Under the next general heading "The Crucifiction," we find first the introduction to a bilingual edition of *Dubliners* by Aubier-Flammarion, entirely devoted to a reading of "The Dead." In that story Cixous identifies the two contradictory movements that also structure Joyce's other works: on the one hand the obstinate effort of the Subject that places itself at the center of the Universe, on the other hand the destruction and expulsion of the same Subject, "either as scapegoat (Bloom, Stephen), or by 'effacement,' by omission (Parnell), or by dissimulation and splitting (Shakespeare)" (290). The cruci-fiction is a machine that Joyce discovered in "The Dead" and that he perfected in *Exiles* and *Ulysses*; it is "the theater of provoked treason" (300), a concept for which Cixous refers to Marcel Mauss's "Essai sur le don" (1966) and Gilles Deleuze's *Logique du sens* (1969) and *L'Anti-Oedipe* (1975). It is from this perspective that she reads *Exiles* in the second section of "Cruci-Fiction." What Richard Rowan does to Bertha, Joyce does to his oeuvre: "The creator wants to be his other, the one who intends to ravish the creation" (306). Joyce wants to have his cake and eat it: he is God the Father, the executioner, and the Son, the crucified. Only in *Finnegans Wake* will Joyce reach some kind of a conclusion, there "the unlimited has multiple 'beginnings,' there is neither gain nor loss, only a kind of fleeting grace; and it is only there . . . that finally phallocentrism loses its hold" (311).

The last section, entitled "Trait Portrait of the Artist in his Other J'Aimot," is a reading of *FW*, 187.24–188.17. It is only here that Cixous loses all contact with Joyce's text; glossing all her misreadings and misrepresentations would take up most of the rest of this book. She follows the text closely and chronologically, offers possible constitu-ents of the puns, translations, and notes. These notes consist of her own interpretations mixed with quotations from passages in the book; one example: "To each parallel signifier corresponds a change of the code which operates in the code, German [*allemand*], French, Latin, the one illuminanding [*s'allumand*] the other, and latin me that, et que ça s'ôte pour que ça transe de votre sens-crie à notre chance-son" (319) which is partly a translation of *FW*, 215.26–27: "Latin me that, my trinity scholard, out of eure sanscreed into oure eryan!" The translations and references are haphazard at best, Cixous thinks that é-chelle is "latter" in English (321); "Burn only what's Irish" is on *FW*, 447, not on page 446; "Brulobrulo" on page 117, not on page 175. Capital letters and punctuation marks are added or deleted indiscriminately. Hélène Cixous has managed to create here a *Finnegans Wake* in her own image, and the coherence and continuity of the passage from the novel that is explicated and of the book as a whole have completely disappeared from her account of it.

An evaluation of the Joyce section in *Prénoms de personne* depends on the sympathies of the reader: if one accepts the book's theoretical premises, it may well be considered a careful and rigorous application of the theories of Lacan and Derrida to the Joycean corpus. If one cannot accept these premises, this text reveals no new insights, it uses questionable translations, inaccurate quotations and shaky biographical evidence and tells one much more about its author than about James Joyce. This observation may be found in most reviews of the book, both in the ones that accept Cixous's general principles and in those that do not. Viviane Forrester writes that Cixous's novelistic instincts (*pulsions*) are freer and more immediate in her critical work than in her novels (1975, 6). Jean A. Moreau describes the references to psychoanalysis, linguistics, and phenomenology not as "intrusions," but as "polymorphous caresses," and he subscribes to Cixous's practice of creative appropriation: "the critical language is the code itself of love" (1975, 298).

The journal *Poétique*, which Cixous cofounded in 1970 and of which she still is a member of the editorial board, devoted its twenty-sixth issue entirely to the papers read at the section of the 1975 Joyce Symposium in Paris chaired by Hélène Cixous. She introduces the volume with a short text "Fort-Sein," written in the new Joycean and untranslatable idiom (*pèrepaixtuer le régime, au moment des id(é)es de Marge*). She quite correctly observes that the attention of the critics collected in this volume goes "in the direction of a certain edge where the double—all/double or quits [*qui-tout-double*] of this text plays. Toward a certain Marge, a verge, a non-maternal femininity" (1976b, 131). Like most of Cixous's puns in this period, the title of this piece opens up an infinite series of echoes. First the Freudian/Lacanian *fort/da*, then the Derridean *seing* of *Glas* (1974) with its Hegelian and Heideggerian connotations (*Sein, Dasein, Seyn*), and then the French *sein, signe, fort, for, fors*, etc. The influence of the *Wake* on this practice must be clear and the style is even more pronounced in Cixous's own contribution to the volume. The beginning of the essay is very poetic (the repetition of *tandis que* and the long sentences) in a deconstructionist fashion that produces nonsensical sentences such as: "the insistence ends up producing its (non)-sense, i.e. its non-sense" (1976c, 240). Like the other texts in the volume "La Missexualité: où jouis-je" is a reading of pages 162–66 of *Finnegans Wake* and its theme is as simple as it is predictable; Marge is the young female who simultaneously fails to fit into the dominating system (family, history, digestion) and who makes it work:

> The margin (not the mother) or femininity as the margin of History, which makes *His-story* waver and oscillate between its poles, revives and neutralizes in the same multiple game the opposition between opposition and sexual difference: hides-breaks [*cache - casse*] the myths with which the unconscious plays during the long slumber of History. (247)

This essay suffers from the same weaknesses as the last section of *Prénoms de personne*: the chronology and the argument of the text under discussion receive less attention than the development of the critic's own writing; quotations are used in a very idiosyncratic way. As a rule few references are given, although those to *Finnegans Wake* are given in italics; but then not all *Wake* quotes are printed in italics and some of the italicized sentences are not to be found in the *Wake*. Because Cixous continually produces her own puns, it is not always clear where a word comes from. Quotations are often inaccurate and translations misleading: when Cixous writes "Just as one will receive the missage with more precision on *Finnegans Wake*, 239, history and all its histories will cease to pass again under the same phallocratic forks the day 'when the new Clitorines shall take their own powers and will be aimancipated'"(246), it is difficult to recognize the original: "When every Klitty of a scolderymeid shall hold every yardscullion's right to stimm her uprecht for whimsoever, whether on privates, whather in publics. And when all us romance catholeens shall have ones for all amanseprated" (*FW*, 239.18–21). The translation of single words is as fanciful and free (a "wop" is "a Mediterranean immigrant who lands in the U.S.A. in 1916"), and we can only conclude that this analysis clearly lies beyond the border that separates interpretation from creative reworking.

Hélène Cixous is not just an English professor at Paris VIII, first in Vincennes and now at Saint-Denis, and a Joyce critic; she is also a prolific creative writer and one of the foremost feminist theoreticians of her country. These last two activities also deserve attention, especially because her reading of Joyce's work and life has influenced both. But this is hardly the place to engage in an extended critique of French feminism, and I will just briefly outline Cixous's position and show some of the relevance of Joyce's oeuvre and her writings on that oeuvre for her project. With Luce Irigaray and, to a lesser extent, Julia Kristeva, Cixous is the most important French feminist thinker. She was involved in establishing the *Éditions des Femmes* and a Women Studies group at Vincennes. With Irigaray's *Speculum de l'autre femme* (1974) and *Ce sexe qui n'en est pas un* (1977), Cixous's books and articles are considered central in the establishment of an *écriture féminine*. That the French kind of feminism differs from its American counterpart is clear for all parties concerned. Irene Finel-Honigman has juxtaposed the two in a short article in reference to the 1979 Barnard Conference on the "Theory of Difference" and the New York University Simone de Beauvoir Conference on "Le Deuxième Sexe—Trente ans après":

The Americans accused the French of arrogance, overemphasis on theory, and a tendency to engage in sterile word games. In response, the French attacked the Americans' supposed false liberalism, "humanisme épuisé," and their inability to absorb ideas beyond nineteen forties' existentialism or to attempt to understand psychoanalytic or linguistic methodology and their relationship to feminism. (1981, 317)

American feminism is pragmatic and action oriented; the French women's movement is theoretical and aesthetic. Cixous's writings cannot be understood outside of the context of post-1968 Paris, just as American feminism is a direct heir to the civil rights movement in the United States. Cixous's approach to the feminist issues can be characterized in a number of different ways.

First there is the antihumanist stance that has been prevalent in France since the end of existentialism and that orginated in the attacks on Sartre's humanist reading of Heidegger by Althusser, Lacan, Foucault, and Derrida (Spivak 1981, 167). It is clear that, in spite of her seminal influence in France and even more so, in North America, Simone de Beauvoir has suffered the same fate as Sartre (168). Secondly, French writing on and by women is indelibly marked by Lacan's psychoanalysis and its emphasis on the Name-of-the-Father and the Phallus. Again with Derrida (in "Le Facteur de la Vérité" [1975]), Cixous opposes Lacan's phallocentric writing and opts for woman's difference (Derrida's *différance* plus sexual difference). As "the most Derridean of the French 'anti-feminist' feminists" (Spivak 1981, 172), Cixous sees woman as the exception, the exiled, the always other. This otherness is both negative because it is *excluded* by a patriarchic, logocentric discourse and positive because it escapes that determination: the female body, female *jouissance* are "the other side of language, an instinctual non-given, pre-name femaleness" (Finel-Honigman 1981, 318). French feminism's attention for the instinctual and the subjective has often resulted in a writing that is unabashedly autobiographical and self-centered.

The distinction between creative and critical writing disappears in the adoption of a concept of *écriture* that closely resembles the one developed by Derrida in *Of Grammatology* (1976): it is a powerful force of change and revolution; it writes what cannot be written, speaks the unspeakable, expresses the holes in language through which otherness can finally manifest itself. Here Cixous and her friends belong to the mainstream of poststructuralist thinking since 1968, where a political and aesthetic revolution go hand in hand, where Mallarmé and Joyce meet Karl Marx. In the States it is this literary practice that has upset feminists most, although Cixous has found support in the "'radical' fringe in French and Comparative Literature departments" (Spivak 1981, 165). Spivak finds it difficult to take seriously the claims about Joyce rising "above sexual identities and bequeathing the proper mindset to the women's movement" (169), but Verena Conley sides with Cixous's practice of creative reading and she even offers some additional puns to Cixous's reading of *Finnegans Wake* 162-66 (1977). French feminists have accepted Cixous's reading of Joyce and have acted accordingly in their own writings: Anne Bernard does not refer to Cixous at all, but she comes to similar conclusions about the role of Joyce's writing in the women's movement. Even more than the poets, the mystics, the romantic writers, the surrealists, and some recent philosophers such as Bachelard, Levinas, and Derrida, Joyce has expressed "the necessity to abandon the domination of male values in order to think and write 'womanly'" (Bernard 1980, 241). Basing herself almost entirely on Colin MacCabe (1978) and Richard Kearney (1980), who are themselves, as we shall see, greatly indebted to French thinking, Bernard writes that Molly represents "the positive and subversive values of the female principle that are repressed and alienated by the rule of the male logos" (Bernard, 242). Nicole Ward Jouve has attempted to confront Molly Bloom in "Tentative de greffe d'une colonne vertebrale sur Molly Bloom," the fourth and last part of her novel *Le Spectre du gris* (Jouve 1977). Only the middle section of this text, "Molly Bloom sens dessus dessous" refers directly to the final chapter of *Ulysses* and, probably, to the peculiar sleeping habits of the Blooms.

Cixous's own creative texts have been less marked by Joyce than one could have expected. Her first book, *Le Prénom de Dieu* (1967a), a collection of stories, is described on the cover as "simultaneously picaresque, fantastic, Kafkaesk and Joycean," but it is in reality a rather late example of the *nouveau nouveau roman*, with its I narrator, its puns, and its sparseness of details. *Dedans* (1969a), published a year after the thesis, is a very personal and autobiographical statement that resembles the stories in the earlier book. *Le Troisième Corps* and *Commencements* were both published in 1970, and they continue the autobiographical project. We encounter Eve, the mother, Georges, the father. The first book is a creative reading of Freud's interpretation of Jensen's *Gradiva* and of Kleist's *The Earthquake in Chile*, the second reads Henry James and Freud's *Essays on Psychoanalysis* and develops much further the radical use of the Wakean *écriture* that will dominate later texts such as *Le Neutre* (1972b), *Tombe* (1973), and *La* (1976a).

As we will also observe in the creative writing of Philippe Sollers, the Joycean inspiration seems to diminish in the second half of the seventies. Although they still contain Wakean puns, Cixous's texts are now turning toward Shakespeare (Conley 1977, 74), and she seems to have found a more suitable model in the works of the Brazilian novelist Clarice Lispector (1925–77). In an essay in *Poétique* (1979b) and in *Vivre l'orange/To Live the Orange* (1979a), Cixous explains how and why she has discovered this new inspiratrix.

After 1979 Cixous returned to Joyce on only two occasions: once at the centenary celebrations in the Centre Pompidou, where she gave an impromptu performance that was published in the Joyce issue of *Les Cahiers de l'Herne,* and in a review of Philippe Lavergne's translation of *Finnegans Wake.* The Beaubourg lecture ("an intervention to a large extent improvised") opens provocatively with a reference to Clarice Lispector, "whose importance is certainly comparable, if not superior, to that of Joyce." From what she considers to be the primal scene in Lispector, Cixous moves on to the first two pages of *A Portrait of the Artist as a Young Man* in which she perceives a similar confrontation with the father and the mother, between the subject and the Law. Dante, the anal mother, sets a test that the boy has to fail: his real mother sides with Dante and makes Stephen apologize in a phrase that for the first time gives the boy his proper name. In the test, which Cixous sees as an essential ingredient of every *Bildungsroman,* the lack of understanding on the part of the child is the necessary basis for a play on the signifier that will engender not only the artist himself but also his entire oeuvre, including *Finnegans Wake.*

In the review of the French *Finnegans Wake*, Cixous covers the same material but here she identifies which elements of the primal scene are relevant for *Finnegans Wake*: like the young boy in *A Portrait of the Artist as a Young Man*, the adult writer is interested more in how words sound than in what they mean: the artist is "the stealer of signifiers, the skilled amateur of the Law because he loves the *sound of the law*" (1983, 429). *Finnegans Wake* is the phoenix of literature, and this bird of paradox appears on three different levels; on the level of Irish history, the Phoenix Park is the site of the two murders that led to the attacks on Parnell for having condoned the murders in his correspondence. The letter in *The Times* can be proven to be a forgery not because Pigott "wrote 'hesitancy' with double t" as Cixous claims (430), but because he wrote "hesitancy." Through this spelling mistake Cixous traces Saint Augustine's *felix culpa* and all its variations. On the mythological level the Phoenix is his own family, much like the incestuous Earwickers and even the book itself is autogenerative: it fails to begin or to end and it always already contains everything. On the linguistic level "the phoenix is the luminous metaphor of what is at work at the heart of the wakean signifier" (432).

With Michel Foucault, the two most influential figures in the French intellectual life of the sixties and seventies are undoubtedly Jacques Derrida and Jacques Lacan. They have left a mark on the writing and thinking of young French intellectuals that can be compared only to the influence of Jean-Paul Sartre on the preceding generation. By a remarkable coincidence the three thinkers asserted themselves just before May 1968, and they were immediately identified with the resulting radical intellectual movements by critics on the right and the left. Foucault published his bestseller *Les Mots et les choses* and Lacan his *Écrits* in 1966, Derrida *L'Écriture et la différence* and *La Voix et le phénomène* in 1967. Foucault became head of the philosophy department in the militantly *gauchiste* new campus at Vincennes, where the department of psychoanalysis, for all practical purposes, was run by Jacques Lacan. Echoes of Derrida's enthusiasm for the *événements* reverberate throughout his "Les fins de l'homme" (1972c). The right-wing press at the time was quick to blame the nihilist philosophers and a number of recent left-wing critics agree. In their critical account of the thinking of 1968, Luc Ferry and Alain Renaut single out Foucault, Derrida, Bourdieu, and Lacan as the master thinkers of *La Pensée '68*, but the choice of Pierre Bourdieu as the representative of French Marxism in the sixties is misleading. Bourdieu never became a member of the French Communist Party in the fifties, and he avoided the radical movements of the sixties. Louis Althusser was much more central and influential, both in the fifties and in the sixties, especially in the poststructuralism that was introduced in the United Kingdom in the mid-seventies. It would even be possible to distinguish between the British and North American kinds of poststructuralism because there is almost no Althusserian influence in the United States at all. But the two thinkers who have been most influential in France, in Britain, and in North America are undoubtedly Lacan and Derrida: their writings have shaped poststructuralist thought and its American counterpart, deconstruction. Both are also readers of Joyce.

Jacques Derrida first read *Finnegans Wake* during a stay at Harvard in the midfifties (Hillis Miller 1982, 4). The first mention of Joyce in Derrida's published work can be found in the introduction to his translation of Husserl's "Die Frage nach dem Ursprung der Geometrie als intentional-historisches Problem," which is dated "July 1961." In a long discussion of the complex interplay between phenomenological reduction, history, and language, Derrida comes to a point where he distinguishes between two solutions for the problem of interiorizing the memory of a culture. Husserl's solution to this problem is clear: to submit the empirical language to a methodical reduction until one reaches "the actual transparency of the univocal and translatable elements" (1962, 105). An alternative is offered by a novelist (Derrida had already pointed to the resemblance between Husserl's theory of language and the poetic practice of Mallarmé and Valéry [58]), and the rival solution to Husserl's method would resemble what Joyce does:

a writing which, instead of excluding it between quotation marks, instead of *reducing* it, places itself resolutely *within* the *labyrinthian* field of a culture that is *restrained [enchaînée*] by its ambiguities, in order to traverse and to assess as contemporaneously as possible the most profound historical distance possible" (104–5).

Joyce interiorizes the memory of a culture (in the Hegelian sense) by repeating the totality of the ambiguous itself, in a language that combines the greatest degree of synchrony with the greatest amount of power in each linguistic atom. Although Derrida does not mention any specific work in which this process is supposed to take place and although he does quote Stephen Dedalus's "History is a nightmare from which I am trying to awake" from *Ulysses*, the description of the processes makes it clear that he is thinking more of *Finnegans Wake*. This early reference to Joyce's philosophical importance is not really developed here or anywhere else, but it is important because, according to Jean-Louis Houdebine, it was this mention of Joyce that made Philippe Sollers get into contact with Derrida (1983, 36; 1984, 184).

There are two more allusions to Joyce in *L'Écriture et la différence*, a motto for "Cogito et histoire de la folie," Derrida's early critique of Michel Foucault, and one with which Derrida closes his essay on Levinas: the two questions that are central in Levinas's work ("Are we Greeks? Are we Jews?") open a whole series of questions at the conclusion of Derrida's essay that ends in "What is the legitimacy, what is the meaning of the *copula* in that proposition of someone who may well be the most Hegelian of modern novelists: 'Jewgreek is greekjew. Extremes meet'?" (Derrida 1964b, 473; 1967a, 228). In a footnote the novelist is identified as James Joyce and the source of the quotation as *Ulysses*, and in the same note Derrida mentions Levinas's dislike of Odysseus but stresses Joyce's interest in Victor Bérard's theory that Odysseus was a Semite. He then places the quotation in its context:

> It is true that "Jewgreek is greekjew" is a *neutral* and anonymous proposition in the sense abhorred by Levinas inscribed as it is on Lynch's headdress. "Language of nobody" Levinas would say. It is moreover attributed to what is called the "female logic": "Woman's reason. Jewgreek is greekjew." (1964b, 473n)

This linking of Joyce and Hegel had originally been suggested by Jean Paris (1957, 56) and has been elaborated since by a great number of critics, among them: Jacques Aubert (1973), Jean-Michel Rabaté (1982a), Alain David (1982), and Geoffrey Hartman (1981). But Derrida's use of the specific quotation from *Ulysses* is extremely questionable. By providing only the rudiments of a context ("inscribed on Lynch's headdress" is not the same as "spoken by Lynch's cap"), he suggests that this statement in some way represents Joyce's philosophical views, while in reality the statement is doubly suspect; first, most obviously, as a sentence in a novel, and, then, even within the context of the fiction. The chapter from which these words are taken ("Circe") deals with hallucinations and the words are spoken by a cap in answer to Stephen's thoughts about the link between poetry and ritual. The full text of Lynch's (or his cap's) reply is: "(*With saturnine spleen*) Ba! It is because it is. Woman's reason. Jewgreek is greekjew. Extremes meet. Death is the highest form of life. Ba!" (*U*, 15.2097–98). Lynch is mocking Stephen's metaphysics and denounces it as mystical hocus pocus. The two sentences Derrida quotes are examples of faulty reasoning, "woman's reason" or oxymoron. Joyce's loyalty to his characters is never unambiguous or outspoken, but it should be clear that Lynch is not a positive figure and that his utterances cannot in any useful sense be taken as an expression of the author's opinions.

The third brief reference to Joyce can be found in the famous seventeenth footnote of Derrida's "La Pharmacie de Platon I" on which Cixous seems to have based the appendix to *L'Exil de James Joyce*. This reference is less straightforward than she suggests: Derrida had mentioned the tradition that Amon-Ra was hatched from an egg, but that at the same time he is the origin of everything, therefore also of the egg. He then writes that it would be silly to ask the "trivial and philosophical" question about the chicken and the egg, "of a logical, chronological or ontological anteriority of cause and effect." This question has been answered "magnifiquement" by inscriptions on Egyptian sarcophagi that claim that Ra is *in* the egg. "When one adds that the egg is a 'hidden egg' (1968a, 17), one would have constituted [but also opened] the system of these significations" (1968a, 22; the words between square brackets appear only in 1972a, 99). Footnote 17 reads in full:

> Cf. Morenz, *op.cit.*, p. 232–233. The paragraph that ends here would have mentioned that this Platonic pharmacy also contains and annotates all of the text by Bataille, inscribing into the history of the egg the sun of the cursed part. The whole of this essay being itself nothing else, as one will soon have understood, but a reading of *Finnegans Wake*. (1968a, 22; 1972a, 99)

First we must note Derrida's characteristically unhistorical reading of Egyptian mythology, which finds fundamental logical contradictions where his sources note only diachronic and geographic variants. The footnote is much more complex than most of Derrida's readers have realized. The prime referent is Bataille, not Joyce; there is the reference to his *La Part maudite* (1949) and more importantly to a rather obscure essay of 1955 that has only recently been included in the edition of the *Oeuvres complètes* (1988), "Hegel, la mort et le sacrifice," and that is mentioned by Derrida not here but in an essay on Bataille published the year before (1967d, 29; 1967a, 379). There Bataille mentions Irish wakes as an alternative, gay reaction to death, and he refers to "Finegan's Wake" [*sic*] (1955, 39) as an example of this custom. Bataille also talks of coffins, but Irish not Egyptian ones. It is therefore quite possible that "this essay" refers to Bataille's text, not to "La Pharmacie" itself.

When one interprets the footnote as most of Derrida's readers have done, and Derrida himself is not an exception, it becomes highly problematic. One of the three mottos of the third section of "La Pharmacie" (*The Inscription of the Sons: Theuth, Hermès, Thoth, Nabû, Nebo*) is taken from *A Portrait of the Artist as a Young Man*, but neither in the rest of the section nor in the remainder of the essay is there any more discussion of Joyce. It is only when taken in the most general of terms—like Plato's pharmacy, *Finnegans Wake* problematizes writing—that the statement makes any sense at all, and in that case it does not really tell us anything we did not know before. That Derrida can hardly be seen as a reliable witness on Joyce is further apparent somewhat later in *La Dissémination*, when, in an unacknowledged quotation from Robert Greer Cohn's *L'Oeuvre de Mallarmé: Un Coup de Dés* (1951, 109–10), the female principle in the *Wake* is described as a triangle pointing down (1972a, 367).

Joyce seems to become more and more important in Derrida's thinking in the seventies. The style and presentation of *Glas* (1974) owe a lot to *Finnegans Wake*, although neither the book nor its author is mentioned (see Hartman 1981, 2). For his introduction to a translation of William Walburton's *Essay on the Hieroglyphs of the Egyptians* (Derrida 1977), Derrida chose the title "Scribble" in reference to *Scribbledehobble* and

> to *Finnegans Wake* which may well be the best reading guide, today, for an *Essay* of which one never knows whether it is signed by a theologian or by a theoretician of the code. Joyce would have said *"for the greater glossary of code"..."Everyword for oneself but Code for us all. . ."* . . . *"Now Gode. Let us leave theories there and return to here's. Now hear. 'Tis gode again."* (1977a, 9)

These quotations, which Derrida found in the article by Jean-Michel Rabaté that he mentions in a footnote on the same page, are all taken from the *Wake* and are repeated verbatim at the end of the preface.

La Carte postale de Socrate à Freud et au-delà, too, would have been impossible without Joyce, but here he is also present in the text itself. In the semiautobiographical first part of the book, Derrida even describes a visit with Hillis Miller and Paul de Man to Joyce's grave in Zürich (1980, 160–61). He also explicitly links his discussion of the postal system with the dichotomy in *Finnegans Wake* between Shem the Penman and Shaun the Postman (154). Shem is H.C.E.'s heir ("which I translate in my own idiom as 'Here comes the person who will have me as a loved body'") who is also "YHWH declaring war by decreeing the de-routing (*dichemination*), by deconstructing the tower" (154). When he juxtaposes pen and sword by taking a number of quotations from pages 307, 3, and 211 of *Finnegans Wake*, Derrida is using Joyce to create his own opposition. He also writes:

> And there, on page 307 of *Finnegans Wake*: "Visit to Guinness' Brewery, Clubs, Advantages of the Penny Post, When is a Pun not a Pun?" Op-

posite, in the margin in italics, the names, you know. Here "Noah. Plato. Horace. Isaac. Tiresias." (155)

Derrida's quotation is incomplete: there is a close connection between the names and the essay titles in the main body of the text: the first link is Noah's drunkenness; the link between "Clubs" and Plato might be the Academy; the next phrase refers to Horace's letters, "When is a Pun not a Pun?" to the etymology of Isaac's name; and Tiresias is mentioned in connection with a title Derrida omits: "Is the Co-Education of Animus and Anima Wholly Desirable?"

One hundred pages later Derrida prepares a lecture on translation and looks up all the references to Babel in *Finnegans Wake*, presumably with the help of Hart's *Concordance* (Derrida 1980, 257; Hart 1974). Derrida is again using the text for his own purposes and he does not seem to be much concerned with an elucidation of the *Wake*. He quotes the text only when it seems appropriate to his own special concerns; on page 255 he stresses that James=Jacques=Giacomo and he quotes the last line of *Giacomo Joyce*: "Envoy: love me, love my umbrella" (but without the comma), presumably in an oblique reference to his own *Éperons* 1978a).

The same process is at work in *D'Un Ton apocalyptique adopté naguère en philosophie*, where he juxtaposes the apocalyptic idea of the prophet who tells the members of his audience that only they are awake and all the others sleep, with the tone of the *"veillée funéraire, of the Wake"* (1983, 70), where at least the capital suggests Joyce's book. Like Cixous, Derrida gave a lecture at the centenary celebrations in Beaubourg in November 1982, which was also published in the Joyce issue of *Les Cahiers de L'Herne* (Derrida 1986), and which has been included by Derek Attridge and Daniel Ferrer in *Post-Structuralist Joyce* (1985). "Deux mots pour Joyce" opens with brief introductory remarks about the two words he will be discussing: "he war" (*FW*, 258.12) and these are followed by the distinction between the two "grandeurs" of the *event* of Joyce's oeuvre (Derrida prefers "event" to *oeuvre*, or *subject* or *author*). The first of these is in an "outrageously simplified" manner the grandeur of he or she who writes "to give, by giving, and therefore to give in order to forget the gift and the given fact, that which is given and the act of giving, which is the only way to give, the only possible—and impossible way" (Derrida 1986, 204–5). The second grandeur lies in Joyce's *hypermnesia,* which always already has in its memory everything that we, as finite readers, can ever bring to the text. We can only endure this when we remember that Joyce himself must have endured it: "He was its patient, and it was moreover his theme, or better his scheme" (205). *Finnegans Wake* is a "little grandson of Western civilization in its circular, encyclopedic, ulyssean and more than ulyssean totality" (206). Derrida claims that although he has never dared to write on Joyce, "every time I write, and even in the most academic pieces of work, Joyce's ghost is always climbing on board" (206–7). He explains that note 17 in "La Pharmacie de Platon" did indeed imply that the essay had already been read in advance by the *Wake* and that "Scribble" (1977a; 1979) refers constantly to *Scribbledehobble. Glas* (1974) "is also a sort of wake" and *La Carte postale* (1980) is "haunted by Joyce" (1986, 207–8).

Joyce's ghost in *La Carte postale* is especially associated with Babel and with the passage at the end of the first chapter of Book II in which "he war" appears. Derrida stresses the biblical echoes in the passage, somewhat to the detriment of the equally clear and genetically earlier presence of Egyptian references. He lists all the possible Hebrew, German, and French connotations of the two words, and he finds that this passage suggests the Hebrew God's confusion of the tongues at Babel. In order to establish this reading Derrida proceeds in ways that resemble Hélène Cixous's: he assembles references to "Babel" from all over *Finnegans Wake,* and he links his findings to his personal preoccupations:

> And as in *Le Soleil placé en abîme* by Ponge, the red-haired whore is not far from the father, in his own bed she becomes one with him, *"In My Lord's Bed by One Whore . . .* (p. 105). It is the long series that starts with *"Thus we hear of, . . ."*. (1986, 212)

At the beginning of I, 6, after an opening prayer to Annah, Joyce lists the many names of her "untitled mamafesta." Half way through the three pages of titles we find "*In My Lord's Bed by One Whore Went Through It,*" with a pun that is more effective in Dublin dialect. Derrida has deleted the last part, probably because he wants to stress the becoming-one (*se confondre*) of the two and not the transient nature of the encounter in the *Wake*.

At the 1984 International James Joyce Symposium in Frankfurt, Derrida delivered a paper on June 12 that lasted two hours. The text was included in 1985 in *Genèse de Babel*, edited by Claude Jacquet; with "Deux mots pour Joyce," it became a separate book in 1987, and it was translated in the proceedings of the Frankfurt Symposium in 1988. Like Lacan at the Paris Symposium eight years before, Derrida spoke French. The audience was half German and half English-speaking, and the opening of the speech thematizes this confusion of tongues. Derrida's first two words are *oui oui*, which can be interpreted either as use or as mention and a decision must be made if we want to translate. From that moment on the text is punctuated by diversions and further explanations that continually break up the argument; Derrida compares this procedure to the circumnavigation of Joyce's texts, which is, paradoxically, the main theme of the paper. A second theme is autobiographical, and Derrida exhaustively documents the circumstances in which he wrote (or dictated) his text. In a third and closely related movement, Derrida links Joyce's text to a philosophical discourse and to his own earlier texts, which he opposes to the Joyce industry, the institution of Joyce studies. In *Ulysses* Derrida already detects the themes of postal difference that will structure *Finnegans Wake*. From the picture postcard and the telegram, the emphasis shifts to the telephone and Derrida claims that Bloom properly belongs to the telephone, that Bloom's Heideggerian *Dasein* (a chapter in *Sein und Zeit* is called *Der Ruf*; *anrufen* also means "to telephone") is an *être-au-téléphone*, a being-on-the-phone. Everything is always already there in *Ulysses*, which is an immense machine, and the James Joyce Foundation is an enormous telephone exchange. At the center of the exchange is Elijah who has the position YHWH occupies in Derrida's reading of *Finnegans Wake*: "All networks of communication, transport, transfer, and translation pass through him. Polyphony passes through Elijah's programophony" (1987, 92). Derrida's reading of single words is as "strong" here as it was in "Deux mots": he reads German *ja* in "Elijah" and French *oui* in A.E.I.O.U. (see also Hayman 1987, 142), but the lecture contains a minor error that does reveal something about Derrida's way of reading Joyce and, since no one challenged it, about the Joyceans' implicit trust. Another reason for the lack of reaction from the floor may be the fact that neither the majority of Joyceans nor the numerous German students had enough knowledge of the subtleties of the French language to understand what was going on. On the blackboard Derrida juxtaposed Bloom's "I. AM. A." (*U*, 13.1258–64) and Stephen's "I, I am I. I" in "Scylla and Charybdis" and compared them to YHWH's self-definition from the burning bush in Exodus (see also the picture in *James Joyce Quarterly* 22 (1985), p. 211). In reality Joyce wrote, "I, I and I. I" (*U*, 9.212), and both in the French and in the English versions the error has been corrected.

Derrida's relationship with Joyce is complex. He has stressed that his interest in literature precedes his philosophical concerns (1983, 37), and the continuing reiteration of Joyce's name in all of Derrida's texts could be used as an argument for the importance of the Irishman in his thought; with the possible exception of Mallarmé, there is no other creative writer to whom Derrida has returned so often. The reasons for this interest have not changed over the years and there is a clear continuity between the earliest references and the more elaborate later analyses: Joyce's project is Hegelian and encyclopedic, and *Ulysses* and *Finnegans Wake* are non-Husserlian attempts to encompass a culture. The only difference in the essays after *La Carte postale* is that this notion is translated in the terminology of electronic communication. Other aspects of Joyce's work that Derrida was bound to be specifically interested in include the privileging of the written over the spoken word (the impossibility of reading *Finnegans Wake* aloud); the deconstructive process at work in the *Wake*, its generalized undecidability, etc.

In order to evaluate Derrida's reading of Joyce, it is necessary to widen the perspective and to look closely at Derrida's hermeneutic.

The problems for such an exercise are obvious: Derrida is an extremely difficult thinker whose style continues to evade all easy identifications of a doctrine or a method. A superficial reading of the writings of some of Derrida's followers quickly proves that point and is, as I will show later, in itself a symptom of an important characteristic of Derrida's work. Although committed Derrideans will undoubtedly disagree, I believe it should be possible to distinguish between the general theory and the hermeneutic. It is clear that Derrida's practice of reading texts, on the one hand, and the underlying theory of interpretation, on the other, form an integral part of Derrida's general project and derive part of their validity from that project, but this does not mean, I hope, that the metaphysical end justifies all practical and tactical means.

In my doctoral dissertation (1984) I have tried to show that French thought was influenced by Heidegger and by an "existentialist" reading of Hegel from as early as Alexandre Kojève's lectures in Paris between 1933 and 1939. Although elements of Heidegger's hermeneutic had reached the public via critical texts by Maurice Blanchot, Paul de Man, and Emmanuel Levinas, Heidegger's radical later works and their application to a specific corpus were introduced in the practice of literary criticism by Beda Allemann's *Hölderlin und Heidegger*, which was published in a French translation in 1959. It represents the first attempt to isolate and present Heidegger's hermeneutic and to apply his critique of metaphysics to *Literaturwissenschaft*, to the study of literature. This genealogy of ideas, to which Derrida and his followers have always strongly objected (Derrida 1972b, 70–76) but which has been confirmed in France itself (Ferry and Renaut 1985), has the additional advantage of providing an explanation for the continuity of French thought between the existentialist fifties and the poststructuralist seventies.

Beda Allemann and to a lesser degree Jean Beaufret, Heidegger's most important French advocate and teacher of a whole generation of French Heideggerians (he was the original addressee of the *Letter on Humanism*), have outlined Heidegger's reading of philosophical texts and his attitude to poetry, more specifically to Hölderlin's work. Allemann's general thesis in *Hölderlin und Heidegger* is that the turn (*Kehre*) between Heidegger's early and later work is mirrored in a break around 1801 in Hölderlin's thinking that the poet has described as a *vaterländische Umkehr* (a national turn, but also a revolution or a conversion). Although the German Hölderlin critics and their colleagues in literary theory were not impressed, the book had a considerable success in Germany and in France, and it lies at the basis of the French Hölderlin revival in the late fifties and sixties.

Hölderlin et Heidegger: Recherche de la relation entre poésie et pensée is divided into four parts. In the first Allemann discusses the turn in Hölderlin's life and work; in Allemann's reading the poet believed that the Gods have abandoned man and that man has to complete the movement by turning away from God. This turn is accomplished in Hölderlin's madness and can be recognized in the paratactical quality of the later works. *Parataxis* is Adorno's term; Allemann uses *harte Fügung*, hard jointing, a term first employed by Norbert von Hellingrath, a student of Friedrich Gundolf and protégé of Stefan George whose edition of the later fragmentary texts by Hölderlin was used by Heidegger. In the second part of the book Heidegger's turn is analyzed and more specifically its relationship with German idealism, from which "Heidegger's thinking is separated by an abyss" (1959, 124). But the last half of the book is most relevant for our present purposes because here Allemann offers an exposition of Heidegger's manner of reading texts and of the difference between thought and poetry. With Heidegger, Allemann distinguishes between "to read one's own ideas into another text" and "a regression toward a more original point of departure," to that which is still unsaid by means of what is said (133). There are two realms, that of identity and difference and that of the Same. The first is the world of logical distinctions, of science; the second in which text and interpretation meet "leads necessarily beyond Metaphysics and the Logic that is inherent in it. The thinking of the poetic word is an essential part of the overcoming of Metaphysics" (135). Although what Hölderlin says as a poet is not identical with what the philosopher may attempt to say as thinker, "the one and the other may, in different ways, say the Same"

(Heidegger, quoted in Allemann, 135). Allemann defends Heidegger's interpretative reading practice: the etymological arguments because in earlier periods of a language's history words name with "a more elementary force" (146); language becomes language only when it is poetry (139), and poems or other texts always turn around a single central word (151). Although he concedes that from a philological perspective Heidegger's readings may be called violent, Allemann adds that their meaning can be looked for only in the aim of Heidegger's dialogue with the text, which is the opening of Being, the uncovering of the dimension of the sacred. It therefore does not make sense to argue that Heidegger destroys the poem's unity in order to replace it by his own coherence, because it is only possible "to see the poem as a creation and as autonomously coherent (the 'unity') on the basis of a previous objectification," which is always necessarily metaphysical (167).

In the last section of his book, Allemann identifies the implications of Heidegger's work for literary criticism and theory. As a science, the study of literature (*Literaturwissenschaft*) can only miss the mark; science is a part, if not one of the most essential manifestations of, metaphysics (244). But Heidegger does not simply leave the sciences for what they are, his preparation for thinking, for the leap out of metaphysics must also prepare for a way out of the sciences; in fact it must "retreat in science to gather momentum and then risk the jump toward a more original thought" (245). By its nature, science can only misunderstand and misrepresent the uniqueness of the sacred word and of the poet himself. The only form of criticism that could amount to anything is that which concerns itself with "the work itself," with the rhythm of the poem; with its vital power that "touches our own vital power, and speaks to it with a depth of contact and urgency that always comes first and that establishes all explicit understanding of the text" (277–78). It is this digest of Heideggerian ideas, together with the subsequently published translations of *Holzwege* and *Erläuterungen zu Hölderlins Dichtung* (both in 1962), that had an important immediate influence on all the protagonists in my story, on Foucault, on the Lacanian readings of the literary text, and even on *Tel*

Quel, which published Michel Deguy's translation of one of Heidegger's essays on Hölderlin.

The strange thing about Heidegger's Hölderlin is that he does resemble Derrida's Joyce; both philosophers are interested in language and especially in poetic language, both make abstraction from the historical and biographical context of a work, and both stress the singular position of the two writers in history in general, but especially in the history of metaphysics, which has, for both philosophers, Hegel and German idealism as its highest achievement. The words of the poet and the novelist are taken out of their fictional and poetic contexts and placed in a philosophical framework in which they acquire a radically different function. Whereas Heidegger has written careful and almost line-by-line interpretations of Hölderlin poems, Joyce occupies only the margins of Derrida's discourse, sometimes as a motto at the beginning of an essay, sometimes in a footnote or at the very end of the text; or Derrida isolates the tiniest fragment or even a single word. Derrida does not read Joyce's texts in the same way as Heidegger reads Hölderlin or even as Derrida reads Heidegger or Freud; Derrida evokes the Joycean text and conjures up Joyce as a tutelary god of radical *écriture.*

A critique of Derrida's hermeneutic can follow a number of different routes; first of all it can address Derrida's concentration on a single word that is supposed to contain the seeds of the text's self-destruction, *pharmakon, supplément,* etc. This technique also owes something to the psychoanalysis of dreams, but in a philosophical context Heidegger is a more obvious influence. Both philosophers have the same problems with their antihumanist hermeneutic; if humanism, metaphysics, onto-theology, logocentrism are indeed as powerful as Derrida and Heidegger claim, how is it then that some writers do manage to escape and that only the philosopher is equipped to recognize and describe their escape? The first question cannot be answered, except by referring to Hölderlin's madness as Allemann does. The second question, too, must remain unanswered, except for silly comments such as Heidegger's statement that he is the most appropriate interpreter of Hölderlin's "Der Ister" and "Andenken" because his grandfather was born in a shepherd's cot in the upper Danube region at the time the poems were written: "The hidden history of language knows no coincidences. Everything is fate" (quoted in Pöggeler 1977b, 31). Over the years Derrida and Heidegger have developed a specific style, which is based on the hermeneutic described here. Its crucial components are the radical etymologies, the puns, the paradoxes, and the oxymorons that, in the end, become explicitly literary. Apart from the obvious question about the authority of the speaker/writer, there is another aspect that needs to be thought through to its logical conclusion, that of the untranslatability of this kind of discourse. This makes perfect sense within Heidegger's philosophy; when he uses etymologies or puns, he is going back to the more original and therefore truer meanings of the words; and when he writes in a Germanic, de-Latinized German, his reasons are very simple: his native tongue is simply a superior philosophical tool:

> I refer to the special intimate relationship between the German language and the language of the Greeks and their thinking. The French confirm this to me time and again. When they start to think, they speak German; they assure me that they cannot do it in their own language. (Heidegger 1976, 217)

The same point was made by George Steiner who writes in an introduction to Heidegger's thought that this kind of philosophy is impossible in English, which is "natively hostile to certain orders of abstruseness and metaphoric abstraction" (1978, 19). Given his distrust of origins and the antinationalist atmosphere of the sixties and seventies, Derrida cannot be that clear, although the same chauvinistic mechanism is there when he hears *aigle* in Hegel or when, in his courses at Yale, he reads Schelling in French.

Like Heidegger's authority, Derrida's never comes into question; both philosophers do not argue, do not try to convince or refute. This is implicitly so in the whole French context; Jean-François Lyotard writes: "The consensus obtained by discussion, such as Habermas proposes? It violates the heterogeneity of the language games" (1980, 8). Again, Heidegger can be more explicit: "All contradicting in the field of essential thought is foolish" (quoted in Krockow 1958, 120), and most of the followers of the later Heidegger seem to accept his special status vis-à-vis *Seyn*, most explicitly David Caputo, who concludes a study of what he calls Heidegger's mysticism with the statement "One of the discomforting things about reading Heidegger's later writings is precisely the realization that the sort of thing that Heidegger does . . . is fully possible only to a few people. . . . It is an endowment, a gift of a higher order, a blessing" (1978, 263).

The width of the field of application of Derrida and Heidegger's thinking—all of Western philosophy from Plato until the present day—and the exceptional status of their own analysis necessitate an exception to the rule; if there were no exception, how could Derrida and Heidegger escape metaphysics/logocentrism long enough to describe it? As Paul de Man writes in an early essay, Heidegger's thought needs a witness ("One is enough, but there has to be at least one") and that witness is Hölderlin (1955, 807). I will not argue that Joyce occupies this position in Derrida's thought—after all there are too many other candidates (Artaud, Sollers, Mallarmé, Jabès)—but Joyce's work has the distinction of remaining a presence in Derrida's oeuvre from the earliest publication in 1962 to the present day.

Jacques Lacan's relationship with Joyce is not too different from Derrida's. His first reference to Joyce occurs in his "Le Séminaire sur 'La Lettre Volée'" in *Écrits*: "*A letter, a litter*, une lettre, une ordure. Somebody in Joyce's group (1) has spoken ambiguously about the resemblance of the two words in English" (1966, 25). Footnote 1 refers us to "*Our examination [sic] round his factification for incamination of work in progress*, Shakespeare and Company, 12, rue de l'Odéon, Paris, 1929." At the end of that book we find Vladimir Dixon's "A Litter to Mr. James Joyce," which was generally thought to have been written by Joyce himself (*JJ I*, 626; Lacan 1971, 3).

The same pun is mentioned in Lacan's article published in *Littérature* in 1971 as "Lituraterre." Although he found support in an etymological dictionary for this neologism, it started with "the ambiguity with which Joyce (James Joyce, I should say) glides from a letter, to *a litter*, d'une lettre (I translate) à une ordure" (Lacan 1971, 3). He goes on to tell the story of Joyce's refusal to his "messe-hain" (maecenas + Mass + hate) to be psychoanalyzed by Jung and adds that Joyce could not have gained anything with it that he did not acquire by himself, possibly with the help of Saint Thomas. Neither here, nor in the *Écrits* does Lacan seem to be aware of the other meanings "litter" can have, except in the expression "faire litière de la lettre" (to neglect the letter) which describes Joyce's creative practice. Lacan's reference to the *Our Exagmination* volume is not accidental; he had been an active partici-pant in the surrealist atmosphere of the twenties and was a regular visitor at Adrienne Monnier's bookshop (Roudinesco 1986, 119).

In June 1975 Lacan read the inaugural lecture at the Fifth Interna-tional James Joyce Symposium in Paris. Of this lecture there are two versions, one printed in the proceedings of the conference, edited by Jacques Aubert and Maria Jolas in 1979, and the other published in 1982 by *L'Âne*, the journal of the new Lacanian movement *Champ freudien* after the dissolution of 1981. In the first version we find Lacan at his most idiosyncratic and even the title is a pun: "Joyce le symp-tôme," symptom + holy man (*saint homme*). Let me attempt to trans-late the first sentences:

> Joyce the Symptom/Holy Man to be understood here as Jesus the Quail: it is his name. Could one expect anything but excitement/in-me [enmoi]: I name. That it makes a young man is a fall-out from which I can only draw one single thing. It is that we are men/zombies?
> LOM: in French it says that which it wants to say well. One must simply write it phonetically: that is faunetically (faun . . .), by its own measure: the eaubscene. Write that eaub . . . [water] to remind oneself that the beau-tiful is nothing else. (Lacan 1979, 13)

In this stream of unconsciousness a few themes emerge: one may be tempted to suppose that Joyce is a Holy Man because he has pushed his art as far as humanly possible; but he is not, he "joyces" too much, his pride is too great. There is no High Road to sainthood, saints are exceptions, they even become saints by renouncing (canonical) sainthood. This makes Bloom a saint, too. The meaning of Joyce the Symptom lies in the fact that one man has dreamed of avoiding the human limitations and of giving the general formula of the "S.K.beau." The surprising thing is that Joyce was able to do all that without having been psychoanalyzed first. The "S.K.beau" is one of those concepts of the late Lacan that are simultaneously all encompassing and used only in one context. I am not aware of any other text in which Lacan uses it. Here it occurs as *escabeau* (stool), also as *hissecroibeau* (*hisser*: to hoist; *croix*: cross; *croire*: to believe; *beau*: beautiful; *corbeau*: crow; etc.) and as *hessecabeau* (*escamoter*: to make away with, to juggle; *escarbot*: dung-beetle; *escargot*: snail; *escobar*: equivocator; etc.). As far as I can make out, it refers to the sum of limitations imposed on man by the fact that he has a body.

The text of the second version of Lacan's lecture (Lacan 1982) was established by Jacques-Alain Miller, "on the basis of notes taken by Eric Laurent." Lacan begins with the statement that he does not feel in top form. He takes the etymological dictionary and finds that *symptôme* used to be written as *sinthome*. Lacan intends not to parody the *Wake* but to show that Joyce's real name is *Joyce le symptôme*. Lacan recounts how he met the writer at Adrienne Monnier's and how he heard the first reading of the French *Ulysses*, a meeting that was accidental. *Finnegans Wake* was written by somebody who enjoyed writing it (Lacan uses the word *jouissance*, which also denotes sexual pleasure), but why did Joyce publish it? Joyce's structuring of the *Wake* with a cross and a circle (Lacan refers to Clive Hart whose *Structure and Motif in "Finnegans Wake"* [1962] he had borrowed from Fritz Senn for the occasion) and that which it produces, the ambiguity of the three and the four, reminds Lacan of his own Borromean knots, and he wonders how Joyce could have missed the notion of the *nom-du-père* that operates the knot of the symbolic, the imaginary, and the real. It is this paternal order that Lacan will study in his 1975–1976 seminars.

Of Lacan's seminars only a few have been published by Seuil, among them *Encore. Séminaire XX* (1975). In the fourth section of the third chapter, "La Fonction de l'écrit," Lacan writes, "the world is decomposing, thank God." With "world" he seems to refer to a unified worldview because he adds: "From the moment that you can add to the atoms something that is called a *quark*, and that that becomes the mainstream of scientific discourse, you have to realize that it becomes something else than a world" (1975, 37). This is a reference to Joyce because the name of the subparticle was taken from *Finnegans Wake*. Lacan's point escapes me completely: he apparently believes that the naming of a new discovery via literature in some way endangers the scientific worldview. He then tells his audience to start reading, not Philippe Sollers ("he is unreadable, like me"), but Joyce:

> You will see there how language perfects itself when it can play with writing. . . . The signifier begins to stuff the signified. It is because the signifiers are fitted in, fashion themselves, are telescoped into each other—read *Finnegan's Wake* [*sic*] —that something is produced, which, as signified, may appear strange, but which is really that which comes closest to what we as analysts, thanks to the analytical discourse, have to read, the lapsus linguae. (37)

Jacques-Alain Miller, Lacan's son-in-law and his sole literary executor, jealously guards the publication of the seminars and the copies that do exist are circulated only among the very loyal few. *Séminaire XXIII (1975–1976): Le sinthome*, which followed the Paris symposium, has not been published in the regular series edited by Jacques-Alain Miller for Seuil, but a number of texts, "established by J.-A. Miller," did appear in *Ornicar?*. On 18 November, Lacan opens with a reference to the etymology of *symptôme*, to Philippe Sollers's statement at the Paris symposium that after *Finnegans Wake* the English language has ceased to exist and that Joyce's works can only be read as *l'élangues*. After a brief analysis of the creation story in Genesis (language belonged to Eve before Adam started to use it), Lacan writes that Eve, as *La femme*, is not mortal: "it is another name for God and it is in this respect that she does not exist" (Lacan 1976a, 5). Against Aristotle who tried to keep the singular out of his logic, Lacan defines woman: "woman is not whole [*toute*] except in the form in which the ambiguous takes away from our empty language [*lalangue*] its point in the form of a *but not that*, as when one says *all* [*tout*] *but not that*" (5). Lacan wants to begin with the *sinthomadaquin* (Saint Thomas d'Aquin), which is quickly followed by a *sint'home rule*. Like Lacan, Joyce is a heretic, the heir of his father, *un pauvre hère-étique* (*un pauvre hère* = a poor devil) and a hero. Slowly the discussion moves to geometry and to Borromean knots, which represent the realm of the symbolic, the imaginary, and the real. The *sinthome* is the fourth factor or the father, because "perversion" is nothing but a "*pèreversion*," a version toward the father (*version vers le père*). Joyce is full of the father, and it turns out in *Ulysses* that Joyce must support by his art not only the father, but also his family, his country, and his race.

This mixture of unconnected remarks about Joyce and a very mystifying discussion of the Borromean knots will characterize all of the seminars in this series. On 20 January (1976e) of the following year, Lacan opens with the statement that his relationship with Joyce must resemble that of a fish with an apple; this is due to his lack of knowledge of English and Lacan therefore asks Jacques Aubert to take over (Aubert's presentation will be discussed in chapter 3). On 10 February (1976–1977a), Lacan describes his work on Joyce as an attempt to sweep away (*éponger*) the vast secondary literature from Joyce's work. Was Joyce mad? What is it that inspires his works? Lacan keeps turning around these questions: when he reads the "dirty letters" (edited by the "priceless Richard Helmann" [*sic*]) or when he asks Jacques Aubert whether Joyce thought of himself as a redeemer. Joyce's desire to be an artist and his obsession with his name are linked to the fact that his father had failed him. Not accidentally, Lacan's obsession with his name shows at the end of this session: he assumes that his audience will have had enough, *avoir votre claque*, even their *jaclaque* and he himself will only add *han*, "an expulsion of breath accompanying a violent action." A week later (1976–1977b), Lacan sees in Joyce's attitude to Lucia's illness a symptom of his own disorder, but the rest of the seminar is taken up by discussions of Borromean knots. In the seminar of 16 March (1977b) Joyce is not a central concern either. The text opens with the observation that nobody, not even Jacques Aubert, not even "un nommé Adams" who has done wonders in this field, has ever succeeded in finding a way of representing Joyce. There is no such way, "Joyce is an *affreud*. And he is an *ajoyce*." Lacan then moves to a discussion of the three dimensions—the symbolic, the imaginary, and the real—and the way in which they are linked. Of these three, the real escapes all determination, "because the stigma of the real is to attach itself to nothing." *Finnegans Wake* is a dream dreamed not by any particular dreamer but by the dream itself, which is what links Joyce to Jung's collective unconscious.

Although his scope is more limited, Lacan's interest in Joyce is similar to that of Derrida in that it tells us more about the interpreter than about Joyce or Joyce's works. His views on Joyce do not differ too much either: Lacan keeps stressing the fact that Joyce was an exception, his work an encyclopedia that always already contains any of our commentaries. About Lacan's knowledge of Joyce's texts, Jean-Louis Houdebine has written:

> Finally, the question is just this: has Lacan ever accepted to enter really, *personally*, into Joyce's work? Personally, I don't think so; saying this, I do not at all disregard the elements of grandeur in the disarray of a philosophy as important as Lacan's before the works of Joyce. (Houdebine 1983, 44; 1984, 191)

This statement seems to suggest that Lacan never actually read the texts, and his repeated misspelling of the title of Joyce's last work also points in that direction, but it is impossible to assess Lacan's attitudes to Joyce without looking at his general theory of language and interpretation and it is necessary to elucidate this aspect of Lacan's work before we can even begin to understand the different ways in which his work has been interpreted by his disciples. I will not deal with the details of the concepts Lacan uses (the relationship among the symbolic, the imaginary, and the real, the mirror stage, the *nom-du-père*, the Other), because these are less central to my present concerns than the thrust of Lacan's hermeneutic itself. The implied theory of interpretation in Lacan's thought is first and foremost Freudian in nature: language is communication, but a statement communicates on two different levels, there is first the manifest content—what the patient thinks he is saying—and secondly there is the latent content, in which something entirely different can be expressed. The analyst must listen carefully for irruptions of the unconscious within the stream of conscious discourse: slips of the tongue, repetitions, displacements, etc. Lacan's dictum that the unconscious is structured like a language makes this linguistic level all the more important, and he even describes the unconscious as "the discourse of the Other."

One of the descriptions given by Lacan of what happens in the psychoanalytical session implies the silence of the analyst, but even then there remains some kind of interpretation of what the patient has said: "That which is central in the analytical discourse, is always this—to that which the signifier expresses, you give another reading than what it means" (Lacan 1975, 37). This implies a knowledge or competence on the part of the analyst that is lacking in the patient: an ability to hear what is left unsaid in what is said. It is also a good description of Heidegger's manner of reading texts: there is a clear parallel between the theories of language of both thinkers. But we must look first at the influence of Kojève on Lacan's thought. Anthony Wilden was among the first critics to point to this connection (1981, 192–96). Lacan's theory of the constitution of the subject is based on Hegel's master-slave dialectic, which was discussed by Kojève in the first chapter of his *Introduction à la lecture de Hegel*, and the idea of a negative quality of language (the word kills the object) is also Hegelian (Kojève 1979, 373–74). But Kojève's reading of Hegel is not exactly a historically faithful analysis; it is a quite deliberate attempt to actualize Hegel's thought and in particular, to introduce in the Hegelian discourse the philosophical innovations associated with the names of Marx and Heidegger. Marxism was important in the discussion of the master-slave dialectic because it is precisely the slave who attains self-consciousness, not the master; and Kojève even claimed at some point that Hegel had made a mistake and that not Napoleon but Joseph Stalin was the man marking the end of history (Pinard-Legry 1981, 110). This eschatological aspect of Hegel's work remains central in Kojève's interpretation, and it leads to a radical antihumanism when he suggests that man will simply disappear at the end of history: "What will disappear, is Man properly so called, i.e., the negating Action of the given and the Error, or in general the Subject *opposed* to the Object" (Kojève, 435). But the text of this note (dating from 1946) was contradictory because according to Kojève posthistorical man would still have art, love, play. In 1968, in the second edition of his book, published shortly before he died, Kojève is even more radical:

> One should have said that the posthistorical animals of the species *Homo Sapiens* (who will live in abundance and in complete safety) will be *satisfied* in function of their artistic, erotic and play-behaviour, because, by definition, they will be satisfied with it. (436)

They will even lose language and philosophy. Kojève adds that this posthistorical stage has already been reached: in 1946 he thought it already existed in the United States, but later he realized that it was only fully present in Japan (437).

The presence of Heidegger in Kojève's philosophy and especially in his reading of Hegel's *Phenomenology* is stressed time and again by critics who have written on this extremely influential philosopher (Wahl 1955, 99; Pinard-Legry, 112; Roudinesco 1986, 154; Wilden 1981, 193). This influence is clearly "existentialist" in that the emphasis is always on death, especially in Kojève's essay "L'Idée de la mort dans la philosophie de Hegel" in *Introduction à la lecture de Hegel* (1979, 529–75). Lacan seems to have borrowed from Hegel the theory about the constitution of the subject, the theme of the power of the negative in language, and the discussion of the *belle âme* (Wilden, 284–90). But there is also a direct link between Lacan and Heidegger in their theory of language (Wilden, 200–201): both see it as preceding man: *Die Sprache spricht.* This results for Heidegger in the opposition between an inauthentic language (*das Gerede*) and an authentic speech, which Heidegger identified in his later texts with the poet's word. The appropriate reaction to the latter form of language implies listening and replying to what language itself says. In the psychoanalytic process we find a similar distinction between what Lacan calls *lalangue*, the *parole vide* (or imaginary discourse) and the liberating full Word, *logos*, which is the real agent of the talking cure. The analyst listens to "lalangue" and identifies in it the full Word, a process that ends in setting the patient free.

A number of critics have analyzed this obvious similarity between

Heidegger and Lacan. Umberto Eco was, I believe, the first to do so in *La struttura assente*. If the unconscious is the discourse of the other, this other speaks in my place: "This Other who presides over parapraxes and over madness itself, just as over the movements of thought in an essay . . ., must be the Logos" (1968, 328). The origin of this idea and of the notion of *absence* is to be looked for in Heidegger: "Although he is not mentioned all that often in the course of Lacan's writings, Heidegger seems to be, more than Freud, the root from which the whole doctrine of absence grows" (339). When we then look at an article by Cornell Mihai Ionescu, "Heidegger 'traduit' par Lacan" (1983) we have to add first that Lacan indeed translated Heidegger (Lacan, 1956), although Ionescu does not seem to realize this. His article is important because it carefully examines the parallels between the two thinkers. Ionescu comes to the same conclusions as Eco: "What Lacan calls 'the universal discourse' really establishes the same trans-subjective system of truth as the 'logos' without authors of which Heidegger speaks" (Ionescu, 95). But whereas Eco had already claimed that "the recognition of man's dependence from something that finds its origin through its own absence, makes that it can only be reached by means of a negative theology" (339), Ionescu refers to the Eleusian mysteries and to John Chrisostomos: "Heidegger's thought and that of Lacan tend asymptotically towards such an apophatic horizon" (106). Similarly Cathérine Clément writes: "Just as Dionysius the Pseudo-Areopagite was able to formulate a negative theology, Lacan defines a negative psychoanalysis" (1981, 167). Three other critics, two of them Heideggerians, find the same parallels between Heidegger and Lacan: William J. Richardson (1980), an important figure in the American Heidegger reception, and Samuel Ijsseling, who claims that Heidegger's unsaid closely resembles Lacan's unconscious because both seem to be primarily linguistic (1969, 287). H. Lang argues that the role of the subject is the same in Heidegger's philosophy as in psychoanalysis and in French structuralism (1977). As in the work of Heidegger and Derrida, Lacan's thought is founded on the assumption that literature *escapes*, that it offers privileged access to what is Other, immediate, nonmetaphysical, unconscious.

This is not the case for all kinds of literature; the three authors limit it to a restricted canon of works that include, in Derrida as in Lacan, the works of James Joyce. The exceptional status of these texts is beyond discussion; it is both a touchstone and a black hole (Schneiderman 1980, 43; Felman 1977, 199).

The problem with Lacan, as with Heidegger, is one of authority. We have seen that the analyst reserves for himself the right to interpret an utterance according not to what it says but to what it fails to say. In the same way as Heidegger, Lacan bases his authority on something outside his own self: the Other or the Logos speaks through the patient or the poet, and the analyst or *Denker* simply listens better than anybody else. If we do not accept this foundation of the thinker's authority, we have to look closely at what Lacan is doing with the texts because in that case his choices become arbitrary impositions: the unsaid is not something identifiable and definite. By definition the "unsaid" is everything the "said" is not, and any statement about it remains necessarily incomplete. Even if we accept that Lacan bases his authority on the unconscious itself, we can still question the analyst's personal authority. In accordance with a traditional Freudian psychoanalytical practice, a candidate must go through a training analysis, and he can only become an analyst when that is terminated. This has as a result that ultimately the authority of each analyst is based on that of Freud, who, alone, attained his position by means of self-analysis (with the silent help of Fliess). In Lacanian psychoanalysis this is not different: Lacan himself speaks of "the privilege which Freud's patients enjoyed in receiving its good Word from the very lips of the man who was its announcer" (1966, 291), and both friends and foes (Stuart Schneiderman and Sherry Turkle [1978] to name only two) have described the strict hierarchy of the Lacanian community in terms of the relative closeness to Lacan himself. In terms of power structures, Lacan was not an enlightened despot; his career is proof of his profound inability on the one hand to accept any authority above or beside him, and, on the other hand, to keep his disciples. The history of the different schisms and quarrels (sympathetically) documented by Schneiderman testifies to that. In his personal life, Lacan was a tyrant: "He was prone to making scenes in public, to being abrupt and rude, to expressing his amorous intentions toward women in flagrant ways" (1983, 12). By 1974 Lacan had acquired almost Napoleonic powers: Stuart Schneiderman tells the story of how Lacan simply took over the psychoanalysis department at Vincennes: nobody dared to intervene, not even the French government itself (41–43). If this is true of Lacan's private life and of his inability to keep his best students, it is equally true on the level of his theory. I believe it would be possible to argue that Lacan kept taking his theory one step further, losing some of his followers but winning others, and it would also be possible to show how the developments in his theoretical positions coincide with problems of authority (e.g., the appearance of the Borromean knots in 1973).

An important aspect of this problem of authority is the fact that Lacan hardly ever wrote anything: most of the essays in *Écrits* are really conference papers and seminars. Lacan was not a constitutional monarch either; the doctrine in the *Écrits* was not binding, at least not for Lacan. He was not even trying to communicate. In the "postface" to *Séminaire XI*, we read "When I wrote "Écrits" (writings) on the cover of the book, I wanted to make it clear that a writing in my sense is made not to be read" (Lacan 1973, 251). His reputation rests almost entirely on the *séminaires* and they remained at the center of Lacan's activity. The relationship he had with his students and collaborators is interesting in itself: when they came to conclusions different from his own or when they refused to adopt the new line, Lacan never engaged in a discussion with them. His commentary on ex-students or people with whom he had had disagreements is usually so indirect and so full of innuendo that it becomes almost impossible to understand except for the people who were directly involved. Some dissidents received an even more insulting treatment: Lacan delegated the punishment to a minor collaborator who speaks in his name. An example is Anika Lemaire's book (1970, with an introduction by Lacan), which was an attack on Laplanche and Pontalis; but the worst condemnation of all was that reserved for Deleuze and Guattari: Lacan simply ignored them completely.

His followers keep to his own interpretation of his authority. Stuart Schneiderman writes:

> Lacan was in fact always true to his own rules, which were neither capricious nor arbitrary. They were based on a Law that cannot be comprised by rules of civilized behaviour, but that determines desire as the basis for action. (1983, 22)

The irony is that Lacan's theory is perfectly applicable to this situation. It is naive to presume that one analyst would be completely free of all feelings of transference. This notion becomes the central concept in François Roustang's attack on Lacanianism:

> While they [the Lacanians] take their distance from Freud, or even, to put it differently, work out their transference with him, they are protected in this by an unanalyzed transference toward Lacan who plays for them the role of the guarantor and trustworthy interpreter. (1976, 36)

Roustang claims that every time a psychoanalyst or a theoretician pretends to know, all of psychoanalysis becomes religion once again (1976, 88) and this description of Lacan's power in religious terms can be found again and again. Cathérine Clément describes him as a shaman, a prophet, a "sorcerer driven by poetry and inspiration" (1981, 13), who teaches by means of an unconscious but efficient language (24); she finally compares his inability to communicate with that of Moses on Mount Sinai (25). This has nothing to do with organized religion, but with the impossible situation of a mystic (81). Clément, and others like her, welcome the final dissolution of the Lacanian movement as Lacan's break with an oppressive community of followers (Benoist 1980, 51), while the opponents, most explicitly François George ("The Lacanian doctrine is a Christianity which has taken a wrong turn" [1979]), also point to the effortless appropriation of Lacan's thinking by Christian theorists (Françoise Dolto and Gérard Séverin's *L'Évangile au risque de la psychanalyse* (George 1979, 91 and 92–93; Dolto and Séverin 1977). Lacan's followers even lose their own identity, a fact nicely illustrated in *Scilicet*, which published all but Lacan's own articles without giving the names of the authors.

The problematic status of Lacan's style is the same as that of Derrida's: it remains one of the prerogatives of the Master. When his followers apply it, it is regarded as either preposterous or ridiculous and most often both. Clément writes: "It is not too different from Lacan. A hair's breadth away. A century away. A rhetoric away. What one person, provided he's a poet, can allow himself to do, others can only imitate at the risk of ridicule" (1981, 47). I believe this is a central critique of both Lacan and Derrida's work: they do not offer a method that can be applied by others, precisely because it presupposes a willful authority over the text that most readers are apparently prepared to accept in Heidegger, Derrida, and Lacan, but not in anybody else. If we do not accept the authority of these writers, all relevance of the procedure disappears. It is only natural that a fundamental critique of Lacan always seems to originate outside of the sociological system he is a part of. The American sociologist Sherry Turkle has analyzed the sociological implications of Lacanianism in Paris (1978); and the German Christa Thoma-Herterich shows in her turn why Lacan is a "pure and original idealist" (1976, 141), and she sets out to identify the historical background of his thought "which today, because it recalls certain unpleasant historical memories, is not evoked anymore" (190). In her search for Lacan's intellectual ancestors, she comes to the conclusions similar to the one I have elaborated: Hegel, Heidegger, and Husserl as philosophers and further the poetical idealism of Baudelaire and Mallarmé and the symbolists in general. It is only when one approaches Lacan from the outside or when one genuinely wants to mediate his influence that one seems to find it necessary to look into his historical antecedents. Anthony Wilden's book (1981) is exemplary in this respect: he shows in considerable detail the influence of or similarities with Heidegger, Hegel, and Kojève, thereby situating Lacan in a framework that transcends the French context alone.

THREE

University Criticism

$\mathbf{A}$part from the other things Lacan and Derrida have in common, they also share a deep distrust of organizations in general and universities in particular; Derrida never wrote a real doctoral dissertation, and his whole project can be (and has been) interpreted as an attempt to deconstruct the institution of the university, while Lacan's difficult relationship with the different French psychoanalytical associations, with the École normale supérieure and with the Sorbonne is well documented, most elaborately in Elisabeth Roudinesco's monumental history of the psychoanalytical movement in France (1986). But French intellectual life differs greatly from that in other countries, and its peculiarities are often essential to understand the dynamic at work in the sixties and seventies. One of the reasons for the revolt in 1968 was the excessively rigid hierarchy, and some of the reforms in the late sixties and early seventies attempted to introduce more flexible structures. In the end, though, the *patrons* have survived 1968: the names have changed, but the structure is still intact.

On the one hand, French culture is extremely centralized; every aspect of education is run directly from Paris, the structure of the programs, the dates of the exams, their content. In his study of the sociology departments at French universities, Terry N. Clark (1973) discovered the same situation on the tertiary level of education. The whole system is strictly hierarchical with at the top one *patron* who runs a complete sector. The center of that web of power is always Paris; that may explain why so many academics may teach in Dijon, Lyon, or Besançon but live in the capital.

On the other hand, this monolithic university does not hold the monopoly in the field of cultural production; French intellectuals have in the Parisian Left Bank a most effective alternative to the university. This goes back partly to the literary *salons* in the eighteenth and nineteenth centuries and maybe also to the mid-thirties when Georges Bataille had his *Collège de sociologie*, which borrowed the name of a university but remained a successor of the different surrealist groupings. This alternative system became even more important in the forties when out of World War II and out of the resistance came a clearly defined antiestablishment existentialism with its own magazines and publishing houses. Régis Debray has even called the period between 1920 and 1960 the "editorial era" (1979).

In the climate of the sixties the opposition between the two groups became very pronounced. In *Critique et Vérité* (1966a) Roland Barthes, who was then teaching at the École pratique des hautes études, which at the time seemed to stand between the two realms, could equate "the system" with the university. The events, a couple of years later, of May 1968, can also be interpreted as a revolt against the centralized academic power structures. Since then the situation seems to have changed dramatically: the campus at Vincennes attracted the unorthodox teachers and students, and representatives of the intellectual avant-garde received the highest academic honors: Foucault and Barthes became members of the Collège de France, Derrida chairman of the Collège internationale de philosophie. But the system itself has remained intact; when Lacan had one of his underlings (wrongly) accuse Paul Ricoeur of plagiarism and when Lacan took over the entire psychoanalysis department at Vincennes, he simply did what *patrons* are supposed to do.

Most of the poststructuralist Joyce critics are such nonacademic free agents; they work for publishers or are independent writers, and they simply do not depend on the university for recognition. But the *anglicistes*, the French university teachers of English, have not been slow in adopting the new paradigm either. The most important essays of these university poststructuralists have been published in *Poétique*. Cixous's thesis can again serve as a landmark: only two critics, Jacques Aubert and Claude Jacquet, were already working on Joyce before 1968, and the new generation of university critics that appeared in the seventies was directly inspired by *L'Exil de James Joyce*.

Aubert and Jacquet have only partially adopted the new paradigm. The former, who is editor of the *Pléiade* edition of Joyce's works, has contributed to the *James Joyce Quarterly* and *A Wake Newslitter*, and he is a trustee of the James Joyce Foundation. In 1971 he defended a doctoral dissertation on Joyce, part of which was published two years later. Apart from a short article in *Change* that can also be read as an introduction to the *Wake* (1972), he has mainly published in university journals and publications.

Aubert's relationship with Lacan is important; in his seminars on Joyce, Lacan repeatedly referred with great respect to Aubert (Lacan 1976a, 3; Lacan 1982, 3). Aubert himself has published in one Lacanian magazine, *Ornicar?* (1977); he was interviewed by another, *L'Âne* (1982b); and he edited *Joyce avec Lacan*, a collection of studies (1987), in the "Bibliothèque des Analytica" with an *imprimatur* by Jacques-Alain Miller. In the article, originally a paper at the "Conférences du champ freudien," a seminar at the department of psychoanalysis at Vincennes, on 9 March, 1976, Aubert looks at Joyce's different versions of *A Portrait of the Artist as a Young Man* and finds at work there a number of factors that can be explained in Lacanian terms. Parts of the discussion that followed the paper were transcribed in *Ornicar?* (1977) but not in *Joyce avec Lacan*: they concern the status of Joyce's writing, which speculates, according to Jacques-Alain Miller, on the symptom, not on the phantasm. Lacan himself adds the observation that Catholics, much like the Japanese, cannot be analyzed "because they have already been molded by a system which the world has tried to outlive by means of Freud's analysis and this makes Freud a shy, discreet Catholic" (Aubert 1977, 17). In the interview with *L'Âne*, Aubert talks mainly about the *Pléiade* edition, which includes Joyce's early work (a second volume with *Ulysses* remains to be published). At this moment, Aubert seems to be drawn between traditional philology and Lacanian theory: "If I may define my feelings about this edition, I would say that I felt myself glide toward a naive historicism, a facile genetic approach . . . I have tried to make up for it in the Introduction, to compensate" (Aubert 1982b, 6). Aubert's introduction opens with a statement of Joyce's central role in twentieth-century world literature, which justifies his place in the *Bibliothèque de la Pléiade*. His presentation follows a traditional Pléiade pattern: Aubert briefly sketches the Edwardian age and the literary scene at the time, the political, religious, and cultural situation in the nineteenth and early twentieth century, and Joyce's relationship with Yeats. Like Cixous before him, Aubert shows the relevance of Joyce's early decisions, the break with the church, the failure of his medical studies. Aubert discusses in great detail the philosophical background of the aesthetics that Joyce developed and that he later attributed to Stephen Dedalus, before presenting the early works one by one. It is only in the discussion of *A Portrait of the Artist as a Young Man* that we encounter the references to Lacanian concepts that will, as we shall see, arouse the ire of Jean-Louis Houdebine.

Introduction à l'esthétique de James Joyce (1973), part of Aubert's doctoral dissertation, is a discussion of Joyce's early attempts at establishing an aesthetic theory. Aubert compares his own approach to that of Umberto Eco in *Opera aperta* (Aubert 1973, 11; Eco 1962a), and he builds on a suggestion of Jean Paris, who had written that Joyce's work has a Hegelian spirit. Aubert has done some very useful work in identifying the exact Aristotle translation Joyce used in Paris and in defining the different stages of the development of the aesthetic. The central thesis of the book is less convincing because there seems to be little basis for a description of Joyce's aesthetics as "Hegelian." Although Aubert proves that Joyce was deeply influenced by Bosanquet's *A History of Aesthetics* (1892), the term "Hegelian" is much too specific, and a more general label such as "neo-Platonist" or "idealist" would have been preferable. The book is also not sufficiently specific when it deals with a very complex genealogy of ideas (Hegel, Schelling, Bruno, Dante, Plotinus, neo-Platonism), which is never really disentangled or properly defined. Aubert also fails to stress Joyce's later opposition to Yeats's philosophy, which pushed him away from the "cultic twalette" and Blake, Swedenborg, Nietzsche, and neo-Platonism.

A brief essay on Joyce's definition of "epiphany," originally read as a paper at the University of Tulsa, is part of Aubert's interest in Joyce's aesthetics (1978a). He shows how Joyce describes the "epiphanies" as phantasms that project the subjectivity of the beholder onto the object and how in this way Joyce attempted to deal with the temptations of an aesthetic Platonism. In 1982 Aubert wrote a brief and very general introduction to Joyce's work, a contribution to a Joyce conference. He is very much the dean of Joyce studies in France and as trustee a representative of French criticism in the James Joyce Foundation. Without him, it seems, there would have been very little academic interest in Joyce.

Claude Jacquet, who teaches at the Université de la Sorbonne Nouvelle, first published a small book on Joyce in which she studied Rabelais's presence in the *Wake* with reference to the VI.B.45 notebook (1972). Two years later she wrote a long essay on Joyce's schemes for *Ulysses* (1974), and after another three years she published her contribution to a conference in Nantes in 1974, in which she looks at Joyce's techniques of word creation in the *Wake* (1977). A year later this was followed by an essay in which she juxtaposed a number of theories of glossolalia (including Freud's) and Joyce's technique of neologisms. Jacquet quotes Lacan and Deleuze but never moves beyond a suggestion of resemblance between Joyce's interest in language and the linguistic preoccupations of structuralism (1978). In 1979 she published an essay on Joyce's manuscripts for the early chapters of *Ulysses* and her contribution to the Paris symposium, in which she claims that Joyce probably derived the theme of water in *Finnegans Wake* I,8 from Jung or Yeats. One year later a study of the Celtic and Breton sources of the two washerwomen in the "Anna Livia Plurabelle" chapter followed (1980). Her next essay looked into the possible influence of Yeats's *A Vision* on *Finnegans Wake*. She finds a lot of resemblances between elements of the two books but admits that the two authors may have been borrowing from the same sources (1981a, 420). Another essay, published in the same year, studies the manner in which Joyce incorporated the epiphanies in *A Portrait of the Artist as a Young Man* (1981b). "Bisquebasque" (1982) is a study of Holograph Workbook VI.B.46, more precisely of the list of Basque words found there. Jacquet gives the translation of the words, their place in the *Wake*, and then some explanation of the function of Basque in general.

Claude Jacquet has continued this genetic work in a number of studies of the development of the texts of *Ulysses* and, more and more, of *Finnegans Wake*. While in *L'Herne* she has a study of the "Circe" chapter, which probably dates from a few years earlier (1986), all of the other essays concern the genesis of the *Wake*. In 1980 Jacquet became director of the Centre de recherches sur James Joyce at the Université de la Sorbonne Nouvelle and of a research program on Joyce that is part of the Institut des Textes et des Manuscrits (ITEM) and that was created in 1982 by the CNRS, the National Center for Scientific Research. ITEM organizes the work of genetic critics with special research projects devoted to the work of four French writers (Flaubert, Proust, Valéry, and Zola) and of Joyce. It collects original manuscripts or microfilms and photocopies, and it promotes the publication of new genetic editions. The Joyce study group has organized annual conferences at the Sorbonne since 1980. Work presented at these meetings has been published in three volumes, all edited by Claude Jacquet. *Genèse et Métamorphoses du texte joycien* (1985a) contains papers read at the conferences in 1980, 1981, and 1982. The second volume (1985b) is devoted entirely to *Finnegans Wake*, and *Genèse de Babel* contains a general introduction and an essay by Claude Jacquet on the development of the text of the "ALP" chapter. In the introduction Jacquet sketches the contours of what a genetic approach to Joyce's work could accomplish: the workbooks and the manuscripts do not contain the keys that will unlock the work once and for all; the unpublished pre-texts are just as mystifying as the final text. What a study of these documents does reveal is *how* Joyce produces certain effects and the emphasis of a genetic approach is centered on the process and not on the product. In the long essay that can be read as programmatic, Jacquet offers an introduction to the specific history of Joyce's text, before suggesting an analysis of the development of the "ALP" chapter, discussing almost all of the existing drafts.

The third volume appeared in 1988, when the *Revue des lettres modernes* published the first issue of a new annual series: *Scribble: Genèse des textes*, which contains a study of the "Eumaeus" chapter of *Ulysses*. Jacquet shows how Joyce in his revisions increases the level of confusion in ways that look back to techniques employed by Flaubert and point forward to the writing of *Finnegans Wake*. In the meantime another essay by Jacquet had been published in a *liber amicorum* for Louis Hay, who is the mentor of *la critique génétique* in France: "Valises ou Chimères" (1985d) discusses the nature of the puns in *Finnegans Wake*. Jacquet refers to specific words in the notebooks or the text of *Finnegans Wake* and analyzes the different components, but some of her examples are marred by misprints and questionable identifications: "zwarthy kowse and weedy brocks" (*FW*, 199.07 has "broeks") is interpreted as English "swerthy cows and weedy brooks" which is translated as "vaches brunes et des ruisseaux herbeux" and as Flemish "Zwarte kousen and widje brocks" ("black socks and shapeless trousers") (1985d, 134). In reality the line describes the typical dress of the Dutch farmer ("zwarte kousen en wijde broeken," black socks and wide or baggy trousers) as McHugh correctly annotated and "zwarthy" can be found in the *Oxford English Dictionary* under "swarthy," which means "covered with grass" or "turfy," or under "swarty," which is still only "dark" or "black," not brown.

Claude Jacquet's work has moved from a general mythological framework that draws on Poulet, Jung, and Éliade to the genetic criticism developed by Louis Hay. Her work in the latter field was seminal, and she has been responsible for the recent move away from purely poststructuralist concerns to a genetic approach in the work of the generation of younger academic Joyce critics whose work I will discuss now.

Jean-Michel Rabaté is undoubtedly the most productive of the university critics; since 1974 he has written more than twenty articles and reviews on Joyce. From his first essay, published not accidentally in

Poétique, he places himself firmly in a poststructuralist context with a reference to *S/Z* in the third line (1974, 75). Rabaté further refers to Lacan, Derrida, the group *Mu*, Jean Paris, and Benvéniste, but he is also well aware of American criticism: he quotes from Adaline Glasheen, Bernard Benstock, Jack Dalton, Michael H. Begnal, and David Hayman. He studies the *Wake* as parody and as polyphonic music and finds quite a number of correspondences. He quotes abundantly from the text of *Finnegans Wake*, but not always very accurately, and his translations are sometimes too limiting: "returnally reproductive of themselves" (*FW*, 298.17–18) is given in translation only as "retournellement reproductifs d'eux-mêmes," whereas "rétournellement reprodictifs" would have been more obvious. Rabaté's ellipses are at times questionably radical, e.g., when he writes: "[Balbus] appears in musical contexts such as on 518.28 where the 'moujique du fouture' brings on 'Thanksbeer to Balbus!', 'Bièremerci à Balbus'" (1974, 76). In the text of *Finnegans Wake* the second phrase comes six lines after the first and has little if anything to do with it. Rabaté's Derridean argument that the text always escapes analysis, that there is no single meaning (the reference to the solar metaphor comes straight out of "La Mythologie blanche") sometimes makes him force the text. His identification of the inventor/theoretician of polyphony in the text of the *Wake* seems to me unconvincing, and his policy of ignoring the coherence of a passage and finding what he wants to find is nothing if not arbitrary. Rabaté has obviously used Hart's *Concordance* in order to find the words he needed: "farce," "order," "trope," etc.; this has as a result that he misses the most obvious references: in "doubleviewed seeds" (296.01), he can see only Derrida's process of dissemination, not "W.C."; "farcing gutterish" (518.25) is for him "to stuff the Irish vulgate (*la langue du ruisseau*, 'gutter,' et l'irlandais 'irish')" (81), without noticing "Vercingetorix" in a context about resistance. Sometimes Rabaté builds a lot on nothing:

> Similarly, to the authority of the Bible (*Eccl.* 4) cited: "Nascitur ordo seculi numfit" (512.36), responds the authority of the wine . . . and of Balbus, the

joker: "In voina veritas. Ab chaos lex. . . ." This is a double gesture which installs the chaos against the order and the hierarchizing exegesis, and which also makes it engender its own law. (93)

First of all, "responds" is too much of a claim: the second quotation comes on 518.31, six pages later. Secondly, the Latin phrase is not from Ecclesiastes but from Vergil's fourth eclogue (line 5 reads "Magnus ab integro saeculorum nascitur ordo"), to which Rabaté refers explicitly in a later essay (1982c, 130). Another example occurs when Rabaté finds confirmation of his analysis in "the Preface of the official *Livre de messe* of the Church of Dublin (the one that Joyce must have used)" (1974, 94) and which turns out to be the *Book of Common Prayer*.

Rabaté has written two articles in one: the first is a general theory of *Finnegans Wake*: that it is a decentered universe in which no single *cantus firmus* can be isolated. This is true, according to poststructuralism, of any text, but the fundamental undecidability of meaning in the *Wake* was being defended even before the book was published. A second article deals with the relevance of parody and the related theme of polyphonic music. This is seriously marred by the doubtful interpretations of single phrases and the occasional disregard for context.

"Lapsus ex machina," read at the Paris symposium, deals with a passage of *Finnegans Wake* different from the passage chosen by the other critics (482.31–483.05), and it tries to show that the *Wake* is a "meaning machine," a self-generating system that does not need an author. Rabaté looks at the notion of code and finds that Joyce thought of his work in terms of an "artefact." He finds the basic form: "a structure which carries four 'homely codes'" (1976, 154) and then introduces Umberto Eco's notion of series in opposition to Lévi-Strauss's structure, in order to show that *Finnegans Wake* uses the scheme of communication and code "in order to better reject them" (155). Rabaté makes here the same mistake as in his first article; he strings together all the references in Hart's *Concordance* to a specific word and seems to suggest that Joyce in some way anticipated the debate between Lévi-Strauss and Eco. In the next section Rabaté bases himself on Austin and Lacan to show that the *Wake* is made up of "lapsus langways," and for his opposition to Austin he refers to "Signature Event Context," Derrida's reading of Austin's speech act theory (164; Derrida 1977b). This article has the same basic movement as the first: it attempts to support the theories about texts developed by Roland Barthes and Jacques Derrida with textual evidence from *Finnegans Wake*. Hart's *Concordance* is used at every step and Rabaté fails to pay attention to context and, as a result, every quotation from the *Wake* is interpreted as self-referential. Different in this article is the style of the critic, which has become more self-consciously deconstructive in its use of clichés and puns: "Il faut imaginer Anna beurreuse" (170), which refers to the last sentence of Albert Camus's *Le Mythe de Sisyphe*: "Il faut imaginer Sisyphe heureux."

In Rabaté's third major article (he also published two shorter texts in 1980), Rabaté offers in English an explicitly Lacanian reading of *Ulysses* and *Finnegans Wake*. This is clear from the outset when he defines fatherhood as a function: "paternity is that place from which someone lays down a law, be it the law of sexual difference, the law of the prohibition of incest, or the laws of language" (1981a, 74). A father is not a problem, but a nexus of unresolved enigmas, all founded on the mysterious efficacy of a Name and the father is defined by his absence. But Rabaté is offering a psychoanalysis not of the father but of "a state of language in its overdetermined articulation with politics, sexuality, and history." The first section deals with *Ulysses*, and Rabaté shows the applicability of Lacan's shift away from the person of the father to his function and his name. He stresses the religious and even mystical dimensions of this idea: "The divine procession of the Logos needs no virgin to encourage believers, but a name is necessary" (84). This is true both of Stephen, who has to write his name down before it can become a signifier, and of Bloom, whose name never acquires the status of a symbolic signifier because it never gets fixed. Molly becomes the only real presence in a world of absent males. The second section focuses on the *Wake*, which is the opposite of the earlier novel because in *Ulysses* "the dead mother is alive—the living father is dead" (93). *Finnegans Wake* also deals with a father, but now one that is truly dead and, according to Lacan, "the symbolic Father is, in so far as he signifies this Law, the dead Father" (96). With reference to Vico's *Scienza Nuova* and Freud's *Totem and Taboo*, Rabaté then looks at the murder of the father and discovers that Joyce goes one step beyond Vico and Freud in interpreting this murder as a rape of the father by the sons, which he illustrates in a close analysis of the "Buckley and the Russian General" episode. The aggression against the mother's language is related to this, and the murder of the father is only "a dialectical climax in this indefinite struggle" (107). Rabaté concludes that the effect of *Finnegans Wake* is the exact opposite of that of *Ulysses*:

> *Finnegans Wake* asserts the primary function of a dead symbolic father who allows for all the substitutions around his name. . . . The living mother Liffey flows on the contrary toward her "bitter ending" when she finally meets Death in the form of her oceanic father at the close of the book. (114)

This article starts from the same premises as the earlier ones, but it is a lot more consistent in its use of quotations; and with some exceptions, Rabaté comes closer to local context than ever before, although our evaluation of his results still depends on our acceptance of the Lacanian premises about language, paternity, symbolism, etc. The weakest point in the essay is the inclusion of biographical references, where Rabaté had explicitly excluded "the author's psyche" from his investigation (74). If the symptoms he wants to read are indeed linguistic effects, any reference to Joyce's own psyche is irrelevant.

In 1982, Joyce's centenary year, Rabaté published no less than six longer essays on Joyce. The first, "De la hauteur à laquelle l'autorité se noue (Joyce, Hegel et la Philosophie)" (1982a), was published in a special issue of *Revue des sciences humaines* devoted to the relationship between literature and philosophy. Rabaté looks at Joyce's writing from the perspective of two philosophers, Derrida and Levinas. Of the former he quotes the end of "Violence et métaphysique" (Derrida 1964b), and he briefly discusses the notions of "infini" and "totalité" in the latter's thought. He then discusses Stephen's theory of the author in "Scylla and Charybdis" and offers an elaborate discussion of

Stephen's "A.E.I.O.U." (*U*, 9.213), which functions as an alternative cogito (I owe, therefore I am) and which can be shown to be Hegelian. In *Ulysses*, Stephen rejects the notion of female (re)production and assumes the position of a self-generating, incestuous, and homosexual God. This Hegelian scheme is replaced in *Finnegans Wake* by a Viconian structure in which the reader becomes the principal character, "no longer an echo or mirror of the writing subject, but its accomplice, its extension and sometimes even its adversary" (Rabaté 1982a, 72). The style of this essay is again more restrained, and only a few puns survive (*auteur-hauteur*), but the content is very daring. The first weakness is again the use of primary texts: the passage of the *Wake* that opens and closes the essay introduces Hegel: "Au fait, Baron du Losador, quel est l'enfant de Hegel qui a écrit toute cette saloperie?" But this is Philippe Lavergne's in this case rather fanciful translation and the original has: "Say, baroun lousadoor, who in hallhagal wrote the durn thing anyhow?" (*FW*, 107.36–108.01). In a footnote we also find a translation of the first seven lines of 108. Lavergne's translation is extremely free: capitals are added indiscriminately; there is a definite change of register between "durn" and "saloperie," and finally there is the inexplicable "l'enfant de Hegel" for "hallhagal." The rest of this passage also has "vision" for "seer" and "démonstrations" for "showers." A second passage (*FW*, 389.9–19) is misrepresented as a parody on Hegel by the deletion of an important section and by obscuring the fact that two different speakers are involved: the second ellipsis deletes "(Johnny MacDougal speaking, give me trunks, miss!)" (11.17–8). A last example is a quotation from a conversation Joyce had with Georges Borach in which he dismissed all modern philosophy: "All the great thinkers of the last two centuries, from Kant to Benedetto Croce, haven't done anything but gardening." Rabaté adds "the mention of Croce must be noted, because he is usually considered a 'Hegelian'" (1982a, 71), and he concludes that Joyce was deeply influenced by Hegel, which is the opposite of what this quotation would seem to suggest. The same is true for the use of secondary sources: Rabaté refers to Aubert's analysis of the early aesthetics and concludes that Joyce "knew Hegel well" (70–71). The discussion of Dante's *Convivio* is interesting in itself, but Rabaté does not show its relevance for Joyce. Most important in this essay is the lucid discussion of the new hermeneutic created by Joyce and for which Rabaté also seeks support from Heidegger. Although, maybe in an echo of Beda Allemann, he warns against "the interpretations that force the texts to fit them into a preexisting scheme" (54), he concludes that the reader, after a long process of reciprocal interpretation of text and subject, must authorize himself to become its reader. This demands an extraordinary mental effort and the resulting authority "excludes radically both mastery and knowledge"; it is "a porous authority, open to the otherness, to the differences of meanings" (75).

Rabaté's second article in 1982 is a review of Seamus Heaney's work and of Glob's *The Bog People* (1969), which also concentrates on "Butt and Taff" in *Finnegans Wake*. Rabaté stresses the importance of the landscape, of tribal mythology, and of violence in the works of Joyce and Heaney. His analysis of "Butt and Taff" links the Freudian interpretation of myth in *Totem and Taboo* with the political echoes and with the importance of the bog, but he exaggerates the importance of the theme in Joyce's work: "The *Bog* signifies here the fundamental meeting place for Joyce, the crucial point where matter wakes up as History" (1982b, 517), which is certainly true of Heaney's poetry. This review reworks the second part of the essay published in English the previous year, interrupted by translations and brief discussions of Heaney's poems.

"Joyce and Broch: Or, Who Was the Crocodile?" deals with Broch's reading of Joyce, but some of the implications are interesting because we have observed them in other essays: the insistence on the autonomy of the reader, on the self-referentiality of the text, and, in the later essays, an interest in the "metaphysical responsibility of any work of art" (1982c, 122), its relation to "the Other, be it God, the Logos as ultimate value, or an Unconscious structured by language." This leads at the end of the essay to a quotation from Maurice Blanchot in which destruction becomes an act of love, a gift of a "boundless empty space" (132).

Rabaté's fourth essay published in 1982 is "Alimentaire et Vestimentaire dans *Finnegans Wake*," which studies Joyce's use of the motifs of clothes and food. Rabaté begins with a look at the notion of epiphany and then studies the ways in which the major characters of the novel react to food and clothes. He finds that the clothes refer to the absence of the All to itself, whereas the food refers to its cyclic reproduction: "The synecdoche of the clothes and the metaphor of food invest the two axes of the process of poetic signification and establish the multiplication of meanings on the absence of Meaning" (1982d, 275). But this descriptive method is a result of the romantic fallacy that sees the body as the supreme truth, whereas the clothes are more important because they are allegories of the work of the text: "A double subjective Moebius-ring, going from the author to the reader and representing the textual infinity, should mask the interaction of the alimentary and the vestimentary" (279). The essay is again more general, and this is evident in the use of the primary texts: "allforabit" is translated as "Toutpourun," and Rabaté also refers to "affidavit" and "Al Farabi" (a tenth-century Arab philosopher) but fails to see "alphabet" in a context about writing. His argument that there is a reference to Baghdad, where Al Farabi taught, probably refers to "bagawards" (18.32) and the scholastic theories he finds, probably in the discussion in lines 24–28, is in reality the Buddhist chain of independent origination. But Rabaté needs Al Farabi for the theme of the unity of the one and the dialectic of the same and the other. Once again our judgment of the article depends to a large extent on our prior acceptance of its theoretical assumptions, which in this case are mainly Lacanian.

Rabaté's fifth article on Joyce in 1982 deals with the notion of "idiolect" in the *Wake*, and it develops an idea from Eco, who had suggested that each individual work of art should be thought of as an idiolect. He discusses Joyce's use of the term *idiotism* to describe "citron-lemon" in "Aeolus" in Gorman's schema and an occurrence of the word in *Finnegans Wake* (299.N.3), but he does not mention the most likely source, which is James Millington's *English as She is Spoke* (n.d.), where a list of idioms appears under the heading "idiotisms."

The use of the word is then described in the force field between the singularity of writing, "a universality which would make oral all idiomatic usages in order to come closer to the perfect enunciation of an absolute Logos" (Rabaté 1982e, 114). The last section of the essay again uses material from the second part of "A Clown's Inquest into Paternity," which makes it the third time we can read the discussion of *fine*, *sept*, and *eric*. This article may be the weakest Rabaté has written: the different passages from the *Wake* he discusses have little more in common than the presence of the word *idiom* or *idiotism* and his textual analysis is incomplete or misleading; he writes "the expression 'idiot' leaves then, in note 4, the word to the mute siglas of the family" (113), which does not make any sense at all. First, there is no expression "idiot" or, as far as I can tell, no idiotic expression on this page; second, if he refers to "idiotism," that word occurs in note 3; third, the sigla are not mute: note 4 reads in full "The Doodles family, ⋔ , △ , ⊢ , ✕ , ☐ , ∧ , ⊏ . Hoodle doodle, fam.?" Also, the square or container does not only represent Dublin (120) but also the title of the book (see *Letters I*, 213; and McHugh 1976, 118). Rabaté's main argument is Derridean here:

> Joyce first gives all rights to a subjugated maternal language, oppressed by the cultural and imperialist discourses, in order to arrive at a reversal of this position later seen as maximally metaphysical, because it ends by assimilating the primacy of the mother tongue over other languages to the primacy of the spoken word over writing. (1982e, 111)

This goes too far: if Joyce really had these considerations in mind, he certainly would not have called it "metaphysical" to believe in the primacy of the spoken word. In a way this is also Rabaté's most Heideggerian paper: the two singularities of the text on the one hand and the reader on the other are mediated by the "universal of a 'we'". This "we" in the text can be described as universal only when we read the text as solely self-referential, because in the context Rabaté quotes from, the pronoun refers simply to the speakers of the passage. The "perfect enunciation of an absolute Logos" seems to give here all interpretative freedom to the reader: Rabaté remarks about "That's U"

(*FW*, 299.N.3), that "the universal escapes the limits of what one will later call 'U English' by the subterfuge of a glance on the part of the reader" (114).

Rabaté's sixth article (1982f) was published in Colin MacCabe's *James Joyce: New Perspectives* (1982a) and deals with *Dubliners*. This translation of an earlier essay (Rabaté 1981c) attempts to place the collection of short stories in the context of Joyce's complete oeuvre and to explain the theme of silence by means of which the "ideological relevance" of *Dubliners* can be ascertained. Not surprisingly, the collection of stories offers a theory of its own interpretation, the initial discouragement a reader is confronted with is "a move which has been calculated by the strategies of the text" (Rabaté 1982f, 45). Rabaté refers to Lacan's theories and uses a largely psychoanalytical framework, but he also mentions Blanchot and Heidegger. In 1983 Rabaté wrote a review of Ellmann's revised biography, of two books of reminiscences and of Aubert's *Pléiade* edition for *Critique* (1983a) and an essay on the "Sirens" chapter (1983b) that again addresses Joyce's text from a Blanchotian perspective, this time staying very close to the chapter's chronology.

A year later a brief article on the *Wake* appeared in the Joyce issue of *Europe* (1984b) and Rabaté's *Joyce: Portrait de l'auteur en autre lecteur* (1984a) was published. The essay is a general introduction to the Wakean processes of lapsus and fall. Rabaté's book is only the fourth French book on Joyce by a single author since Cixous's thesis, and it is based on his own doctoral dissertation (*Lectures critiques de James Joyce, Ezra Pound et Hermann Broch*), which had been directed by Hélène Cixous. In the introduction Rabaté describes the perspective he has adopted in his book as "the ineluctable modality of the readable." Joyce's texts turn the reader into a writer of his own reading, a reading which involves him in the play of the text, the mysteries of naming and of family ties. The locus of the Father cannot be occupied by a critic who holds an absolute authority:

This reading will appear as a decision to authorize one-self in the converging of operations effected by the presuppositions, the signifying effects and the relationship to the unconscious of the text, with the appearance of remarks that issue from my unconscious. (Rabaté 1984a, 16)

The philosophical implications of Joyce's position are similar to those in Hegel's *Phenomenology*: an emphasis on an absolutized perversion (Rabaté 1984a, 18). Most of the chapters in the book have appeared elsewhere in some form, except the third and fourth, which interpret "Circe" and "Penelope." The main themes of the book come together again at the end when the ambiguous role of criticism (always already written into the text itself) is discussed. If Roland Barthes has distinguished between the *lisible* (the readable) of the classic text and the *scriptible* (the writable) of the modern text, the *Wake* hesitates between the *scriptible-illisible* and the *lisible-risible*, while the criticism of *Finnegans Wake* tends toward "the unstable mixture of *the scriptible-risible*, the pure pleasure [*jouissance*] of a signifier beyond meaning" (158).

Some of Rabaté's essays published after his book date clearly from an earlier period: his article in the *L'Herne* volume (1986a) originally dates from 1977, and it shares the clearly Lacanian concerns of Rabaté's early work. In the proceedings of the Frankfurt Joyce Symposium, Rabaté has a paper in the panel on "deconstructive criticism of Joyce," which is a version of "De la hauteur à laquelle l'autorité se noue," and he contributed to the discussion on Lacan and to the panel on paternity. Rabaté's essay in *Genèse de Babel* (1985c), on the other hand, represents a decisive step in the direction of the genetic approach: most of the entries in the workbooks that are cited and commented on are picked from VI.B.19, one of the notebooks that the French researchers have chosen to work on. Claude Jacquet and Rabaté were the only Joyceans who contributed to the volume in homage of Louis Hay and the essay signals the latter's shift toward the genetic paradigm. It opens with an autocritique; in his early work on Joyce, ". . . concepts borrowed from rhetorics or from a modernized version of formalism were not sufficient to account for Joyce's work, its play with meanings and quotations, its linguistic creativity" (1985d: 108).

The scientific rigor of the work on manuscripts, combined with the theoretical sophistication of new hermeneutic critics such as Roland Barthes and Gérard Genette, has given rise to a new approach that functions on four different layers. The first three involve the establishment of the historical facts, the elaboration of the conceptual apparatus that is implicit in the work, and the empirical analysis of drafts and notes. On the fourth and most important level one attempts to relate the gesture of writing to the rewriting that is demanded of the reader. This essay can be read as a rewriting of "La 'missa parodia' de *Finnegans Wake*": the presence of the linguistic theories of Marcel Jousse can be confirmed on the basis of notebook evidence, that of the inventor of polyphony could not.

Rabaté's contribution to *Joyce avec Lacan* escapes from this trend toward a genetic strategy: it tries to elaborate on Lacan's statement in the unpublished seminar of 13 January 1976 that *Exiles* represents a privileged access to Joyce's central symptom: "that there is no sexual relation" (1987b, 98). The play and especially the accompanying notes hinge on a dialectic of doubt and desire that is definitely not psychotic and that alone can enable the writer to do to language what Joyce has done in *Ulysses* and *Finnegans Wake*. Rabaté's most recent article concerns the period in the middle of "Penelope," and it makes a case for its reinsertion in Gabler's edition.

From his first publication on Joyce, Jean-Michel Rabaté has placed himself in the context of a poststructuralist approach to the literary text. Independent, like the other university critics, of sectarian *groupuscules* such as *Tel Quel* and *Change*, he has developed an impressive amount of poststructuralist readings of almost all of Joyce's oeuvre. His reference to poststructuralist thought does not distinguish between Lacan and Derrida, although we can see in his work an evolution, not uncommon in France in the late seventies and early eighties, away from Lacan toward Derrida and Heidegger, Levinas, and Blanchot. In a second movement Rabaté has joined the cooperative effort of the genetic research group in Paris led by Claude Jacquet.

This evolution is even more obvious in the career of Daniel Ferrer, who belongs to the same generation of young Joyceans; like Rabaté he read a paper at Cixous's panel on Burrus and Caseous at the Paris

Symposium. In "Hissheory ou le plaisir en trop" he discussed this section of the *Wake* in Lacanian terms (Ferrer 1976); Ferrer sees in Professor Jones's parable two opposite forces at work, a first that is based on the Law, on science, and that establishes the paternal order, and a second that undermines any kind of authority and places the reader in the position of the implicated listener analyzed by Freud in *Der Witz* (1972a) (Ferrer even suggests that the professor is Ernest Jones, Freud's biographer). After an analysis of the phonetic components of this passage with concepts developed by Kristeva in *La Révolution du langage poétique* (1974a), he concludes that the fight between Shem and Shaun can be interpreted as that between the semiotic and the symbolic aspects of language. Eight years later Ferrer published a text on the "Sirens" chapter of *Ulysses* in which he briefly discusses the Linati and Gorman schemes and he proposes a reading of the chapter on the basis of its perversion of representation (1984). In 1986 another Lacan-inspired essay appeared in *L'Herne* that had figured the previous year in the volume of French Joyce essays published by Ferrer and Derek Attridge. "Circe" is read as a dream in which Freud's *Unheimliche* plays a central role. "Circe" is a dream, a distorting mirror in which the characters' neuroses are reflected and distorted, but a mirror that is an integral part of the book and that cannot be separated from it. In this chapter Joyce returns not to the referents in the earlier chapters but to the texts themselves. Another essay that exists in an English and a French version signals Ferrer's move toward the genetic approach, although Ferrer manages to combine the new and the Lacanian inspiration: in VI.B.19 he identified several pages of quotations from the third volume of Freud's *Collected Papers*, and he shows how chapter 4 of Book III of *Finnegans Wake* may be indebted to the case study of the Wolf Man (1985b; 1985c).

"Hemingway aux sources de la Liffey" (1985a) is a brief companion piece to the essay on Freud (1985b) in which Ferrer identifies the source of a number of notes in VI.B.19 as Ernest Hemingway's *In Our Time* (1925), and a year later he gave these findings a more general and theoretical framework (1986a). He returned to "Circe" in 1988 with a closer look at the early stages of the chapter that confirms his earlier findings, and the proceedings of the Frankfurt Joyce Symposium contain an essay on the decentralization of character in the *Wake* (1988).

André Topia also participated in Cixous's panel at the Paris symposium in June 1975. "La Cassure et le flux" identifies, once more, two movements in Joyce's writing: fragmentation is the primary technique in *Ulysses*, unification in the *Wake*. The first novel is marked by a complete lack of synthesis in its heterogeneous components, which Topia shows at work in "Aeolus." Surprisingly, he refers not to Lacan's notion of the objectified body, the *corps morcelé*, but to McLuhan's writings, although he does speak of the book's basic movements as one of deconstruction/reconstruction. To this "generalized heterogeneity" in *Ulysses*, Topia opposes the coexistence of "a semantic organization which goes in all directions" and a "rhythmical and phonic texture which imposes an oral and linear reading that precedes any other reading of the *Wake*" (1976a, 142). With Barthes in *S/Z*, he then tries to show the book's readability (145). The *Wake* is not unreadable in itself; it becomes unreadable when the reader concentrates on single words instead of on syntax: "The polysemia turns into an undecidable to-and-fro, the reading becomes an abyss, the text becomes a monster and the *Wake* is unreadable" (146). Critics have too long emphasized the monstrosity of the book, instead of stressing the fact that it *can* be read. Topia's aim is to discover "the modalities of a reading practice of the *Wake*" (145). In this, and in his statement that *Ulysses* is far less radical in its fragmentation than *Finnegans Wake*, Topia differs from most French Joyceans who agree on the basic ambiguity of the text.

An article in the next issue of *Poétique* was included in the collection edited by Attridge and Ferrer (1985); it tries to develop a theory of parody in Joyce on the basis of the theories of Mikhail Bakhtin. Topia finds that there is in *Ulysses* and especially in "Cyclops" a radicalization of parody in which any sense of an original disappears and in which everything is already a cliché or stereotype (1976b). Topia's next article (1982) is a review of Bernard Benstock's *James Joyce: The Undiscover'd Country* (1977), and Kenner's *Ulysses* (1980), in which he follows closely the arguments in both books and does not seem to add any of his own ideas, and in the first issue of *Fabula* Topia wrote an extended analysis of the novelistic form in Joyce's work, in which he discussed the most important American and English Joycean critics and the reactions of the early reviewers. He comes to the conclusion that it is in Bakhtin's critical work about the novel that we can find the most relevant definitions of the kind of works *Ulysses* and *A Portrait of the Artist as a Young Man* really are (1983). In Claude Jacquet's *Genèse et Métamorphoses du texte joycien*, Topia contributed an essay on "Circe" in which he shows a movement at work from the visual towards the auditory, from the impossibility of imagining the hallucinations to the phonic patterns used to describe them (Topia 1985a). *L'Herne* contained an essay on the difference between the "Ithaca" chapter and the novelistic techniques of Robbe-Grillet (Topia 1986). Topia's contribution to the first volume of the new "*Scribble*" series is a Jakobsonian study of the stylistic effects in "Sirens" (1988).

In all, Topia is one of the most open Joyce critics in France: he uses both French and American sources, and he does not restrict his attention to any one of the French cliques: he refers to Kristeva and Derrida, to Cixous and the writers of *Change*. He is the only academic critic of this generation who has not adopted the genetic approach.

Rabaté, Ferrer, and Topia were not the only participants in Cixous's panel; Claude Condou's essay is also clearly deconstructionist; he does not identify his quotations, refers to Lévi-Strauss and Nietzsche, and builds his argument on the familiar thesis: "The text therefore stages the incarnation, the materialization of the culture, its consummation by itself in the incessantly reproduced annulment by which it is constituted" (1976, 175). Condou describes the basic movements of this text, which are those of decomposition-recomposition and which result in a mutual annulment of fragments of meaning that reiterate the fundamental impossibility of meaning. He also makes numerous textual errors—Brian Bora [*sic*] is "a character from Scandinavian history" (Condou, 175)—and a large number of very doubtful or one-sided interpretations—in "demilitery" (*FW*, 166.04) he sees "une laiterie," in "athemisthued" (*FW*, 167.10), "atheist, atomist, amethyst and Themis" (175), while neglecting the more obvious *Gr* athemistos: illegitimate; in "national cruetstand" (*FW*, 165.16–17) "the signifier works, produces the French word *croûte* (crust), which hesitates, looks for and finds itself in English and in the expression 'a fragment of the true crust,' of the true cross" (177). He does not seem to be aware of the primary English meaning of the word or of the fact that Londoners used to call the newly built National Gallery the National Cruet-Stand. In an attempt to show a Lacanian view of the absent father in the text, Condou interprets "Persic-Uraliens" (162.12): "the father is fundamentally a stranger to himself (Ur: German prefix that marks the origin), he always comes from somewhere else than from his own self, and it is this elsewhere that is his origin." The term refers in reality first to Persse O'Reilly and then to the Ural Mountains, which are part of his "Coucousien oafsprung." Condou reads "Ostiak" as "a nomad, Finnish, somebody who belongs nowhere" (177), whereas Ostiak Vogul is a district in Siberia that again fits in a whole Russian subtext: Ural, St Petersburg, Caucasian, Tobolsk (a Siberian town), and in the framework of Napoleon-references: "*champ de bouteilles*" (162.11), "Coucousien oafsprung" (via German "Aufsprung": Corsican upstart). At the end of his article Condou comes to the conclusion that Marge signifies the impossibility of the passage from nature into culture, "and that is why Burrus has to exclude her on principle: 'I, having quite got the size of that demilitery young female.'" In reality it is Professor Jones, the narrator of the story, who is speaking here. Although Condou shares the general theoretical frameworks about the passage with almost all of the members of this panel, his lack of concern for the integrity of the primary text cannot even begin to demonstrate his point.

Also in *Poétique* no. 26, Michael Beausang, a North American Irishman who teaches in Paris, offers a deconstructive reading of the text that concentrates on the concept of the limit and its transgression. Beausang seems to belong both to the French and the North American context: he quotes from American sources (Jane Harrison, Francis Cornford, Norman Brown) and his essay is "traduit de l'anglais par Jean-Paul Martin and l'auteur" (1976, 231). On the other hand, he quotes from Marie Delcourt, Émile Benvéniste, and Deleuze and Guattari's *L'Anti-Oedipe*. The essay is similar to Cixous's in that it concentrates on the figure of Marge, who is the mediatrix between Burrus and Caseous. Shaun is Hermes, God of the limit and its transgression, and Marge becomes the incarnation of the Law, "as *violavit*, transgression of the law and the taboo" (224). Antonius is the father-authority who will decide between the two warring brothers: "In short, the historical survey of Jones . . . inscribes the history of the unconscious and the unconscious of history: the murder of the father, incest with the mother, fulfillment of a forbidden desire" (226). The basis of all doubt in this passage is the inability to establish a personal identity. In the notion of comedy, which is social in nature and based on the absolute relativity of everything, and in the absence of any fixed position in a world in flux, Beausang finds the synthesis that reunites the marginal and the world. In this notion of a synthesis, he differs from most deconstructionists who refuse to endorse any kind of reconciliation. Beausang has pursued this investigation in contributions to *L'Herne* (1986), to *Genèse et Métamorphoses* (1985) and to *"Scribble"* 1 (1988).

"La Condensation" by Jean-Paul Martin (1976) offers a detailed close reading of a tiny fragment (*FW*, 162.01–11) and attempts to juxtapose Joyce and Freud. Martin refers to Cixous, to earlier works by Joyce, and to Freud. He suggests that condensation is the major technique of Freud's dreamwork and Joyce's favorite artistic device in *Finnegans Wake*. Joyce's text has a number of different effects, some musical, others seductive or frightening. Martin distinguishes two sides: the side of the father, of Shaun, of obsessional paranoia, and the side of the mother, of Shem, of hysteria and of the flux of life.

Laurent Milesi is the youngest academic Joyce critic and his work belongs from the beginning in the genetic field. His first long article on the languages in the *Wake*, subtitled "Recherches thématiques dans une perspective génétique" (1985), is a careful and erudite study of the different languages in the notebooks. In *"Scribble"* 1 (1988) Milesi published an essay on the relationship between the linguistic theories of Marcel Jousse and those in Vico's *Scienza Nuova*.

Quite a number of other French critics have written on Joyce from Lacanian or Derridean perspectives: Jacques Trilling has published only one article on Joyce, a 63-page analysis of "matricidal writing" that was published in *Études freudiennes*, the journal of the Société psychanalytique de Paris, the non-Lacanian "official" organization of Freudian analysts (1973). The essay is a remarkable combination of literary analysis and autobiographical writing. The author uses both the traditional sources of Joyce criticism (Ellmann, Stanislaus Joyce, Stuart Gilbert) and almost all of the French Joyce-criticism available at the time: Paris, Cixous, Heath, Butor, and of course the theoreticians of psychoanalysis and post-structuralism: Barthes, Kristeva, Freud, Lacan, Derrida, Beaudry, Leclaire. Trilling does not seem to belong to any particular group, but his essay is a synthesis of the different ideas that were current in the early seventies: pro Lacan and contra Jung; the power of writing and the decentralization of the speaking subject; the opposition between the law of the father and the occult law of the mother. Quite a number of followers of the later Lacan have attempted to apply Lacan's intuitions to Joyce's texts: Serge André (1988) shows that if Joyce is a symptom, Victor Hugo is a phantasm. In *Joyce avec Lacan* (Aubert 1987) three analysts who belong to the faction of psychoanalysts that remained loyal to Lacan and to his son-in-law after the dissolution of the École de la cause freudienne in 1981 focus on different aspects of Joyce's work. Annie Tardits (1987) looks at Joyce's attitude to heresy and to the theology of Stephen's aesthetics. She confronts the theological discussion about the Trinity with Lacan's writings about paternity, and she seems to belong to the faction of the religious Lacanians. Cathérine Millot was, with Stuart Schneiderman, one of the six new teachers who replaced dissidents when Miller and Lacan took over the psychoanalysis department at Vincennes. In her contribution to *Joyce avec Lacan* Millot discusses the relationship between Joyce and the mystics: both encounter the Lacanian "real," that which is radically different. Whereas mystics attempt to symbolize this Other by means of metaphors, Joyce works with metonymies (1987). A shorter version of this paper was published in the proceedings of the Frankfurt Symposium (Benstock 1988). In his contribution to the Frankfurt Symposium and to *Joyce avec Lacan*, Jean-Guy Godin, too, stays close to Lacan's analysis of the *sinthome*, to the point of simply repeating the main ideas of the seminar on Joyce.

Ultimately all of these orthodox Lacanian critics read Joyce's texts as nothing more than a symptom; Joyce has always already known what Lacan would teach and one can only agree with Elisabeth Roudinesco when she writes of one of Lacan's few essays of literary criticism that it is full of "de formidables banalités" (1986, 527) and that "the Lacanians are incapable of seeing in literature anything more than the confirmation of their doctrinal positions" (532).

The group of Derridean critics at work on Joyce is smaller. This has much to do with the fact that, as a philosopher, Derrida is less important in France than he is made out to be in the States. By the end of the seventies, Joyce had reached a status similar to Friedrich Hölderlin's in the sixties, and this resulted in a radical use of Joyce's texts (or fragments of them) for purposes other than the interpretation of Joyce. Two articles by Alain David serve as illustrations of this phenomenon: the first essay in which he mentions Joyce is a reading of Levinas that concentrates on the problem of Jewishness in general. David tries to show that there is always an outside, and that this is, in the Western world, Jewishness. In the philosophy of Hegel, this is all the more clear, and David looks in some detail at its analysis of Jewish thinking and claims that anti-Semitism lies at the root of all Western thought. Jewishness is the radical Other, that which cannot really exist: "language without the verb to be holy, Hebrew language. Literature" (1980, 49). Joyce's role is minimal: David starts his article with a quote from "Ithaca": "He thought that he thought that he was a jew, whereas he knew that he knew that he knew that he was not" (*U*, 17.527–31). David concludes, "In this way non-Jewishness is the motif of all knowledge and of the knowledge of knowledge; Jewishness is, for the person who lives it, an opinion of an opinion, less than an ignorance" (43). This is simply not true: the "encyclopedic" perspective of "Ithaca" makes such a reading impossible. David reads this phrase completely out of context and makes of it a fundamental philosophical insight. He underestimates the complexity of the passage: in reality the two answers deal exclusively with what Bloom thinks about Stephen, the Jew about the Gentile. The second essay, originally "a presentation in 1980 for Jacques Derrida's seminar in the École normale supérieure at the rue d'Ulm" (David 1982, 161), deals mainly with the relationship between Hegel and Kant, which is expressed at the end of the essay in a familiar fashion:

> What, reduced to their simplest reciprocal form, would have been Kant's thoughts about Hegel's thoughts about Kant, and Kant's thoughts about Hegel's thoughts about Kant's thoughts about Hegel?
> He thought that he thought that he was a jew whereas he knew that he knew that he knew that he was not. (174)

But not all university *anglicistes* write in the poststructuralist tradition; studies are still being published that remain within the limits of prestructuralist criticism: Louis Bonnerot's *"Ulysses" cinquante ans après* (1974) assembles American, Irish, and French studies that are, except for an essay by Hélène Cixous (section B.1 from "Les Hérésistances du sujet" in *Prénoms de personne* [1974b]) traditional (Guiguet, Jacquet, Mayoux, Vitoux, Bonnerot, and Aubert). The same can be said about most of the contributions in the Joyce issues published by *Études irlandaises* and *Europe* (Cortanze [1984a, 1984b], Stéphane [1984], Lemaire [1984], Dauphiné [1984], Minière [1984]) and even those in Jacquet's *Genèse et Métamorphoses* (1985a) (Noel, Monod, Lojkine-Morelec, de Labriolle). Most of the traditional academics tend to publish in journals devoted to Irish literature: *Gaéliana* (Caen), *Études irlandaises* (Lille), *Études anglaises*, and *Cahiers du centre d'études irlandaises* (Rennes); and they are generally more interested in Joyce's Irishness than in his (post)modernity, the studies by Nelly Gensbourger (1976), Jacqueline Genet (1981), Claude Fierobe (n.d.), Jean-Claude Bouffard (1984), Michel Bariou (1982), Jacky Martin (1982), Danièle Sallenave (1972), and many others all belong in this category. One could even claim that the approach followed by most French *anglicistes* remains traditional and that it is only when a wider audience is reached that the poststructuralist bias gets stronger.

The first significant confrontation between the international Joyce industry and the French Joyce took place at the Fifth International James Joyce Symposium in Paris in June 1975. After the puzzling opening lecture by Lacan (at which indignant or simply bored Joyceans who decided to go for a stroll through Paris found they couldn't leave the room because the doors had been locked), the visiting Joyceans were confronted with the additional problem of having to distinguish among no fewer than three different French Joyces: one based on an academic application of Lacan's theories, one on the political reading of *Tel Quel*'s Philippe Sollers, and finally the equally political interpretation of the members of the *Change* collective. *Tel Quel* will be discussed in chapter 4, here I will present the work of Jean Paris, Jean Pierre Faye and Mitsou Ronat.

Even to a careful observer, the difference between *Tel Quel* and *Change* is not all that obvious: both use an explicitly Marxist and Freudian rhetoric, both refer to structuralist and poststructuralist thinkers and both consider Mallarmé, Saussure, and the Russian formalists as precursors. Although both groups were active in May 1968, there are political differences, too: *Change* never became Maoist and did not join the *nouveaux philosophes*' condemnation of Soviet Russia as early as 1976 when *Tel Quel* did. *Change*'s politics are close to Chomsky's, of whom they also borrow the transformational grammar, which is described by their opponents in the jargon of the day as "the anarchizing technocratic ideology of an imperialism reaching its breaking point" (*Tel Quel*, no. 38 (1969), iv). Both groups were close to the French communist party, which had had a turbulent relationship with its intellectuals for most of its history. Central in the discussion in the sixties was Louis Althusser who became "caïman" (director of studies) in the École normale supérieure, where he deeply influenced several generations of intellectuals. Until the mid-fifties the *parti communiste* had followed Moscow's anti-Freudian doctrines, and when Stalin died in 1953, the general liberalization also altered the party's attitude toward Freud and to structuralism. In the wake of the de-Stalinization Althusser attempted to introduce a structuralist and nonhumanist Marxist philosophy. From the early sixties he and his assistants, Jacques-Alain Miller and Pierre Macherey, taught structuralism at the École normale supérieure and in 1963 Lacan's work became the focus of Althusser's teaching. Althusser marked the beginning of a theoretical conjunction of Marxism, structuralism, and psychoanalysis in 1964 with an essay on Lacan in *Nouvelle Critique* (1976), the journal of the Parti Communiste intellectuals, and a new structuralist reading of Marx in *Lire le Capital* and *Pour Marx*. The official party ideologues, who had just effected a break with the Stalinist tendencies, resented the return to a revolutionary Leninism and especially Althusser's interest in Mao and China. A break became inevitable between, on the one hand, a party that was intent on forgetting its Stalinist past and that wanted to show an interest in problems that had little or nothing to do with the class-struggle—sexual liberation, contraception, feminism, etc.—and, on the other hand, a radically antihumanist tendency that branded as "revisionist" all attempts to compromise the revolutionary legacy. Not accidentally the break occurred in the student group at the *Rue d'Ulm* and a pro-China student organization was created that would become, after May 1968, *la gauche prolétarienne*, the Maoist Marxist-Leninist movement. In 1967 attempts were made to bridge the gap between *Nouvelle Critique* and *Tel Quel*, which had been drifting toward Althusser's position and maoism. The go-between was Jean-Louis Houdebine, a member of the party. As good Maoists, the *telqueliens* believed that with the science of writing they had developed "a single proletarian line" in aesthetic matters, while their opponents defended a pluralism of aesthetic forms because they saw in the single line a return to Stalinism. In the following few years *Change* opposed *Tel Quel* from a more liberal and open position.

That the two journals have so much in common is only normal: Jean Pierre Faye was a member of *Tel Quel*'s editorial board until the autumn of 1967, when he left after a quarrel with Sollers. The first manifesto of *Change* was proclaimed in Havana on 8 January 1968, and the first issue appeared in the spring of the same year at Seuil, the publishers of *Tel Quel*. Of the founding members of *Change*, three had contributed to *Tel Quel*: Faye, Jean Paris, and Maurice Roche.

Because of the very aggressive attacks and counteroffensives between the two journals, Faye was forced to leave Seuil and take *Change* to Seghers/Laffont. Like *Tel Quel*, the new collective also started a series of book-length studies (the Collection *Change*).

Jean Paris is the dean of Joyce studies in France: his *Joyce par lui-même* (1957) and especially his statement that Joyce is a "Hegelian" had an enormous influence on nearly all French Joyce critics. Since 1957, Paris had published a short sketch on *Ulysses* (1962) and another on Hamlet in which he discussed the psychoanalytical interpretation offered by Stephen in *Ulysses* (1966). His essay in one of *Tel Quel*'s Joyce issues (no. 30, 1967) refers both to Mallarmé and to the Russian formalists whose ideas had just been introduced in France by Tzvetan Todorov. In 1972, Jean Paris also edited *Change*'s Joyce issue (no. 11), and in 1975 he published two earlier essays in his *Univers parallèles*. In 1984, finally, *Europe* had an essay by Paris that is described in a footnote as a "fragment of an essay in preparation: Ulysse(s) since 1945" (64) and that discusses the history of the *monologue intérieur*.

Jean Pierre Faye also published on Joyce in *Tel Quel* 30: a short introduction to Philippe Lavergne's translation of "Shem" (Faye 1967). Faye is an extremely prolific writer on an extraordinarily wide spectrum of subjects. He has published to date nine novels, four collections of poetry, plays, several books on literature and on language, a book on pre-Nazi totalitarian writers in the Weimar republic, a book on the revolution in Portugal and one on Prague, a book on Jewish story-telling, etc. He is also extremely active in writers' organizations and has been a member of the Russell Tribunal. Faye had joined *Tel Quel* in 1963 after having published novels and poetry with Seuil since 1958. In that year he published the first novel of the series he later called "Hexagramme," *Entre les rues*. Two more novels, *La Cassure* (1961) and *Battement* (1962), were to follow, before in 1964 he published his *Analogues: Récit autocritique* (1964a) in Sollers's "Collection Tel Quel." The series of novels was completed with *L'Écluse* (1964b) and *Les Troyens* (1970). In *Analogues* Faye prefigures Sollers's experiments in *Lois* (1972a) and *H* (1973a) by introducing other voices in his text, among them fragments of texts by Hölderlin and Joyce. After a quotation from Dante's *Purgatory*, we read "Eins within a space and a weary wide space it wast ere wohned a Mookse" (Faye 1964a, 54). At the end of the book this is identified as a quotation from "Finnegan's Wake" [*sic*] (268).

Faye claims to have been at the origin of *Tel Quel*'s interest in Russian formalism, and after the break with Sollers in 1967 he placed his new journal, *Change*, under the aegis of both Joyce and Althusser, from whom the two mottos of the first issue were taken. Also included in *Change*'s first issue is Lavergne's translation of the first chapter of *Finnegans Wake*. The eleventh *Change*, subtitled "l'Atelier de l'écriture" and edited by Jean Paris, is a rather heterogeneous collection of essays on Joyce: it retains *Tel Quel*'s interest in verbal experimentation and in the godfathers of that type of writing (Mallarmé, Joyce, Hölderlin), and it remains interested in linguistic structuralism, political revolution, and the practice of writing. In his introduction, Paris distinguishes the "new critical space" of the volume from "a certain structuralism, whose publicity-triumph does not hide its sterility anymore" (1972, 9). To the "frozen structures" structuralism attempts to find he opposes an interest in the underlying processes of change. Joyce is considered as somebody "who prophetically and intensely poses the great problems of contemporary linguistics and criticism." In this problematic, *Change* always stresses the historical and diachronic aspect of a phenomenon and its potential for change, whereas the traditional structuralists' work retained a strictly synchronic perspective.

A first section of this 1972 issue, subtitled "Hypothèses," deals with the elaboration of the theoretical foundations of the pun in the works of Rabelais, Lewis Carroll, and Joyce. The second section, "Séries," assembles a few notes on Joyce by Eisenstein and a selection of remarks on Joyce by Gilles Deleuze. Philippe Boyer applies Deleuze and Lacan in a very general discussion of the effects of the *Wake* and Pierre Beaudry describes in *Ulysses* and in *Finnegans Wake* the movement of a book "which searches itself through autorepresentation" (71). Beaudry's choice of quotations is very selective and manipulative, and the critic seems to be discussing private concerns, in this case a quite Heideggerian interest in the *between* and in self-referentiality (via Foucault and Blanchot).

The third section is called "Finnegans" and contains Paris's translation of the "words" section of *Scribbedehobble* and two articles in translation by David Hayman and Northrop Frye, the former taken from the introduction of *A First-Draft Version of "Finnegans Wake"* (Hayman 1963) and the latter from *Fables of Identity* (1957). Jean Paris himself then looks in detail at the workings of the pun, basing himself again on Deleuze and on American transformational linguistics.

This volume of *Change* is more interesting as an introduction to Joyce than most of the special issues *Tel Quel* devoted to the writer: the suffocating presence of one critic's views is lacking here, and Jean Paris includes translations from relatively traditional North American critics and from thinkers and artists such as Eisenstein and Deleuze. On the other hand, the concern with a linguistic and transformational approach does dominate and is developed in later issues.

Mitsou Ronat had only become a member of the collective in 1971 (*Change*, no. 8), and in *Change*, no. 11 she published an essay in which she offers a transformational-generative approach to the problem of the pun in Carroll and Joyce (1972). Three years later the essay was reprinted in *La Langue manifeste: Littérature et théories du langage*, a collection of linguistic and critical studies (1975). Two years later, she read a slightly different version at the Paris Symposium: Ronat refers constantly to studies published in the different issues of *Change* and to Saussure and Chomsky. Her conclusions are surprising: she finds that from a linguistic point of view, *Finnegans Wake* is less progressive than *Ulysses* because in the former book Joyce seems to have worked on the basis of the assumption that meaning is exclusively assigned to words, whereas syntax is far more important in the production of meaning (1979). Mitsou Ronat works primarily as a linguist, and she bases her approach on the theories of a transformational generative grammar developed by Noam Chomsky; she has collaborated on the *Hypothèses* volume published by *Change*; she has edited a book on transformational generative grammar and published a study of the works of Jean Pierre Faye in the *Cahiers CISTRE* (1980), which is more an autobiography by Faye than a critical study by Ronat.

Jean Pierre Faye's paper at the Paris Symposium belongs to a kind of criticism that does not have too many adherents in France although some of the later essays by Sollers move in the same direction; Faye studies a number of tiny fragments from *Ulysses* that all refer to the parallels between the history of the Irish people and that of the Jews. The previous year he had published a book on the diaspora (1974), under the influence of the works of Edmond Jabès (Faye 1980, 215), and Faye now connects the discussion between Mr Deasy and Stephen about Ireland and the Jews, a brief mention of a sewage sluice in "Wandering Rocks," a passage about Old Troy in "Cyclops" and especially the arguments between Bloom and the Citizen. The lack of page references hides the fact that two consecutive lines in a quotation may be separated in *Ulysses* by six or even more pages. He then quotes one of the question-and-answer sets in "Ithaca," which deals specifically with the parallels between the Irish and the Jews. He observes that "Ithaca" responds to "Cyclops" when the same names of famous Jews are given, a fact only partly true. Faye concludes that there is a link between migration and narration and that Joyce remained "too linearly odyssean" (1979, 28). The difficulty of this essay is due mainly to the fact that Faye does little more than juxtapose quotations and suggest connections between them. The only real connection is the critic himself: he includes the quotation from "Wandering Rocks" only because the word *écluse* appears in the French translation of the book. It also happens to be the title of one of Faye's novels (1964b). If we look at the other quotations, we discover other allusions to books by Jean Pierre Faye in the work of James Joyce: the reference to Old Troy recalls Faye's *Les Troyens*, and the phrase "Hell upon earth it is" his novel *Inferno*. When Faye is not finding autobiographical echoes, he is busy looking for Lacanian references, as when he quotes a reference to Bloom's father: "the *name of the father*, it is that which poisoned itself," whereas the English, though idiomatic, is quite clear: "the father's name that poisoned *him*self" (*U*, 12.1639-40, my italics). In April 1979, Paris, Faye, Mitsou Ronat and Marie-Odile Faye held a discussion published in *L'Herne* in which earlier statements are made more specific. It becomes clear that Faye's interest has shifted to the French and Irish revolutions, and he even suggests that Parnell knew Marx via James Connolly (Collectif "Change" 1986).

Jean Pierre Faye occupies in *Change* the same central position as Philippe Sollers in *Tel Quel,* and the break between the two groups seems to have been as much due to a clash of personalities as it was to irreconcilable political differences. Both writers began their careers as young representatives of the *nouveau roman;* both wrote first against Sartre and in favor of a formalist science of literature; both hailed Foucault, Lacan, and Derrida as prophets of a new episteme; and both became actively involved in the political discussions during and after May 1968. As Philippe Sollers is in *Tel Quel,* Faye is the spokesman and the main inspirator in *Change,* and his creative work is always at the center of the discussion, but he has never become as important as Sollers, who has succeeded in remaining at the center of Parisian cultural life for more than twenty-five years now.

FOUR

Joyce and *Tel Quel*

To tell the story of *Tel Quel* is to write a history of the mainstream of the French intellectual avant-garde. This formulation is not as paradoxical as it sounds; in a way, as Jane Kramer wrote in the *New Yorker*, *Tel Quel* really is the Yves Saint-Laurent of intellectual fashions in France (quoted in Sollers 1980b, 10). Sollers has succeeded in remaining the chief spokesman of the avant-garde for more than a quarter century, and his interest in Joyce is almost as old. *Tel Quel's* very birth was controversial; while Jacqueline Risset coyly writes that some of the members of the original editorial board belonged "to the left" (1982a, 9), Jean Pierre Faye recalls Jean-Edern Hallier's boast in 1958 that he was going to start a right-wing periodical at Seuil (Faye 1980, 69). The name does suggest a solidarity with the writers of the *nouveau roman* against a Sartrean *littérature engagée*. In the second issue of *Tel Quel*, Philippe Sollers published a short essay, "Sept propositions sur Alain Robbe-Grillet," which functions as a kind of manifesto and as an explicit siding with the *nouveaux romanciers* (1960).

Joyce's work appears for the first time in *Tel Quel* two years later: Umberto Eco published two extracts from his *Opera aperta* (the French translation had been published by Seuil in 1965) in issues 11 and 12 under the title "Le Moyen-âge de James Joyce." It may be a coincidence, but between the tenth and the eleventh issue Jean-Edern Hallier has been replaced by Marcelin Pleynet as "directeur gérant" of *Tel Quel*, a disappearance that is later described as an "exclusion." A more important break occurs in *Tel Quel* 17, which contains the discussions at the *Décade de Cérisy* organized by the journal in September 1963. The original editorial board has been replaced by Jean Pierre Faye, Marcelin Pleynet, Denis Roche, and Jean-Louis Baudry; and from this moment on, the majority of the articles will be written by the members of this group. The first effects of structuralism have registered in the year preceding this break: in *Tel Quel* 13 there is a reference to Derrida's translation of Husserl (Derrida 1962), and Jean-Louis Houdebine later writes that it was Derrida's reference to Joyce in his introduction to that book that sparked Sollers's interest in the philosopher's work (1983, 36). In the next issue, Sollers describes Foucault's work (*Folie et déraison* had been published in 1961); in *Tel Quel* 15 Foucault himself contributes an essay (1963), and in the next issue texts appear by Roland Barthes, Maurice Roche, and Jean-Pierre Richard. In the autumn of 1964, Sollers reviews Deleuze's *Proust et les signes* (1964) and describes Proust as an end and Mallarmé, or Joyce, as a beginning. *Tel Quel* 20 has Derrida's "La Parole soufflée," and no. 21 a motto by Joyce. In the next volumes the references to Lacan, Saussure, Jakobson, and Barthes have multiplied, and in *Tel Quel* 22 Hélène Berger-Cixous publishes an essay on "A Portrait of the Artist" and a translation, with Jean Fuzier, of that text.

In the autumn issue of 1965, Sollers publishes "Dante et la traversée de l'écriture," in many ways a manifesto of *Tel Quel*'s views on literature at this point. The essay was reprinted in *Logiques* in 1968, where it follows "Programme" (1967) and an earlier programmatic essay, "Logique de la fiction" (1962), and again in *L'Écriture et l'expérience des limites* (1971a), where it opens the collection after a short text, "Écriture et révolution" (1969), and "Programme." In the text, part of an issue devoted to Dante, Sollers offers an interpretation of the *Divine Comedy* that not only points forward to his own *Paradis* (1981a), but confirms the central importance of Dante in his own creative works. In her book on Dante, Jacqueline Risset has described this essay as "a turning point" in the French complete lack of interest in the poet and as the beginning of a "diffuse presence" of Dante in recent French writing (Risset 1982b, 232, 234). It also marks, after

"Logique de la fiction," a new theoretical and practical discourse which lies at the basis of most of *Tel Quel*'s later theoretical and critical practice.

Sollers emphasizes neither the content nor the form of Dante's work, "but the profound affinity of Dante with writing." The *Divine Comedy* is the first great work conceived as a *book* by its author (Sollers 1968b, 45). It is turned toward a reader who, alone, makes its writing possible between the two poles of a complete unreadability and an absolute transparency. Where the insistence on the book is based on Blanchot and Mallarmé, Sollers's literal reading of Dante is founded on Saussure and Lacan. The *Divine Comedy* is a "passage into a third dimension," "*Dante posits himself as the writing of Dante*, as a passage of this writing without limits or end" (63). The *Divine Comedy* contains an impossible totality, it is everywhere and nowhere: "Its circumference is everywhere, its center nowhere" (64). Dante's poem is also an example of a new kind of radical writing whose ambition can be compared only to Sade's project and to Mallarmé's, which is what makes of Dante "somebody who speaks to us today most clearly" (47). Sollers mentions Joyce twice in this text, first briefly with Pound as two Danteans who have stressed the poet's microscopic project, and second as somebody who is, like Dante, preoccupied with the myth of Babel. It is clear that Joyce ranks with Dante, Hölderlin, and Mallarmé as the most interesting protagonists of new reading and writing strategies.

In *Tel Quel* 30 Jean Pierre Faye introduces Jean Paris's "Finnegans, Wake!" (1967) and Philippe Lavergne's translation of "Shem" (1967). The first part of "La Pharmacie de Platon" with its famous footnote (Derrida 1968a) is published in *Tel Quel* 32, again an important moment in the history of the journal because Jean Pierre Faye has disappeared from the editorial board, and Houdebine sees as one of the reasons for this exclusion Kristeva's work (1967) on Saussure's "paragrammes" (Houdebine 1983, 43). Faye starts his own collective and accuses *Tel Quel* of being idealistically preoccupied by the signifier and Derrida of being a Heideggerian and, by implication, a Nazi. Before *Tel Quel* can answer, May 1968 interferes. *Tel Quel* 34 (Summer 1968) announces "La révolution ici maintenant" and the establishment of a *Groupe d'études théoriques* consisting of almost all of the regular contributors. *Tel Quel* becomes explicitly Marxist-Leninist; no. 38 has a motto taken from Lenin's writing, and Sollers speaks about the philosophical works of the Russian revolutionary at meetings of the *Groupe d'études théoriques*. The same issue contains *Tel Quel*'s version of the split with Faye and a defense of Lacan and Derrida. Chomsky, whom *Change* had wanted to pit against *Tel Quel*, is "not a materialist, not a Freudian, not a Marxist, not a Leninist." The controversy continues in the next issues, while the tensions with the Communist party grow; *Tel Quel* 40 publishes Sollers's translation of poems by Mao. In the autumn of 1970 (*Tel Quel* 43) the attack against Faye spreads over seventeen pages; his name will not be mentioned in *Tel Quel* again. Here it is claimed that Faye "had to leave *Tel Quel* (at the end of 1967) because he was not able to move into the new phase of our work: an accelerated transformation of the fictional text, a theory of writing and Marxism-Leninism" (90). He is also quite simply a bad writer (88). Maurice Roche, who had left *Tel Quel* to help Faye found *Change*, is back at *Tel Quel*; together with Roland Barthes, François Wahl, and Jean Cayrol, Roche publicly supports Sollers against Faye. New schisms follow each other rapidly: *Tel Quel* quarrels with *Change*, with the French Communist party, with the *Union des écrivains*, and with the *comité d'action écrivains-étudiants* led by Marguerite Duras and Maurice Blanchot.

In *Tel Quel* 47 the break with the Communist party is made official and *Tel Quel* becomes openly Maoist. The occasion is the publication of *De la Chine* by Maria-Antonietta Macciocchi (1971), and the result is the creation of a new group, with the same collaborators, "the movement of June '71." Both Cixous and Lacan are attacked; by the next double issue (48–49) China has become the major focus; and, this time without explanation, Ricardou and Thibaudeau disappear from the editorial board. Strange as it may seem, this is also when, after an absence of almost two and half years, Joyce reappears on the scene, not in a text by one of the regular contributors but in two long essays by Stephen Heath, a student of Raymond Williams and Terry

Eagleton. In *The Nouveau Roman: A Study in the Practice of Writing* (completed in 1969 but only published in 1972) Heath had already set up *Finnegans Wake* as the *terminus ad quem* of the *nouveau roman* and based this position on statements by Sollers, Barthes, Foucault, Lacan, Faye, Hallier, and Derrida (the introduction to the Husserl translation). The order of the chapters (after a definition of the "practice of writing," a chapter each on Sarraute, Robbe-Grillet, Simon, and Sollers) suggests a logical conclusion of the movement of the *nouveau roman* in Sollers's novel *Lois* (Heath 1972a; Sollers 1972a).

If the Joyce essays that appeared in *Tel Quel* before 1972 had been rather reserved in their application of the new methodology to the texts of *Ulysses* and *Finnegans Wake*, Heath's "Ambiviolences" is the first *telquelian* reading of Joyce. Squeezed in between the second half of an essay by Joseph Needham, the first part of which had appeared in the previous double issue on China, and the rest of the dossier on China, entitled "Chine (2)," "Ambiviolences" belongs, from its first motto (Kristeva's etymology of *lire* in *Sémeiotikè* [1969]), to the *Tel Quel* tradition. The quotations and references to Lautréamont, Pound, Barthes, Nietzsche, Sollers, Flaubert, Eco, Foucault, Mallarmé, Freud, Proust, Derrida, Saussure, Paris, and Starobinski confirm this impression. The first half of the essay deals with a number of different topics; in the discussion of each subject, Heath chooses a decentralized, deconstructed reading against the two complementary Anglo-American strategies of dealing with the *Wake*: rejection or reduction, whereas "the writing of *Finnegans Wake*, work *in progress* ('wordloosed over seven seas,' *FW*, 219), constitutes itself as a fundamental incompleteness; the text produces a decisive [I assume "dérisive" is a misprint] hesitation of meaning whose final revelation is always postponed until 'later'" (Heath 1972b, 22). Heath further argues against the supposed continuity of the text and even against the use of the word *style* in dealing with Joyce's writing, because there is no possible connection between the work and the man (25), a fact that does not stop Heath from using statements by Joyce about his authorial intentions in writing *Ulysses* (29). He further writes that *Finnegans Wake* tries to destroy the 'real world' or, better, the common sense view of the world we all inhabit, by "infinitizing the fictions": context becomes intertext. The book breaks through our ordinary notions of rhetoric, parody, and even language itself, which is radically changed by the text's continuous interrogation, "a kind of 'Rückfrage' always to be started again, the elaboration of a hesitative writing that changes from one language to another and that will posit itself in its detour on the scene of the production of meaning and of the subject" (42). The second part of the essay develops these themes: the "story" of the *Wake*, the basic myth of the fall, is interpreted with reference to Hegel as a fall into language and limitation. The text breaks through the barriers of language as communication in a "play of the signifier" and attains in the "wake" the "in-between" of Derrida's *différance* (Heath 1972c, 65), which can also be identified with ALP as flux, although HCE remains the key to the book, because "obviously it is the letters of the 'HeCitEncy'. . . that link forgery to a strategy of hesitation . . . and that reflect the vacillation of the subject and 'its' meaning caught in the game of letters" (68). Via the works of Marcel Jousse, Joyce effects in the *Wake* a dramatization of language with the help of two strategies: the "optic hearing," which stresses the collision of word and writing and makes a reading out loud impossible, on the one hand, and "a kind of 'vacillation' of the negation starting from a confusion of contradictions" (72), which results in the suspension of the principle of noncontradiction and which finds its theoretical foundation in Freud's "Über den Gegensinn der Urworte" (Freud 1972b) and in Derrida's work, on the other. Stephen Heath is well aware of Joyce's earlier works and of the traditional criticism, especially the biographical work by Ellmann, the letters, and the reminiscences. He always quotes in full and identifies his sources. His central theme is deconstructive: there is no identifiable single meaning; the text is its own interpretation; all readings are violent acts. Although Houdebine does not even mention these essays in his survey of *Tel Quel*'s interest in Joyce (1983), Heath's ample use of textual material makes them very important. The central themes were further elaborated in an essay on Joyce and Sollers in the magazine *Discours sociale* (1973a) in which Heath anticipates the central thesis of Colin

MacCabe's book (1978) and in the same year Heath published an introduction to the translation of parts of Book IV of *Finnegans Wake* he made in collaboration with Philippe Sollers (1973b). The latter essay does not differ in style or in theoretical framework from the earlier ones. Heath still refers mainly to Kristeva and Freud, but he has exchanged Derrida for Lacan, maybe as a result of the increasing tensions between *Tel Quel* and the philosopher. First Heath explains that the text is not a translation (already in "Ambiviolences" he had shown that a translation would be impossible), but a "brutal, risky transformation" (1973b, 5). He rejects André du Bouchet's attempt at a translation of a section of *Finnegans Wake* for its lack of intertextual consciousness, and then he describes a number of different aspects of the text. First the nature of the "entre" between night and day, sleep and waking; then, the different clusters of Christian references, elements of Irish mythology, and of Eastern systems of belief. Third, the notion of origin and its Freudian consequences in the references to Morton Prince's *The Dissociation of a Personality*. Again Heath quotes extensively and accurately, and he always gives full references, although he occasionally does forget to give sources for some of the interpretations he borrows from Hart and Atherton. Heath's last essay in *Tel Quel* is a discussion of Sollers's texts, in which he stresses their similarities to Joyce's work: "Sollers's text revives the writings which have surely, and for obvious reasons, been 'forgotten' (Hölderlin, Joyce)" (1974b, 125). He also identifies two places in *H* (Sollers 1973a) in which Joyce is mentioned.

In the meantime *Tel Quel* 54 and 55 had had a "Joyce in Progress" section; the first included Heath's "Trames de lecture" (1973b) and Sollers's "Argument" (1973b), introductory statements to the translation of parts of the last chapter of the *Wake*. *Tel Quel* 55 had an essay by Umberto Eco (1974), which is a translation of a chapter in *Le Forme del Contenuto* (1971), and a paper by Jacqueline Risset on Joyce's own reworking of "Anna Livia Plurabelle" into Italian (1974). The spring issue of 1974 (no. 57) signals the final break with Derrida and Althusser, who have joined the "Union de la Gauche," the historic agreement between the French socialists and communists to coordinate the left-wing opposition to the conservative government. *Tel Quel* is now completely isolated; it has written against every possible ally on the left: against Faye, against the French Communist party, against Jean-Edern Hallier's *La Cause des peuples* (1973), against Blanchot, Duras, Derrida, and Althusser; in the subsequent issues it will also attack Ponge, Hallier, Clavel, Lardreau, and Jambet. It remains faithful only to Barthes, Lacan, and the literary avant-garde. With the final exclusion of Derrida and Althusser, there remain four imperatives for *Tel Quel*: to elaborate Lacan's "intervention," to fight philosophical Marxism, to oppose academic Marxism, and to continue the literary avant-garde (Sollers 1974, 137). In that avant-garde practice Joyce has a central role to play, with Artaud and Hölderlin. In an interview with Jean-Louis Houdebine published in *Promesse* as "Littérature et révolution: Vérité de l'avant-garde," Sollers and Pleynet make that abundantly clear; Sollers even claims that the new form of epic that will replace both poetry and the novel will be called "*du wake*" (Houdebine 1973b, 33).

Marcelin Pleynet is with Sollers the only one of the early collaborators to survive all the different purges. His poetic beginnings fit perfectly into the Heideggerian atmosphere of the late fifties and early sixties and his first three collections of poetry, *Provisoires amants des nègres*, *Paysages en deux* and *Comme* contain clear echoes of his reading of Hölderlin. Another early *telquelien*, Jean-Edern Hallier, had described Pleynet's poetry under the title "Descendance hölderlinienne" (1962). The first section of *Provisoires amants*, "Le petit déjeuner sous l'herbe," opens with "I thought of the wild animals who walk in their cage alongside the sea" (Pleynet 1984a, 17), which is a reference to Wilhelm Waiblinger's account of a visit to the mad Hölderlin in 1822 (Pleynet 1981b, 16); the second section, "La Cave natale," has a motto from Heidegger. In *Paysages en deux*, Pleynet closes his poem "Bouquet" with a reference to Hölderlin, and in *Stanze*, his first truly *telquelian* work, the mad poet again appears, this time with two quotations in German, one acknowledged in the notes at the beginning of the fourth canto. In the margin, between square brackets and in capital letters, we read "HE HAD / BUCK / GOAT / PAPS ONES /

HIM SOFT / ONES FOR / ORPHANS" (1973, 120). These enigmatic words can be found in a slightly more comprehensible form in *Finnegans Wake* as "He had buckgoat paps on him, soft ones for orphans" (215.27–28). In the notes at the end of *Stanze*, Pleynet points to different influences on his work in progress (*Stanze* has only four of the total of nine cantos that the complete work will contain), from Mao, to classical Chinese philosophy, Pound, Lautréamont, and Artaud, but above all to the relationship between the magic square and

> the extract from a letter in which James Joyce defines for Miss Weaver what one could consider as the blazon of *Finnegans Wake*: "I am making an engine with only one wheel. No spokes of course. The wheel is a perfect square. You see what I am driving at, don't you? I am awful solemn about it, mind you, so you must not think it is a silly story about the mooks and the grapes. No, it's a wheel, I tell the world. *And* it's all *square*." (Pleynet 1973, 165)

The square wheel itself makes its appearance in the poem a number of times (89, 91, 97). Pleynet's claim about this influence has already been challenged by Robert W. Greene (1977, 140); Pleynet's puns (*hainemie, la question et conne homme hic*) and his references to Catholic liturgy (among them an answer to Buck Mulligan's first words in *Ulysses*: "it te mousa est la mèse est finie" [Pleynet, 80; *U*, 1.5]) and to Bruno and Vico cannot hide the fact that the *Wake* functions only as a very general paradigm. This is the same in Pleynet's critical writings, in *Art et littérature* (1977a) and *Transculture* (1977b). In his journals Pleynet describes meetings with Sollers and Houdebine in which they talk about Joyce and his work, but Pleynet never actively participates in the discussion (1981a). The collection of poems and essays *Fragments du choeur* (1984b) contains a limited number of references to Joyce: *Ulysses* and *Finnegans Wake* mark the crisis of the novel; Joyce is quoted in a long essay on Shakespeare entitled "Shakespeare in progress"; and Joyce is opposed to Eliot as a writer who does face the paternal question, among other things by borrowing from *Troilus and Cressida* the homeric framework.

Although officially he was never anything more than a member of the "comité de rédaction," Philippe Sollers is undoubtedly the most important figure in *Tel Quel*; his name has almost become synonymous with the journal. Sollers's documented interest in Joyce comes relatively late with the publication of his and Heath's translation of sections from Book IV of the *Wake* in 1974; but even in the sixties it was Sollers who published almost all of the French Joyce critics, and in 1966 he functioned as a representative of the younger generation in an homage to Joyce organized by *Le Figaro Littéraire*. His essay, "Une Oeuvre extraordinairement réfléchie" appears under the notice: "The writers of the 'nouveau roman' recognize Joyce as one of their precursors. One of them, Philippe Sollers, situates Joyce's 'literary adventure' in this perspective" (1966a, 9). In this short text, Sollers deplores the superficial mythologies that have been built around Joyce's name by an *"avant-hier-garde"* in league with conformism, while the truly revolutionary power of Joyce's work lies on two distinct levels: that of language breaking radically with any preestablished rhetoric and that of the "totality" of our world and thought being radically questioned. Sollers praises the width of this work in progress and claims that France is incapable of looking beyond classicism and therefore of understanding Joyce's central importance. Although Sollers here announces that Joyce will become central in the future of the French avant-garde, he does not yet express which aspects of the Joycean oeuvre will become important.

A partial answer to this question is given in the first text by Philippe Sollers that was fully devoted to Joyce, "Argument," an introduction to the translation of parts of Book IV of the *Wake*. It is written in very short sentences and it describes briefly what happens in the translated text and offers another interpretation of the initials HCE (*Hic Est Filius Meus*: the book is baptized by the father in the mother)(1973b). The translation itself (of *FW*, 593.01–594.09; 596.34–598.16, and 626.35–628.16) follows the original closely although some aspects are emphasized more than they were in the original; especially sex and language: "breeding bradsted culminwillth" becomes *génitortf bâlitard communencumuls* and "lifelike thyne of the bird" becomes *c'te langue d'oisie*. Inevitably other aspects are lost: when translating "Mehs" into "Moahs" the translators change "me" into "moi" but lose the opposition between Nuahs and Mehs, which is that between the inverted Shaun and Shem.

It is clear at this point that Joyce will play a part in the sexual and political revolution *Tel Quel* is propagating. The exact nature of that role is definitively expressed by Sollers in his contribution to the Paris Symposium in 1975. The circumstances of the address (frictions between the American and French Joyceans and between the different French factions) are relevant for the style of the paper; as representatives of the academic establishment, as capitalist and imperialist Americans and as supporters of an anti-Freudian ego-psychology, the Joyceans are three times damned. Sollers begins by stating that "since *Finnegans Wake* was written, English no longer exists" (1975a, 3) and that Joyce dreamed of a book "that will be inseparably dream and interpretation, ceaseless crossing of boundaries—precisely a *waking.*" *Finnegans Wake* is a political act, since to the virulent nationalism of prewar fascism Joyce opposes a "transnationalism." His interest in religion makes the *Wake* "the most formidably antifascist book produced between the two wars." In the most fundamental struggle of the twentieth century, that between Jung and Freud, Joyce takes Freud's side against Jung, who represents "the set of spiritualist or para-occultist resistances to psychoanalysis; the hope of a possible 'beyond,' something that the surrealists, for example, did not fail to clutch at; in short, in relation to the sexual question radically affirmed by Freud, [it represents] a metaphysical counter-investment" (5). The English-speaking countries are Protestant and puritanical and therefore almost by nature Jungian; that this includes most of Sollers's audience cannot have escaped his attention. Joyce's word always includes a factor of annulment (Dante's fourth level of interpretation), of *jouissance,* and this turns Joyce into an anti-Schreber: "He writes and speaks in that impossible place where there ought not to be anything speaking or writing" (12). It is also the reason for the ferocious *Verneinung* his work had to undergo and still undergoes today. This essay is more a provocative statement of purpose than an analysis of a text. Sollers does not add much to the ideas articulated in Heath's "Ambiviolences"; he only reinforces their political and psychoanalytical consequences.

This is even clearer in the proceedings of the symposium, where, under the title "Joyce et l'aventure d'aujourd'hui," we find a discussion among Michel Butor, Sollers, Nathalie Sarraute, François Aubral, Jean-Yves Bosseur, and Jean-Claude Montel. Sollers repeats the main points of his paper but stresses the fact that "we have produced a certain work in 1973 on *Finnegans Wake* and this work has not been read, cannot be found in this discipline" (Butor 1979, 60). This is only one symptom in the history of the enormous resistance on the part of the academic establishment against Joyce. Even more interesting is the discussion about Joyce's politics: Sollers once again repeats the main thesis of his paper, but now he is opposed by Leslie Fiedler, who feels that Joyce, as a political prophet, is "simply wrong, wrong, wrong" (Beja 1979, 112), and by Seamus Deane, who looks at the Irish dimension of Joyce's politics. Paul Delaney agrees with Fiedler that Joyce's modernist politics is an elitist politics, but he shows that Joyce was the only one of the five most important writers of his time (Joyce, Eliot, Lawrence, Pound, and Yeats) who was not contemptuous of ordinary people and who did not flirt with fascism. The difference between these critics and Sollers is that the former deal with Joyce in his historical context and the latter deals with the writer's revolutionary potential in the current climate:

> *Sollers*—(Placing a book on the table): Je vous montre une révolution.
> *Translator*—He shows you one revolution.
> *Beja*—That is a copy of *Finnegans Wake*. (107)

And it does not come as a surprise when Sollers is carried away in his presentation of that potential:

> *Sollers*—. . . The first books to be banned are those by Freud. (111)
> *Member of the audience*—Is it true that Freud's books were the first to be banned by Fascism?
> *Sollers*—The first? I didn't say the first. I mean that no fascist regime can allow Freud's thought to take root . . . . I did not say the first. (117)

Jean-Louis Houdebine, since the mid-seventies a regular contributor to *Tel Quel*, has written a short essay on the history of the journal's involvement with Joyce. He, too, dates the serious attention to Joyce to the early seventies, and he particularly mentions Sollers's creative work, from *Lois* (1972) onwards. This novel represents an important stage in Sollers's writing in its "paroxysmal punctuation, which echoes Céline but also Joyce" (Houdebine 1983, 41); on the same page Houdebine quotes a number of lines from *Lois* as proof: "Away! Debout! Debout! Write it! Write it all down! Farewell ezra! Welcome jimmie! Away! Je vous l'avais bien dit que je reviendrais! Pas si fou! Éternel détour! Avec mon carnet carbone! Juif érin!" (41). I am not sure what Houdebine is trying to show here, because this is a collage of a number of short quotations instead of one single one. "Away! Away" occurs twice on page 82 of *Lois*; "Debout! Debout!" three times (77, 78, 80); "Write it! Write it all down!" occurs ten pages earlier (69) and is a quotation from *Giacomo Joyce* (*GJ*, 16); and the last five sentences can be found forty pages later (125). The carbon notebook is *Giacomo Joyce* itself, which was published by Richard Ellmann in a carbon-colored facsimile edition, and "Juif érin" refers to Joyce's answer when he heard that his application for a visa had been turned down by the Swiss *Fremdenpolizei* because they thought he was Jewish: "Je ne suis pas Juif de Judée mais aryen d'Erin" (*JJ II*, 736), which is very much the opposite of what Sollers here writes.

Compared to *Nombres*, published in 1968, *Lois* is indeed very Joycean: although the book still has a geometric overall structure similar to that of the earlier novel, it introduces the use of puns, of seemingly gratuitous and unacknowledged quotations, and the continuous onslaught on clichés that will characterize Pleynet's *Stanze* one year later. Sollers has told David Hayman in an interview published in *Vision à New York* (Sollers 1981b) that he rewrote *Lois* completely after studying *Finnegans Wake*, and this is evident all over the book. Just a few examples: "Gloria patri et panfilio" (1972a, 39), "mezzo sopracammin en solo" (27), "Iena, iena, sombre saale!" (93), "Il ne valse pas, ne lévite pas sur du flonflon strauss" (109). In other passages Sollers quotes literally from *Finnegans Wake*: on page 41: "Sandhyas! Sandhyas! Sandhyas!" (*FW*, 593.01) and "aquaface" (003.14); page 43: "Sacer esto? Semus sumus" (168.14–5); page 47: "fireland" (021.16–

17); page 64: "Sinsinsinning since the night of time and each and all of their branches making and shaking twisty hands all over again in their new world through the germination of its gemination from ond's outset till odd's end. And encircle him circuly. Evovae!" (505.09–13), for "making" read "meeting" and "ond" and "odd" should be capitalized; page 64: "Order is othered!" (613.14); page 76: "Wipe your glosses with what you know" (304.F3); page 85: "You never made a more freudful mistake, excuse yourself!" (411. 35–36); page 112: "Tell!" (the beginning of I, 8, quoted by Sollers in his *Figaro* article [1966a, 9]); page 123: "Preausteric man and his pursuit of pan-hysteric woman" (266.R1), and "Totam in tutu!" (397.32–33). Transla-tions or variations of phrases in the *Wake* are on page 41: first of the opening paragraph (003.01–03), then of the opening of Book IV (593.01–08), and then of "Father Times and Mother Spacies" (600.02–03); page 43: "perçoreille-la," which is Persse O'Reilly; page 45: "le nonprincipiant nous a-t-il lâchés? le verbus en panne" refers to "Verb umprincipiant" (594.02–03); page 76: "l'étym" (353.22); page 89: "Gulls. Gulls. And gulls. Groax, groagk, gkekgxkg!" refers to "Whish. A gull. Gulls" (628.13), and "Brékkek Kékkek Kékkek Kék-kek! Koax Koax Koax!" on 004.02. More indirect references to Joyce are on page 47: "O jimmie aveugle auréole en spires"; page 68: "Triste becquette mise à la place de jimmie"; page 70: "Ralbloum" may refer to Bloom; and, finally, on page 95: "Sound the trumpet. Saaound. Till araound" is a rather obscure reference to Joyce. It represents the voices of a duet for tenors from *Come ye Sons of Art* by Purcell, which Joyce was trying to find on his radio set when Jacques Mercanton first visited him (1967,11).

As carefully constructed books, *Lois* and *Stanze* are clearly related; both have a very deliberate structure; Pleynet explains in his post-script ("Le Bandeau d'or: Notes") that the cantos are organized around the nine words of the sentence "Si on connaît les commence-ments on connaît les fins." These words always appear in bold types at the opening of the canto, just as Sollers prints six words at the beginning of his six chapters ("NE-; FACE; A FACE; NIANT; LA MEMBRANE; L'ENTREE"), which represent the book's first sentence,

"nié face à face, niant la membrane, l'entrée" (5). Pleynet also introduces a historical progression from the "pre-Asiatic, postimperialist"
first canto; to the Asiatic Egyptian second; the third devoted to slav-
ery and Greece; the fourth to antiquity and Rome; the fifth to feudal-
ism and Christianity; the sixth to precapitalism and the Italy of the
renaissance; the seventh to capitalism, England, and France; and the
eighth to the supreme stage of capitalism and imperialism, to the
United States (1973, 156–57). Similarly, Sollers describes his six chapters as six *chants*, of which the first is "cosmo-theogonic" and deals
with Hesiod and prehistory; the second discusses Greece and Christianity; and the following chapters deal with the modern capitalist
period. The use of puns, the reformulation of clichés, and a heterogeneous intertextual reference that includes Chinese ideograms in
both works confirm that observation. But it may go too far to refer to
Joyce for all of these innovations; in Pleynet's case there is the more
obvious and obtrusive reference to Pound's *Cantos*, and Sollers bases
his use of puns theoretically on Freud's work.

Sollers made a more far-reaching technical discovery in the year
Lois was published; in the last issue of *Tel Quel* in 1972 he published
"Das Augenlicht," a text that was later incorporated in his novel *H*.
The text has lost all punctuation marks and capital letters and is called
"Travail en cours" (1972b, 30). The most obvious models are of course
Molly's monologue in *Ulysses* and the prepublication of *Finnegans
Wake* as "Work in Progress." The first reference to Joyce in this first
part of *H* is "ce qu'on voit est parfois tout près de ce qu'on écoute limit
of the diaphane why in diaphane adiaphane if you can put your five
fingers through if it is a gate if not a door shut your eyes and see c'est
curieux ces coïncidences" (1973a, 23). The English is taken from Stephen's interior monologue in the third chapter of *Ulysses*, although
apart from the punctuation, a few words have been distorted: "in" is
missing between "diaphane" and "why" and the second "if" should
be "it" (*U*, 3.7-9). Another phrase, "o libidinous god" (58) is taken
from *Giacomo·Joyce* (*GJ*, 11), "sillage" (88) is immediately followed by
its translation, "wake," and ten lines down we find "hithering waters
of" from the end of the Anna Livia Plurabelle chapter (*FW*, 216.04–

05). The anecdote of Joyce trying to find a Purcell concert on the radio (90) is taken from the first page of Mercanton's book and had already been referred to in *Lois*. Further on, Sollers evokes the first words of the *Wake* (95), after the opening sentences of *Don Quixote* and of *A La Recherche du temps perdu*, and still further, the battle between the sexes is described in terms of that between ALP and HCE, "la vieille nana moribunda pluramoche cherchant herr coït everywhere." On the next page we find an account of Joyce's last days, taken from the end of Ellmann's biography (*JJ II*, 733), and on page 128 Stephen Dedalus's *non serviam*. *Finnegans Wake* itself is mentioned on page 151. On the last pages we find "the west shall shake the east awake fantasy fantasy on fantasy amnes fintasies" (184), which is taken from the end of the third chapter of Book III in the *Wake*: "The west shall shake the east awake" (473.22–23) and from the next chapter: "Fantasy! funtasy on fantasy, amnaes fintasies!" a variation on *Eccles* 1:2 (493.18). Sollers also continues the use of stylistic parody in a Wakean vein: "au nom du père du fils ou du monoprix" (75), and he even uses single Wakean words such as "pfuitt" (Sollers, 116; *FW*, 033.34) or "comme dit jimmie etceterogène" (Sollers, 133), which borrows from Cixous the habit of referring to Joyce as "Jim" or "Jimmie" and which translates "etceterogenious" (*FW*, 595.23). More difficult to spot is another reference to Joyce in "et voilà dagda avec sa massue et le jeune lug avec son javelot" (168). The reference is to Book IV of the *Wake*, where both mythological figures appear, at least according to Stephen Heath: "the inexhaustible cauldron and the harp of Dagda ('dag si', 607), the sword of Nuada, god of fertility ('the word of Nuahs', 593), the lance of Lug, god of thunder and lightning ('Lugh the Brathwacker', 594)" (Heath 1974b, 7).

Written and published at the height of *Tel Quel*'s Maoist phase, *H* represents radical *écriture* at its most revolutionary. Sollers's comments on the back cover of his book begin with the claim that to explain why the book cannot be introduced would probably require as much space as the book itself, the reader must simply relax and read. Sollers's novelistic production had already been studied by important critics such as Derrida, but now Roland Barthes and Julia

Kristeva published essays on *H* that can be read as side panels to the novel. In "Par-dessus l'épaule," Barthes implicitly posits *H* as a modern text, *scriptible* in the terminology of *S/Z* (1970), *texte de jouissance* in that of *Le Plaisir du texte* (1973). *H* cannot be recuperated by means of critical notions of any kind; it contains a "suffocation," an excess of beauty, of languages; the text does not have "an atom of rhetorical fat"; the absence of punctuation is a challenge to religion; the novelty of its language is the result of the pluralization of the old language. Barthes's description of the different types of readers *H* can have inevitably leads to a proposal that may shock followers of the Barthes who had announced the death of the author but that makes perfect sense in the context of *Le Plaisir du texte*:

> When will we have the right to institute and practice an *affectionate criticism* without running the risk of being called biased? When will we be free enough (free from a false notion of 'objectivity') to include in our reading of a text the knowledge we may have of its author? Why—in the name of what, for fear of whom—should I cut from my reading of Sollers's novel the friendship I feel for him? (1979, 78)

Kristeva opens her "Polylogue," her contribution to an issue of *Tel Quel* devoted to Sollers's creative work with a statement that seems to echo Barthes' point:

> *H-*: music that writes itself in language and that reasons with itself, without stopping and until the saturated, overflowing, vivid meaning is exhausted. . . . *H* takes you with it: takes you from the place where you sit, blows you a whiff of vertigo, but lucidity returns immediately with the music. . . . *H* takes you in analysis, and you take the author as the pole of your transference, character in your Oedipus. . . . You pass from *H* to Sollers, from Sollers to *H*: who is what? (1974a, 19)

Like Barthes, Kristeva is much more personal in this essay than one would have expected from the author of *Sémeiotiké: Recherches pour une sémanalyse*: "To put things bluntly, I speak in French and about literature because of Yalta and I do not just mean that because of Yalta I had to marry to obtain a passport and to work in France" (20). Kristeva omits an important part of the story; she married Philippe Sollers, author of *H*. Like Barthes, she develops a binary opposition, in this case the symbolic and the semiotic, which Sollers transcends by placing one against the other:

> The novelty of *H* lies in playing the contradiction between the two; in being neither one nor the other. . . . In *H*, . . . all the strings of the wonderful instrument that language is play together and simultaneously: no process is halted, repressed or put aside to give the other free rein. (29)

The result is not a totalization but an "infinite, interminable fragmentation: an 'exterior polylogue'" (32).

The message is the same for Barthes and Kristeva: *H* is heterogeneous, plural, new, different. The function of "Sollers" in his own text is for the two critics both crucial and problematic. Poststructuralism, and especially the *Tel Quel* variety, had abolished the humanist and bourgeois notion of subject, Sollers himself in almost every text of this period (1973c, 11), Kristeva in essays such as "Le Sujet en procès" (1972, 1973) and "Sujet dans le langage et pratique politique" (1974b), in which she elaborates the opposition symbolic/semiotic (here equated with *doxa* and *chora*), a dichotomy that threatens the very existence of linguistics:

> Because also the science of linguistics, in league with this political idealism, offers us a systematic view of a language full of meaning, without emptiness, without process, without practice: therefore without a subject in process. (1974b, 23)

Why is it then that the *subject* Philippe Sollers occupies center stage in the reading of *H* offered by Kristeva and Barthes?

The answer lies in the text itself; like Molly Bloom's monologue, it is impossible to read *H* as an enunciation by more than one individual speaker. In the case of *Ulysses*, its status as the final chapter and its multitude of references to already established fictional information make it impossible to read the text as anything but originating in Molly Bloom. In *H* the context and therefore also the fictional world are absent: the only "je" available is the name of the author on the cover. Sollers refuses the notion of a single-voice matrix in the book itself: "j'oppose au monologue intérieur le polylogue extérieur" (1973a, 42), to which can be objected that clearly somebody is writing "je" in this sentence, too. The omnipresence of autobiographical references, the distinct voice we know from the essays and interviews and the reiteration of the author's name in the text make it difficult if not impossible to come to any other conclusion. There are reasons to assume that the autobiographical bias of the book came relatively late in the process of writing the book: "Das Augenlicht" (1972b) had no references to Sollers's name (although it does refer to a "je"); when it was incorporated into *H*, it was preceded by a discussion of Sollers's *nom-du-père*, Octave Joyaux, and of his own names, Joyaux and Sollers, and he also added two words "jew jewel" (1973a, 29). "Jewel" is *joyau* in French. The openness about autobiographical material and the two critics' plea for a corresponding affectionate criticism both point ahead to a new phase in *Tel Quel*'s history following a new break in the autumn of 1976.

The early *Tel Quel* reception of Joyce's work remains at a superficial level and does not transcend tactical name-dropping until a number of theoretical essays are published: Eco's two studies remain marginal but Heath's form the basis of all subsequent discussions of Joyce. Little has been published on this particular Joyce interpretation: Tudor Olteanu wrote a review of issues 54 and 55 in 1974, and five years later Jennifer Levine published a short article in the *James Joyce Quarterly* that attempted to introduce the "other Joyce" (1978–79). She briefly discusses *Tel Quel*'s project in general, especially its anti-establishment position; she describes the movement in which the unreadability of the *Wake* is taken as the starting point of the interpretation and as a paradigm for the critical *écriture* of the writers of *Tel Quel*, which is self-referential and metaphorical. In the interpretation of Joyce's writing Levine identifies three major themes: the deconstruction of totality, that of the codes, and that of the subject. The common denominator is another sense of the production of meaning, away from identity and toward activity. Levine fails to emphasize the ideological and political breaks in the history of *Tel Quel*, but her article remains important for its attempt to mediate between the two enemy camps at the Paris Symposium.

What Levine and most of the American and English critics who wrote on the French Joyce had missed was that Sollers's performance in Paris had been the intellectual equivalent of an admittedly loud whistling in the dark; *Tel Quel*'s virulent Maoism was already on the way out. This became official only in the winter issue of 1976, which closed with a brief note:

> Reports continue to appear, here and there, on the 'Maoism' of *Tel Quel*. Let us therefore make it clear that although *Tel Quel* has indeed, during a certain time, attempted to inform the public about China, especially in order to oppose the systematic disinformation of the French Communist party, this need not be the case today. . . . The recent events in Peking will finally open even the most reluctant eyes to what one should no longer hesitate to call the 'Marxist structure,' the sordid consequences of which on the level of the manipulation of power and information can from now on be verified. We must return to it, and in depth. It is time to rid ourselves of these myths, of all myths.
>
> *Tel Quel*, October 1976

In *Délivrance*, a series of discussions with Maurice Clavel broadcast on the national radio station France-Culture, we can almost witness Sollers's conversion; in the July talks the two men are *face à face* and the France Culture journalist who introduces the discussions presents the two as adversaries: Sollers had attacked Clavel's ideas "very violently" two months before. Maurice Clavel belongs, especially with his books *Ce que je crois* (1975) and *Dieu est Dieu, nom de Dieu* (1976) to the earliest group of *nouveaux philosophes*, more specifically to the Catholic branch of the religious faction. When the first critical history of this latest of Parisian intellectual fashions was written by François Aubral and Xavier Delcourt in 1977, the two authors could still dismiss the phenomenon as a "storm in a theological glass of water" (120), as a typically Parisian fad that would have failed miserably anywhere else and that will soon be replaced by something else. But the opposite seems to have been the case. Bernard-Henri Lévy ended ninth on a list of the most influential French intellectuals in a poll organized by the magazine *Lire* in 1981, before Beckett, Aragon, Althusser, and Sollers; and André Glucksmann, Bernard-Henri Lévy and their fellow travelers are still at the center of the intellectual scene today.

It all started in the spring of 1976 when Christian Jambet and Guy Lardreau published *L'Ange*, which represented the beginning of yet another intellectual revolution. For the first time in a long while, political revolutionaries exchanged the purity of a radical Marxism-Leninism for metaphysics in a more or less explicit return to Heidegger. Under the attacks of Derrida and *Tel Quel*, metaphysics and its twin, onto-theology, had been the enemy to be analyzed and exposed. While Jambet and Lardreau embraced metaphysics, Maurice Clavel went a step further; for him, and for Philippe Némo, metaphysics remains within an atheist framework. On the part of God there has been a Revelation and man's only adequate answer can be Faith.

This message had already been disseminated by Clavel in *Ce que je crois* and in his work as a journalist for the socialist weekly *Le Nouvel Observateur*, but according to the dynamics of intellectual fashions, the movement still needed a name before it could become really influential. In June 1976, Bernard-Henri Lévy edited a dossier in *Les Nouvelles Littéraires*, which he called "Les Nouveaux Philosophes." The dossier is symptomatic: first of the orchestrated media impact, of the narrowness of the base of the 'movement' at this point and of the attempt to set itself up as a legitimate child of poststructuralism. The first thing Lévy does, as Aubral, Delcourt, and many other early commentators point out, is to create the impression that these new thinkers are being prosecuted. The problem is that there simply wasn't such a thing as a new philosophy yet and certainly not in this dossier, which centers around *L'Ange*. The only real *nouveau philosophe* who is present here is Jean-Paul Dollé, and all the others are only marginal figures. As usually happens with such movements, the label had only just been invented when it was already dismissed as misleading, and Lévy himself would, a couple of months later, attack the name he had introduced himself as "an invention of the media" (quoted in Aubral and Delcourt 1977, 15). The dossier itself contains a letter from

Barthes and interviews with Lévi-Strauss, Desanti, and Michel Serres, who are definitely not new philosophers; and it carries dedications to Heidegger, Freud, Lacan, to China, Foucault, Barthes, Serres and "the Nietzscheans." Aubral and Delcourt simply dismiss this as a futile attempt to recuperate the "old" philosophers, but I am afraid they are wrong. The links between structuralist and poststructuralist thought, on the one hand, and the new philosophy, on the other, are quite clear. Jean-Marie Benoist was Lévi-Strauss's assistant; Jean-Paul Dollé follows closely Heidegger's writings; and Guy Lardreau, Christian Jambet, and Philippe Némo apply Lacan's late theories.

A number of the ideas of the new philosophers are simply borrowed from poststructuralism: literature is the most dangerous enemy of the State (Dollé); the repression of the state is pervasive and functions especially through language; on the level of theory the weapons of the State are rationalism and positivism, both children of the Enlightenment. In addition Heidegger resumes the important role he had before 1968. In the early sixties, Jean Pierre Faye had exposed the political conservatism of Heidegger's philosophy, and Heidegger's name had subsequently become taboo. But this does not mean that his philosophy did not have an influence on poststructuralism, which developed precisely at the time the philosopher's name was being repressed. Lacan, Derrida, Michel Foucault, and Gilles Deleuze all have clear Heideggerian echoes in their writings, either directly or via the strictly Heideggerian interpretation of Nietzsche popular in France in the sixties. The idea that literature, and especially difficult avant-garde literature, escapes the foils of metaphysics remains pervasive, and even critics of the new philosophers such as Delcourt and Aubral do not escape from it: in the conclusion of their critique of the new philosophy they write that the idea of literature with which the new philosophers work is a literature of dreams:

> for them, the imaginary is reduced to the soporific, which allows one to forget the discomforts of the real by sinking into paltry superstitions. . . . The 'new philosophy' is to fiction what photo novels are to the works of Joyce or Borgès. To be against the 'new philosophy' also means to be in favor of fiction, in favor of literature. (324)

The idea of the special status of literary language itself is directly related to Heidegger's *Denken* and *Dichten,* and especially Dollé's *Haine de la pensée* (1976) is full of references to Heidegger and Hölderlin: "The Angel will not survive, but the poet, in these times of need" (quoted in Aubral and Delcourt 1977, 32). Dollé also follows Heidegger, and with him every single poststructuralist who has written on Hölderlin, in pitting the poet against his friend Hegel, which is now considered to be one of the weakest points of Heidegger's interpretation of Hölderlin (Jamme 1984, 215). Dollé distinguishes two reactions to the Real: either the Real makes you weep, like Hegel and Wagner, or you make the Real weep, like the inventors of a language and the passionate thinkers such as Hölderlin and Nietzsche (Dollé 1976, 167). Jean-Marie Benoist sees Hölderlin as a protostructuralist à la Lacan (1975, 335), and Glucksmann even explicitly excludes Hölderlin from his list of master thinkers whose totalitarian philosophies are responsible for everything that has gone wrong since the beginning of the nineteenth century (1977, 126).

The new philosophers do not challenge either their precursors or the intellectual inspirators of their godfathers; on the contrary, they simply elaborate their theories and scrape away the materialist varnish that covered the Heideggerian heritage in France, a movement that was probably accelerated by the German philosopher's death in May of 1976. The only master thinker who does not survive is Karl Marx, not yet in *L'Ange,* which is still Maoist, and not yet in *La Cuisinière et le mangeur d'hommes,* in which Glucksmann carefully distinguishes between Marx and the Marxists, but most explicitly in a book like *Karl Marx: Histoire d'un bourgeois allemand* by Françoise Lévy (1976) and in various comments about Aleksandr Solzhenitsyn and the gulag by Maurice Clavel and Bernard-Henri Lévy. Marxism is now analyzed as the totalitarian political twin of fascism, and the gulag is shown to be already present in Marx's writings. In concretely political terms, things escalate accordingly; although Jambet, Lardreau, and Clavel called themselves left wing, they opposed the Communist party, which as Maoists they had already disagreed with anyway, and they also oppose the Union de la Gauche, the agreement between

French socialists and communists that would bring them to power in 1981. The only alternative in real-life politics is Valéry Giscard d'Estaing and there are even a few nostalgic references to Charles de Gaulle.

Politically, these thinkers base themselves on Foucault's concept of an omnipresent power of surveillance that expresses itself in language and that controls every aspect of life. This power is personified in the figure of the leviathan, *le Maître*, simultaneously discovered by Jambet, Lardreau, Némo, and Bernard-Henri Lévy. Whereas the Master in *L'Ange* seems to be a Foucauldean Big Brother with a complete control over sex and language, Némo borrows his concept from the four structural positions Lacan had distinguished in his *Séminaires*, the Hysteric, the Academic, the Analyst, and the Master (1975, 21).

Sollers shares the basis from which the *nouveaux philosophes* start: a Maoist Marxism-Leninism that became increasingly difficult to reconcile with the realities of China and Solzhenitsyn's gulag. It is highly symptomatic of the power of the written, literary word in France that after half a century, Stalin's camps were accepted as a reality only when a writer, Solzhenitsyn, had described them. Second, Sollers accepted Foucault's interpretation of the omnipresence of power and Althusser's view that political structures resemble linguistic ones. *Tel Quel*'s work was furthermore based on an unavowed Heideggerian notion of the privileged access via literature to the Real and an interest in all forms of irrational transgression. One proof of this common ground is André Glucksmann's genuine surprise when he calls the questions Kristeva, Sollers, and Houdebine ask him about *La Cuisinière* "sympas voire sympathysantes" (1975, 72).

But in July 1976, Sollers is not ready yet, which is clear in the France-Culture discussion with Clavel: in the regular sessions Sollers opposes Clavel's interpretation of the events of May 1968 as an irruption of religion or "a return of the human autotranscendence" (Clavel and Sollers 1977, 40). This is in keeping with *Tel Quel*'s policies: Clavel himself had been accused by Maria-Antonietta Macciocchi of belonging to "the whining fringe" (1975, 64), and *L'Ange* would be ridiculed in the autumn issue of 1976. But in a sixth talk between Clavel and Sollers, taped in October and not broadcast, a new confrontation reveals that the latter has changed his mind after the recent events in China (Mao's death). Sollers explains that his interest in Marxism dates from 1966: "It was in 1966, precisely as a result of the Cultural Revolution, that I became interested in Marxism. I may not have become interested otherwise" (132). But this was a mistake; Mao had only managed to prolong the life of the "Marxist illusion": "One thinks one is surpassing religion and one reinstates it under its most repressive form" (133). This becomes obvious when we look at the phenomenon of the mummification of Lenin and Mao, where the revolutionary message is turned into a quotation, "justifying any-thing" (137), and which becomes "the transformation of the letter into a dead letter, into a stereotype which has force of law" (146). The alternative lies in Christianity itself—"The stroke of genius of Chris-tianity is that there is no mausoleum of Christ, that nobody has seen Christ rise" (139)—and in political terms, the Great Man: "But I also defend the Great Man, Clavel, in the sense in which Nietzsche, in a magnificent saying, claims one must always defend the strong against the weak" (137–38). It even allows statements such as "Mao and de Gaulle are only great and will continue to exist because, in politics, they looked for . . . something else" (138).

It is clear that Sollers has adopted Clavel's point of view, and this new attitude will dominate *Tel Quel* from now on. Sollers's "conver-sion" can therefore be dated between the end of July and the end of October, after the publication of Lévy's dossier but before the New Philosophy happening organized by Jérôme Bindé and Henri Ronse at the Théâtre Oblique. In November, Sollers followed Julia Kristeva to the States, where he delivered a lecture at Yale and where he was interviewed by David Hayman; the conversion also changed *Tel Quel's* attitude to the United States. Whereas in the sixties, Kristeva had for political reasons refused the professorship René Girard had offered her (Kristeva 1983b, 43), in the seventies she regularly went to Colum-bia to teach, and judging from the holiday pictures published in *Tel Quel*, her husband followed her. In 1983 she looks back at the time when she was "warmly welcomed by a generous American Univer-sity, which was free and encouraging by its curiosity and its intellectual naïveté" (53), a rather ambiguous compliment she could only begin to express in 1977 when the political line had changed. First Sollers published in *Tel Quel* 69 "Deux interventions aux Etats-Unis," in which he observes: "America is born at the same time as writing as an experience of limits: a question asked about the limits of the species" (1977a, 7).

Tel Quel 70 has an essay by *nouveau philosophe* Philippe Némo (1977a), and next is a triple issue, entirely devoted to the United States of America, that opens with a discussion by Sollers, Kristeva, and Pleynet about their reasons for such a venture. The United States is nonphilosophical and non-Greek (Kristeva will later compare New York to decadent Rome [1983b, 53]), the signifiers of sex and money are reproduced more openly there than anywhere else, and New York is the world's computer center (Kristeva, Pleynet, and Sollers 1977). The French contributions to this special issue include the second part of Némo's essay on Job (1977b) and a paper on Plato by a follower of Jambet, Gilles Susong (1977). *Tel Quel* 77 has a contribution by Bernard-Henri Lévy (1978), and no. 78 announces the establishment of a "Comité des Intellectuels pour l'Europe des Libertés." The initials spell *CIEL*, "heaven."

Some of Sollers's new ideas are comfortably close to the old doctrines: the interest in the exceptional individual is simultaneously an elaboration and a perversion of a general antihumanist stance in (post)structuralism that had already been diagnosed by Sartre, an elaboration that can be found in the *nouveaux philosophes* and that is at least partly based on ideas in Lacan's psychoanalysis. For *Tel Quel* and the new philosophers, Lacan's inability to keep a school together became a characteristic of all (good) psychoanalysis: "The analysis, basically, dissolves every possible community" (Sollers 1975b, 25). Even the most striking shift in Sollers's thinking, from an antimetaphysical, antireligious stance to an explicitly Catholic position, is less radical than could be inferred from the discussions in *Délivrance*. Sollers had already been interested in mysticism, in Dante, and in the Bible since the sixties, especially in what he then called "l'expérience des limites," a kind of mystical experience that Sollers finds in the life and works of writers such as Artaud, Bataille, and Lautréamont. It is this religious dimension that continues to characterize the works of the new philosophers and that helps to distinguish them from the New Right, a movement that dates from the same period but should not be confused with it. The *nouvelle droite* is explicitly antireligious, either from a Celtic, Breton, or other pagan point of view, or from the perspective of a Greek and Nietzschean atheism that blames all the ills of the Western world on the Judaeo-Christian heritage, an attitude that is also reflected in its anti-Semitism and opposition to the state of Israel. The new philosophers are explicitly pro-Israel: Maurice Clavel was from very early on; he even volunteered for the 1956 war. For the others, the support for Israel, like that for Solzhenitsyn, seems to have come relatively late.

We do not have enough evidence to support the claim that Sollers was converted by Clavel; Sollers himself never offered reasons for his change of mind, and it seems to have been the result of the kind of *coup de foudre* that Clavel describes in *Ce que je crois*. This book is very interesting, also for its peculiar attitude to the Catholic church, to philosophy, and to politics. The similarities between the ideas in this book (and even its autobiographical form) and Sollers's new stance are striking and fit into a long tradition in French Catholic thinking. The French church has always been conscious of its role as the "eldest daughter" of the church of Rome. There has always been a link between conservative politics and one segment of the French church, from the works of novelists such as Barrès and of poets such as Péguy to more recent phenomena, such as the movement in support of Monseigneur Lefèbvre, who leads the opposition against the modernist innovations introduced by the second Vatican Council. Ex-leftists such as Clavel and Sollers do not sympathize with the worker-priests; on the contrary, they support the explicitly reactionary positions of Lefèbvre and Pope John Paul II. This Catholicism is antiliberal and antimodernist; the enemy is the French revolution and the capitalist, bourgeois society it engendered. That is why Clavel's attempt to enlist Kant in his camp is so provocative. Kant has always been seen by these right-wing Catholics as unpoetic, anticlerical, and philosophical. But Clavel takes only one sentence from the introduction to the first *Critique* in which Kant writes that he wants to limit science to make room for religious belief; and Clavel discards the rest of Kant's work and even philosophy as such, which is, according to Sollers, the handmaiden of Protestantism. The Catholicism of Sollers and Clavel is basically anticlerical and sides with the mystics, the Gnostics, and the saints, not with the church as an institution or as a community of believers; in Jean-Marie Benoist's terms, not the church of Peter, but that of John (1980, 55), which would explain the special role the fourth gospel plays, both for Clavel (1975, 286) and for Sollers.

This passionate and ecstatic religion implies a sexual dimension that relates these conversions to those of Baudelaire and Huysmans. Sollers places himself in a tradition within decadent literature, which has been analyzed by Mario Praz in *The Romantic Agony* (1978), which originates in Chateaubriand, and which includes Barbey d'Aurevilly, Josephin Péladan, Villiers de l'Isle-Adam, Paul Verlaine, Maurice Barrès, Léon Bloy, Henri Millon de Montherlant, and Dostoyevski. Praz also mentions an indictment of these 'neo-Catholic' writers from the orthodox perspective in a chapter of Father Laurence Janssens's *Summa Theologica* entitled "De sensuali mysticismo recentioris cuiusdam scholae pseudo-catholicae" (Praz 1978, 409). It is only within a tightly hierarchical and even authoritarian church that we have a strict set of rules and regulations. In a secularized modern world the limits between good and evil are vague at best and transgressions are rarely scandalous. In the ultramontane church the ordered universe of morality offers the determined sinner a greater potential for transgression and scandal. Not only can one break the rules by sinning, one can also obstinately adhere to the rules positively in the asceticism and self-immolation of saints and mystics or negatively in the torture and death of martyrs. This drew Bataille both to Catholicism and to Chinese and Japanese cruelty, and, conversely, it attracted a violently anti-Western Japanese nationalist such as Yukio Mishima to the iconography of Saint Sebastian's martyrdom. The theme continued to be important in France: we had Barthes's juxtaposition of Sade and

Loyola, and the whole phenomenon of the popularity of Sade and Artaud's works; there is Lacan's work on the mystics, on Bernini's Saint Theresa, etc. In Sollers's novels the theme gives rise to the combination of sexual explicitness and reflections on religion in *Femmes* (1984), *Portrait du joueur* (1984), and *Le Coeur absolu* (1987). Clavel compares the Revelation to the struggle of a frigid woman to liberate herself and be liberated by a man; it turns out that his interpretation of the Ten Commandments and of Kant's Second Critique leaves something to be desired when he writes that his categorical imperative has always been "to commit adultery, but never to lead somebody into it" (Clavel 1975, 240).

Tel Quel was very early in its openness to the *nouveaux philosophes*; most of the other leading French intellectuals either ignored or rejected them without too much discussion, although all seem to have come to terms with them by 1980. In the same issue in which "A propos du maoïsme" appeared, Denis Roche translated Pound, a writer who had disappeared during the Maoist years, and a new interest in Hölderlin is announced in Jean-Louis Houdebine's translation of some unpublished fragments by the German poet. Houdebine had been a fellow traveler of *Tel Quel* ever since *Théorie d'ensemble* (Foucault et al. 1968), but his role became more central in 1971 when, as an editor of *Promesse*, he interviewed Derrida (the talks were later included in *Positions* [Derrida 1972b]), and later Sollers and Pleynet (Houdebine 1972b). In the following years, his contributions to *Tel Quel* follow the strict Maoist line: attacks against surrealism (1971a; 1971b; 1972), against Jean-Edern Hallier's *La Cause des peuples* (1973a), an essay on *Lois* (1974). Most of these texts are shorter essays and book reviews, and ironically, it is precisely in the issue that announces *Tel Quel*'s break with Mao that Houdebine publishes the first part of "L'Impasse du langage dans le marxisme," which is part of a book called *Langage et marxisme* (1977a). The embarrassment of publishing this still Maoist study at the beginning of the new era can be read between the lines of the preface Houdebine supplies: "what can a title like this, *Language and Marxism*, mean in 1976? *Which* Marxism are we dealing with?" (1976c, 81). In the spring of 1977 the second half of the essay is published (1977c) with another study by Houdebine (1977b), this time on Zhdanov's attack against Joyce at the first Congress of Soviet Writers in 1934. In the historical survey opening the latter essay, Solzhenitsyn's *Gulag Archipelago* (1974) figures prominently as a source, and Joyce is presented as the natural enemy of a repressive political system such as Stalinism and of socialist realism as the cultural symptom of such a regime: "From the literature of 'socialist realism' to the O.G.P.U. [the Stalinist secret police] and the gulag, the link is clear" (Houdebine 1977b, 47). In an appendix Houdebine also attacks Aragon for not defending Joyce and for having remained an accomplice of the Stalinist French Communist party. As the official writer of the French Communist party, Aragon had already been a favorite target of the maoist *Tel Quel* and this continued to be the case in the next decade (Macciocchi 1983, 294–95; 342–43).

In an essay published in 1979, Houdebine addressed Joyce's texts, this time in a discussion of socialization/exclusion procedures from which there is only one escape, Kristeva's *polylogue*. Houdebine's examples are *Finnegans Wake* and *Paradis* (1979a). In the autumn of the same year Houdebine published two more essays on Joyce, and once more Sollers is a central presence. The first opens with "Starting from one of Sollers's remarks. . ." (1979b, 52) and is punctuated by remarks such as "and which Sollers translates very well as . . ." (53), "Sollers has already remarked about another subject. . ." (54), "(see also the very beautiful analysis of the fragment of 'Anna Livia Plurabelle' by Sollers)" (56), "Sollers defines the operation very well. . ." (58), etc. The text itself is heavily indebted to Sollers's "Joyce and Co" (1975a): the Dantesque superposition of four levels of meaning, the long quotations on page 58, the difference with surrealism, with Jung, with Gertrude Stein; and the idea of the infinite and transcendental ("trans-nomination" [62] marries two Sollersian concepts: "l'élangue" and "transnationalism"). Finally, Houdebine stresses all through the essay the evolution from Mallarmé to Joyce and Sollers. He also refers to the same remarks about *Finnegans Wake*, and he even uses the same quotations. Houdebine's own use of the text is debatable: he suggests a relationship among three different fragments: "the return of the

Verb umprincipiant through the trancitive spaces is punctuated by the carillons of Easter returning from Rome to Botany Bay, *sicut campanulae petalliferentes, in whole clangalied* ([FW] 615)" (1979b, 53), where these three different phrases occur respectively at *FW*, 594.02–03, 601.16, and 601.20 and have very little in common. Houdebine does the same thing a bit further on: the square wheel of the *Wake* "turns back on its tracks, though they are never altogether the same; *in that multimirror megaron of returningties, whirled without end to end* (582.20– 21), and each time *with a little difference* (581.35)" (Houdebine 1979b, 58). The two phrases have no textual connection in the *Wake* at all. A special problem is the link between Hölderlin's *Sprachverwirrung* and Joyce's use of the Babel theme. Houdebine writes:

> But, and here as much as elsewhere, the "James Joyce" strategy is insepar-
> able from the experience which takes place in the *Sprachverwirrung* Höld-
> erlin spoke of, this "confounding of languages" signified by Babel, of
> which the "furnace" (*ein Brand*) darts its flames amidst all the *tribab-*
> *balbutience [sic] hides* (309), *babbelers babeling, babbling, bubbling* (*passim!*).
> (Houdebine 1979b, 57)

The reference to Hölderlin is unfairly obscure (the words occur in a late fragment "der Vatican" [1943, 253]: "Oft aber wie ein Brand / Entstehet Sprachverwirrung"), and I completely fail to see what the *Wake*'s joyous *babbling* has to do with the horrendous experience described in Hölderlin's late text.

Although Heath had still quoted Jung without comment in "Am-biviolences," Houdebine picks up Sollers's suggestion in "Joyce et Cie" that Jung was bound to misunderstand *Ulysses*, and he takes it one step further: "I do claim that C. G. Jung's interpretation of *Ulysses* in 1932 is a Nazi reading" (1979c, 65). But Houdebine's basis for such an accusation is extremely narrow: first he points to the resemblance between Jung's interpretation and Radek's and then claims that Jung anticipated the current psychiatric practice in the Soviet Union by doubting Joyce's sanity. Rather predictably Houdebine finds that Jung's reading tends towards polytheism and the eternal female and that it is anti-Catholic and anti-Semitic. This is another element of

Sollers's new worldview in which, maybe partly under the influence of William Burroughs, women are blamed for everything that goes wrong with the world. Politically this analysis follows the new philosophers' insistence on the fundamental resemblance between fascism and communism: both inevitably lead to the suppression of individual freedom, to censorship, and later to anti-Semitism and concentration camps; both have their sources in the works of nineteenth century German master thinkers. The only force that stands up to this unholy alliance of feminism, Jung, fascism, atheism, polytheism, and paganism is the Catholic and Jewish belief in one male God and the application of this insight in the art and literature of Freud, Picasso, Joyce, Lacan, Dostoyevski, and Shakespeare.

This idea is further developed by Houdebine in an essay on Picasso in which he links Jung's rejection of Picasso to the typically psychiatric "denial of the exception" (1981b, 54) that is also at work in the sociological, Marxist, socialist and, of course, fascist analyses. This new interpretation of Catholicism is more pronounced in "Jung et Joyce" (1979c) than in "La Signature de Joyce" which was probably written earlier. In the latter, Houdebine mentions the Catholic element twice in rather vague terms, although he does not hesitate to add that it plays an important role in Joyce (1979b, 53, 57). This is what distinguishes *Tel Quel* at this late stage of its development from other *nouveaux philosophes*: whereas Maurice Clavel stresses the Christian element and Glucksmann and Lévy the Jewish dimension as antidotes against the totalitarian threat, Sollers and *Tel Quel* combine the two, Sollers by reclaiming the Catholicism of his youth, Kristeva by searching for Jewish ancestors. This shift toward an openly religious dimension can be followed in Sollers's writings: in *Délivrance*, during the regular sessions, Sollers still bravely opposes Clavel's transcendentalism by pitting the Bible against Catholicism, while in the October session he has adopted a position that is much closer to Clavel's. The book ends with the statement of Clavel (who was to die soon afterward): "In one word, let us be ready for that which is preparing itself! I will try to *tame* the apocalypse. Help me. And soon, maybe, replace me" (Clavel and Sollers 1977, 153).

The same shift can be observed in Sollers's writings about his own creative work. The note on Maoism was preceded by a short text "Vers la notion de 'Paradis,'" in which he described the Bible as "the book that most frightens all moderns, that scandalizes most and shocks most deeply their incredible decency" (1976b, 103). A sequel to this essay, in the form of a radio interview with Pleynet in 1976, was published two years later; here Sollers elaborates on the relationship between *Paradis* and the Bible. Just as God's "I" in the Bible cannot be traced to a single source, so Sollers's "je" in *Paradis* appears "in the points of effervescence of language where the subject speaks each time from a position that cannot be reduced to the identity of this or that author, while there obviously is an author" (Sollers 1978c, 95). His writing is directly inspired by his reading of the prophets, and *Paradis* derives from them an apocalyptic discourse that insists that something is resuscitated, that a father is alive,

> In other words, the thing that most frightens mankind, its most important repression, is the fact that a father should be alive in the form of *I say*. That is what they call God. What do you want, it's their problem. While me, I am just interested. (97)

Culture, civilization even, is based on the notion that the father is dead, that the mother is made to remain a virgin, and that she experiences inexpressible pleasures, which make her the addressee and holder of language. From this maternal matrix, few manage to escape: "For the twentieth century, I see only one who is great enough and that is Joyce, to whom I return often" (98). This text goes further than the first, but Sollers is still holding back.

In a text read at a conference in Milan in November 1977 and also published in *Tel Quel* 75, Sollers proceeded to attack the two foundations on which *Tel Quel*'s Maoist phase had been built: "It is no longer a secret for anybody that, in the final analysis, Marxism and psychoanalysis do not have anything to say about art and literature" (1978a, 56). The resemblance between fascism and communism is analyzed again and in passing Lacan is chided for having praised a Stalinist poet. But is psychoanalysis really the antidote to the Marxist repression as Sollers still seemed to think in 1976? "On all other levels the Marxoid and the analytical deliriums seem to exist on completely opposite sides. But I think more and more that in their constant desire to refute the aesthetic exception the two positions, nodally, meet" (58). This explains the title: "Marxism Sodomized by Psychoanalysis, Itself Raped by God-Knows-What": both Marxism and psychoanalysis have as a model the Catholic Church, "Isn't that Church built on the impossibility of really admitting a history of a word-made-man which results in the same impossibility of imagining a reverse side which would be a man-made-word?" (59). Art and literature are not even human and cannot be grasped by merely human means. In the next essay, Sollers again goes a little bit further: the central question is whether a language needs a body. Because this question remains unanswered, the Church can always rise from its ashes. In our Christian culture the question has been addressed only by the mystics: "hundreds, thousands of people all through the centuries have had adventures with this story of the Holy Ghost and the Word" (1978b, 88). Witnesses are Saint Bernard, but also Freud's Schreber, Artaud, Bataille, and Joyce.

Finally, in an interview published in 1979, Sollers claims that really great art "releases the religious neurosis" (1979b, 11), and he now stresses the alliance of Jews and Christians (i.e., Catholics).

> If I would be a pagan, if I would be violently opposed to all questions about monotheism and the Bible, if I would therefore be, by definition, anti-Semitic, anti-Jewish, anti-Christian—because that is the same thing—in other words if I would be a Nazi today . . . I would try to prevent by all means the reconciliation between Christians and Jews. (14–15)

The Catholic Church and Pope John Paul II represent the lesser evil, the institution that is the least repressive in its surveillance of exceptions: "The exception is not self-evident. I am a Catholic then, like Matisse. Or, if you want, like a Pole today" (17). In addition he defines his position as Gnostic because he believes that the world has been created by an evil God, who is no other than the Great Mother herself.

The relevance of this radical shift in Sollers's thinking and, consequently, in the editorial policies of *Tel Quel* on the interpretation of literature and more specifically of Joyce's oeuvre is minimal. Although a shift from Mao to John Paul II, from Lenin to Nietzsche, and from a Marxist-Leninist communism to the Holy Catholic and Apostolic Church of Rome would seem to necessitate an equally radical shift of literary allegiances and although Joyce may at first sight seem rather difficult to enlist in the Catholic ranks, Sollers does manage to retain *Ulysses* and *Finnegans Wake* at the center of his attention. In almost all of the essays I quoted from and in other texts from the same period, Joyce's name keeps cropping up. Not that Sollers's conversion is surprising—after all he had already moved through quite a number of different phases; what really shocks the observer is how little this radical turnabout seems to have affected Sollers. Although he has exchanged one church for another, he has not altered his style of writing and speaking, or his attitude toward sex, writing, women, music, art, and even politics. We should not forget that the Communist and Socialist parties had already been the deadly enemies of the Maoist *telqueliens*, much more even than Georges Pompidou or Giscard. *Tel Quel*—and this also goes for other ex-Maoists such as Glucksmann and Bernard-Henri Lévy—did not have allies in France, especially not in concretely political terms.

At the center of this puzzle is Sollers's attitude to literature and especially to the select group of writers *Tel Quel* had adopted as patron saints in the sixties: Artaud, Bataille, Joyce. Most of them survive the two most radical breaks, and the only exceptions are the writers who are still alive and who come in and move out of orbit for more obscure and maybe more personal reasons. Hölderlin is only apparently exceptional: although he was not mentioned in *Tel Quel* between 1971 and 1976, the German poet is much more present in *H* and *Lois*, the only creative products of the period, than in any other of the novels Sollers wrote. The same can be said of Dante, Mallarmé, Sade. Sollers himself is adamant about this point and repeatedly stresses the continuity in his thinking. This is why the word *conversion* may be badly chosen: a conversion is a radical and intimate change in the deep structure of a personality; it involves an equally radical change in a person's allegiances, a burning of idols, and, most importantly, a humble submission to another authority. Humility is not one of Sollers's prime virtues; and it is important that despite the chameleonic changes Sollers goes through, he fundamentally remains the same person. This is evident in the rhetoric of his critical and theoretical writings; although some of the authorities have changed and some new enemies have been identified, *écriture* remains an experience of the limits, a mystical state of grace that is as scandalous as a sexual perversion. Neither the university, nor psychoanalysis, nor even politics can begin to interpret this radical form of literature. From 1976, Sollers proceeds to exclude from his analysis of texts the last remnants of the marginal kinds of politics and psychoanalysis that he had deemed useful before. They are replaced by Jewish and Catholic theology and doctrine.

What does all this mean for Sollers's Joyce interpretation? In an interview with Frans De Haes, a Belgian critic who has taken Houdebine's place as his favorite interviewer, critic and hagiographer, Sollers tackles Joyce directly by reading "The seim anew" (*FW*, 215.23), not just as "the same anew" because he believes that the word "anew" does not exist in the English language, but "as French pronounced with a heavy English accent" and then we hear "sem" (semite, seed) and "agneau" (lamb). "Always the same semite lamb, mystical lamb. . . . It is maybe simply Christ" (Sollers 1979a, 44). This indicates the direction *Tel Quel*'s reading of Joyce will take from now on and it is confirmed in another special Joyce issue in the spring of 1980.

This dossier, edited by Houdebine and entitled "Joyce: Obscénité et Théologie," presents a number of translations (of the University of Padua essays and of Joyce's letters to his wife Nora and to Martha Fleischmann), two long talks between Houdebine and Sollers, and an essay by David Hayman published in the *James Joyce Quarterly* three years before (1977a). In the interview with Sollers, Houdebine immediately introduces the notion of the "Catholic element" in Joyce's work. Sollers stresses, once again, the exceptional nature of Joyce's achievement: "Joyce closes one cycle of Catholicism and he announces another" (Houdebine and Sollers 1980a, 37). The scandal lies in the relationship between the Old and the New Testament: the sensational novelty of *Ulysses* is due to the lifting in that book of the taboo on the Jewish origins of Catholicism by a critique on both the earlier forms of Catholicism and on the form of the Jewish exile. This central insight, which continues to haunt our own age, was arrived at by Joyce when he was writing *Giacomo Joyce* and *Ulysses*, where, from the beginning, Joyce opposes Greek culture (and therefore also nature) in the person of Buck Mulligan to something else, something incomprehensible to a Greek, natural mind. Stephen's refusal to kneel at his mother's deathbed is a religious act because it is a rejection of the "maternal, pagan substantialism" in Catholicism: "it is nothing less than the rejection of all that harks back to paganism in Catholicism" (41). Buck Mulligan represents a belief in nature, in the mother as holder of the phallus; he is a heretic, a Protestant, and a servant of women, "la femme parodisée." Stephen's reaction is one of horror and this represents a link to Shakespeare—to *Hamlet*, *Macbeth*, and *King Lear*—but with references also to the Bible. Mulligan also represents heresy and for Joyce there is only one, that of Arius, which also happens to be the source of Protestantism. The problematic status of the Trinity is central in every type of heresy, and a heretic will claim that the Father is alone, that the Word is not a person, or that Christ was only a man, sanctified by the Holy Ghost. All these heretics have a woman behind them, usually an empress who wants to reintroduce a religion dedicated to the service of the Great Mother. The answer of the Catholic church to this conspiracy was the dogma of the Immaculate Conception:

> Catholicism, with a magnificent symbolic mechanism, continues to reintegrate the elements of a fundamental obscenity, which constitutes the species and which is not that of the birds and the bees, although from time to time an important (ground) movement, of Woman, would have us believe that. (51)

Joyce himself was "very orthodox" (54), although he had to leave the church in order to remodel it. That is why *Ulysses* ends with Molly's monologue; Molly gives birth to a *yes*, "She gives birth clearly to what Joyce indicates he has made himself capable of producing, *Finnegans Wake*" (55).

The second part of the interview "La Trinité de Joyce" deals with the scandalous and obscene part of the Catholic experience, which cannot be analyzed by the Reformation or by its handmaiden philosophy, which is in itself "a secularized theology, the passage of all the points of a theology to something resembling an abstraction which will be called the field of philosophy" (1980b, 64). The scandal that Joyce and Sade have uncovered is the notion that a natural sexuality does not exist and that what we think of as sex is "nothing but an effect of language" (65). This insight heralds the end of the Reformation in our time.

In *Finnegans Wake*, HCE is *Hic est*, the voice of the Father recognizing the Son, a God who integrates the demoniac, the sexual, and the horrible, and it is here that we must situate Joyce's failure. Although he does not belong to humanity, "or at least he tried to escape from it" (74), he fails to cross the limits of mysticism, "I mean by that that Joyce's humor maybe fails to address a certain dimension of horror" (80). His hesitation before the central insight of mysticism that there is no world at all, gives rise to a "joycisme de convention" (84).

This dialogue is the most complete exposition of the last phase of Sollers's interpretation of Joyce. This reading is very simple; two forces are involved: first, the Jewish and Catholic theologies that posit the Trinity and manage to include the demoniac and sexual aspects of reality, and second, the opposite force, which is female, body and death, and which is expressed in pagan matriarchy, in Greek thought, in Rome ("Rome, c'est Maman"), in the Reformation, in philosophy, in feminism, in Jung, in Marx. Joyce represents the first tradition and this makes him, like Hölderlin, an exception: "Il fait interruption" (85). Sollers's comments also contain the usual number of inaccuracies: a remark by Mr. Kernan in *Ulysses* that America is "the sweepings of every country" is attributed to Joyce himself (49); Houdebine writes that Joyce opposes "Tiberiast duplex" to "Oedipus complex" (67), which is unlikely enough, but he adds "alluding thus to the reign of Tiberius, during which the other arrives there, in Palestine," a statement that is equally unlikely and not even true. Neither is it accurate that the Gospels were written at the time of the end of the Roman empire (82). A last element that needs to be mentioned is the autobiographical bias of the comments by Houdebine and Sollers: "ERIN, GREEN GEM OF THE SILVER SEA," a quotation from "Aeolus" (*U*, 7.236) is followed by "we must hear here something else that brings us close to this James Christ Joyce"; gem is *joyau* in French. A little later Sollers says about Professor Bassine, a Russian psychoanalyst who had attempted to introduce Freud's discovery to Soviet psychology by referring to Lacan and who is treated by Sollers as an agent of the KGB: "His first name is Philippe. . . . Irony! Because who knows if that is not a sign!" (68).

Paradis was published the following year (Sollers 1981a). The book was described by opponents and supporters alike as the ultimate in avant-garde writing and it even made the front page of *Le Monde*. This time every episode of the book had been published in *Tel Quel*, starting with no. 57 in the spring of 1974. The last episode dates from the winter of 1980 (no. 84) and this *"oeuvre en cours"* did not appear in issues 64, 66, and 74. Sollers continued to publish sections after 1981, first in *Tel Quel*, later in *L'Infini*, and in March 1986 Gallimard published *Paradis II*. The continuity with Sollers's earlier works is beyond question; there is hardly any thematic or stylistic difference between *H* and *Paradis*; in fact the latter picks up where the former leaves off. The last sentence of *H* reads ". . . toute chair est comme l'herbe l'ombre la rosée du temps dans la voix"; the first sentence of *Paradis* in its 1974 version is "voix flower c'était la dernière cascade jetée dans le noir." Against this continuity speaks the caesura of 1976, and there are traces, though very few, of that political change of ideas. In *Tel Quel* 58 Sollers had described Augusto Pinochet's coup in Chile, ". . . spain congratulates the chilean army with its coup the soldiers . . ."; in the book this becomes "the army succeeds in its coup the soldiers . . ." (1981a, 34); the next four lines, which describe a poet dying (presumably Pablo Neruda), are simply deleted. A page further on he also deletes ". . . israel recognizes the junta immediately and so does franco well he is still here that one protest from the jewish students they at least understand france recognizes too . . .," and in the text published in *Tel Quel* 61 Sollers also deletes "moroccan tunisian" after "frontier," and after "over there" he erases "oran algiers constantine," thereby de-particularizing the passages and making them more universally applicable. But for the most part, Sollers leaves the text as it was before 1976, and the break cannot really be observed in the text of *Paradis*, which again confirms the continuity in Sollers's thinking and writing. At the same time, Sollers's interest in Joyce seems to have diminished; the three references to his work all occur in sections that were published in 1974: "the waker is thunder" (13); "roll on thou deep and darkblue ocean roll" (17) (taken from Byron's *Childe Harold*, but it may have been borrowed via Joyce's *Wake* [385.35]) and a bit later a tree and a stream resemble the stem and the stone at the end of the Anna Livia Plurabelle chapter: ". . . speak louder I can't hear you with the noise of the highway . . ." (Sollers 1974, 31).

But Sollers did not forget Joyce; in the centenary year he wrote an introduction to Gisèle Freund's *Trois jours avec Joyce* (Sollers 1982a), in which he recapitulated the themes in "La Signature" and he wrote a similar piece for *Le Nouvel Observateur* (1982b). The next year Sollers effects another radical break; he cuts himself off from Seuil, abolishes *Tel Quel*, founds a new journal at Denoël with a new title but with the same format, letter type and frequency of publication, and publishes a 570-page traditional *roman-à-clef* (1983a).

In a way Sollers's decision to leave Seuil mirrors the political paradox in France, where the first seriously right-wing intellectual revival since World War II coincides with the first socialist government and president. Seuil is a Catholic publishing house that had tolerated Sollers's antics and had published, in addition to the journal itself, ten of Sollers's books and more than fifty titles in the "Collection *Tel Quel*." The editorial of the first issue of *L'Infini* has a motto by Hegel ("The infinite, the affirmation, as negation of the negation . . .") and is written in dialogue form with one speaker unmistakably Sollers, the other an incredulous outsider. *L'Infini* will continue where *Tel Quel* left off, with the same godfathers (Borgès, Blanchot, Lautréamont,

Levinas, Artaud) and the same program, in John Duns Scotus's words: "Theology is the science of the individual being whose essence is individualized by means of infinity" (quoted in Sollers 1983b, 4). The clean break does not represent a change of ideas and it probably has more to do with personal or financial differences.

Although Sollers simply continued the publication of *Paradis* in *L'Infini*, he managed to shock even more people by publishing another novel, *Femmes* (1983a), in Gallimard's series "NRF," after a quarter century with Seuil. This is all the more surprising when we read what he said in an interview with Jean-Jacques Brochier only two years before: "There is also the phenomenon that I will call 'n.r.fism.' The institution Gallimard has arrived at an extreme point of exhaustion in its conception of the staging of literary characters. Céline already violently put into question the institution Gallimard/NRF" (Brochier 1981, 51). Unexpectedly, Sollers produces a readable novel, with an "I" narrator who is called Will and who is writing the novel in English. The book will later be translated by a French friend called S., who is writing a book called *Comédie*, who comes from the southwest corner of France (Sollers is from Bordeaux), and who is described as "That conceited son of a bitch who thinks he is the new Joyce" (Sollers 1983a, 160). Again: "One probably recalls that, in his laborious *Comédie* without any punctuation, the most unreadable gibberish that has ever been produced, S.—not really famous for his modesty—thought he was Joyce" (269). There are characters in the novel called Werth (Roland Barthes); Fals (Lacan); Lutz (Althusser); Flora, a Spanish woman anarchist, who is really the Italian ex-communist Maria-Antonietta Macciocchi; Deb, the narrator's wife, a Bulgarian refugee, psychoanalyst and part-time teacher at Columbia ; Boris Fafner, a very publicity-oriented public figure (Jean-Edern Hallier); Alfredo Malmora (Alberto Moravia); Elissa, an Egyptian, editor of *Thoth*, a university journal (Hélène Cixous and *Poétique*). The references to Joyce in this novel do not offer new insights; Will's son is called Stephen; Joyce is often mentioned in conversation, with Malmora-Moravia, with S. and even with Pope John Paul II (386). The visit to the Vatican described in this novel did take place; in her memoirs Macciocchi tells of a visit to the Vatican library by a whole group of French intellectuals, among them Bernard-Henri Lévy and Sollers. Needless to say, they never even came close to Carol Wojtyla himself (Macciocchi 1983, 479–82).

In *L'Infini* Sollers does not lose sight of Joyce; in an interview with Frans De Haes in the second issue, he still compares *Paradis* to *Finnegans Wake* (Sollers 1983e, 18), although Joyce is not mentioned in a second talk about *Femmes* and *Paradis* in which, strangely enough, Sollers now openly uses the Heideggerian "being-toward-death" and refers to Hölderlin once more (1983f, 35, 41). Sollers repeated his performance one year later with an admittedly shorter but very similar novel, again published by Gallimard, *Portrait du joueur*. The narrator of this novel, author of *Femmes* (1984, 87), resembles also in other respects the writer of the book: his real name is even Sollers; his pseudonym is Philippe Diamant; and he even contemplates calling himself "joyaux" (224). "Will" has completely disappeared but Fafner is still there; there are also a best-seller called *La Rose Innomable*, an "Éditions de l'Autre," a Sophie who is not Diamant's wife, but who has become his mistress. The two met in Tübingen, in Hölderlin's tower, and she sends dirty letters to him. De Haes quite rightly points out that these letters are related to the ones that Joyce wrote to his wife Nora and that were translated in *Tel Quel* 83 (De Haes 1985, 100). Other references to Joyce can be found in the title; like Joyce's it is a "portrait of *the* player," and Sollers even compares the mistake of one of his critics in calling the book *Portrait d'un joueur* to the famous apostrophe in *Finnegans Wake* (1985, 92). There is also a "Non serviam" (77); a quark is mentioned (168); and Quinet's sentence in the *Wake* and in Hemingway is discussed (218–19). This is not different in *Le Coeur absolu*, Sollers's latest novel, which contains just a few little references to Joyce as when the narrator dreams that he meets the Irish writer (1987, 200). In *Théorie des exceptions*, finally, a collection of essays and articles (1986a), Sollers publishes a text on Joyce's voice that has not been published before. Joyce's recording of the end of Book I, 8 of *Finnegans Wake* is a mass for the apocalypse, and Ellmann's biography one of the best novels of all time. Sollers emphasizes the fact that Jung hated Joyce because his name means the same thing as that of Freud, in French *Joyeux* or *Joyaux.*

In the meantime Jean-Louis Houdebine had continued his theoretical work on Joyce. In 1981 he published in *Tel Quel* an elaborate review of Robert Boyle's *James Joyce's Pauline Vision* (1978), and he opens it with the characteristic tribute to Sollers for his discovery of the Catholic theme in Joyce (Houdebine 1981a, 41). He observes that the analysis of the literary experience can now come from only two sources; one is psychoanalysis, especially its reformulation by Lacan, to whom we owe "one of the rare important contributions to the understanding of Joyce's work" in France (46). Boyle, situated in the English-speaking cultural context, knows of psychoanalysis only the Jungian "(per)version" and he therefore chooses the second source, theology itself (47). But the one cannot be used productively without the other: "In short, let us say that if one does not take an *analytic* leap, theologian or not, Jesuit or not, one runs the risk of falling back . . . on Jung! Elementary, my dear Father" (47). Father Boyle and with him all "licensed Joycean commentators" make the mistake of reading Molly as the Third Person in the Trinity (49) and they thereby fall victim to the Jungian mythology of the Great Mother Goddess. This does not make sense, not on the level of theology, not on that of Joyce's text itself. Theologically speaking, there is no place for a woman in the Trinity, neither for a man; on the contrary, the Trinity commands "the logic of a truth *that does not at all belong to a natural order*" (49). Boyle is wrong when he posits the Trinity as a symbol of all generation and regeneration:

> No. This is completely wrong: there is no form of "regeneration" whatsoever in the Trinity. . . . the exact opposite is true: every form of human "generation and regeneration" is itself nothing else than the indefinitely failing metaphor ("something fails us") of that which Catholicism has registered as the Trinitarian operation and the drama of the Incarnation. (50)

On the level of his experience as a writer, Joyce's writing must be seen in the context of a radical experience of what is *symbolic* in humanity, and of the "(literal) enormity which the emergence of *language* makes appear in the cycles of an animal nature" (51). In Lacanian terms, Houdebine argues that Catholicism has most thoroughly investigated the logic of the insertion of the symbolic into the knot of symbolic/imaginary/real that constitutes each speaking subject, and it is therefore necessary to follow Joyce's theological argument to its logical conclusion. In "Ithaca" we witness a "general movement of *effusion* of the invisible" (55), and "Penelope" is a parody of "some of the essential dramatic elements that are proper to the evangelical scene of Incarnation" (56). The reflection of Molly's lamp on the screen of roller blind is the Annunciation, the sighting of the meteorite Epiphany, and "Ithaca" itself resembles the *Summa Theologica*. "Penelope" on the other hand is human, sexualized nature, which cannot be understood if one ignores the dimension of horror and abjection. Molly is not a prehuman, phallic mother; she represents a passage into something that is decidedly posthuman; she is the Virgin Mary through whom the Word can become flesh. With help from medieval theologians and mystics, Houdebine shows that Joyce stresses the obscenity of sexuality and its relationship with language: "it is impossible to understand obscenity (whether Joyce's or anybody else's) if one does not begin by recognizing that it is essentially a gesture of *language*" (68); sex is not natural at all. The Third Person of the Trinity must be Joyce himself, who has indeed disseminated his name all through *Finnegans Wake*.

In a last essay on Joyce in *Tel Quel*'s final issue, Houdebine has written an introduction to the *Tel Quel* interpretation of Joyce, originally intended as a preface to an American translation of *Tel Quel*'s Joyce essays (1983). Houdebine stresses *Tel Quel*'s resistance against any kind of academism and its adoption of a new concept of the subject, but he concentrates on Lacan's contribution to the discussion: Sollers has gone further than Lacan by stressing the transcending power of *écriture*, which has escaped psychoanalysis (and Lacan) completely. Whereas the latter has stressed the subjugation of the subject to *lalangue* (the empty word), the former has suggested a passage *through* the subject of the unconscious by the subject of writing that results not in *lalangue* but in *l'élangues* (both *les langues* and *l'élangue,* something that escapes language).

In 1984 Houdebine published, in Sollers's "Collection *L'Infini*" at Denoël, *Excès de langages (Hölderlin, Joyce, Duns Scot, Hopkins, Cantor, Sollers),* a book that contains studies on these authors published earlier in *Tel Quel* and *L'Infini* (Houdebine 1974, 1976b, 1977b, 1979c, 1981a, 1981b, 1983). The first sentence of the introduction of Houdebine's book is already written in the later Catholic style:

> It lies in the destiny of all languages that one day somebody, always, armed only with his freedom of speech, manages to formulate the demand for a transcendence, for a tearing away from the world, that beats contradictorily at the heart of each single language. (1984, 9)

Every language is a possible filter for all languages,

> an opening to practice in the enigmatic, *infinite* whole, which contains all, and which, although it does not exist (of course), is no less there, eternally ready to manifest itself to one or the other in the absolute urgency of an eternal Pentecost. (10)

It is this experience that entails an excess of thought and that can be found whenever literature becomes great art. Houdebine looks at the implications of this insight for the works of the writers he mentions in his title; in the first section he considers the works of Hölderlin, with a remarkable insistence on the later poems, and in the second he offers a reformulation of the ideas in his book on language and Marxism (1977a) in an essay on the problem of language faced with totalitarian revolutions, i.e., Soviet communism. While the fourth section deals with Duns Scotus, Cantor, Hopkins, and Sollers, the third and largest section is devoted completely to Joyce's works; it contains slightly revised versions of all the essays Houdebine published on Joyce in *Tel Quel.* In addition, there is also a text about *Our Exagmination Round his Factification for Incamination of Work in Progress* and an essay on "the second birth of James Joyce." The former opens with the statement that Joyce's work was "far, very far from having received in France the attention it deserved for its importance to all forms of modern literature" (1984, 161), although a more favorable climate was present in Paris than in Zürich or Trieste. That Joyce did not make a mark on French literature and thought and that efforts to introduce or even to interpret his works are still being thwarted are both due to the combined efforts of surrealism and Marxism, which have formed the cultural *doxa*. Breton, Aragon, and Jolas, too, have completely rejected Joyce's "lonely adventure," and it is precisely these two elements—the loneliness and the avant-garde adventure—that cannot be perceived by either Marxism or surrealism. After this summary of his earlier statements, Houdebine introduces and translates the two "letters of protest" that were added to *Our Exagmination*. The latter text once more articulates Joyce's Catholic opposition to the pagan worship of the Great Mother; Houdebine's remarks seem to be based almost entirely on the material developed in the two interviews with Sollers in *Tel Quel* 83 (Houdebine and Sollers 1980a, 1980b), which were not included in *Excès de langages*.

The allegiance to Sollers is the most distinguishing characteristic of Houdebine's critical work; I believe it would be difficult to isolate one thought that is original or one idea that contradicts or even challenges the Sollersian doctrine. This book is paradigmatic of Houdebine's allegiance: it opens and closes with essays on Sollers's creative work, and there is scarcely a page without direct reference to Sollers's writings or sayings. Like Marcelin Pleynet and, more recently, Frans De Haes, Houdebine has a very peculiar position within *Tel Quel* and *L'Infini*; although the magazine has always presented itself as a collective, it is clear that both endeavors are very much controlled by Sollers himself. One can only wonder about both Sollers's enormous influence on the people surrounding him and the intellectual integrity of his collaborators, who seem prepared to follow him again and again through all of his chameleonic changes.

This is also the case with the work of a number of other critics: Philippe Muray's *L'Opium des lettres* has an introduction by Sollers, and the critic keeps referring to the same authorities: Sade, Mallarmé, Lacan, Kristeva, Freud, Bataille, etc. In his book, Muray analyzes the presence of a philosophy of the One, which is the explicit code and the natural language of literature, and he offers an alternative, a kind of writing that escapes the "terrible submission to the One and the multiple." After sections on Mallarmé, Saint Paul, Rabelais, and Zola, and after a presentation of the Gnostic philosophies as an alternative to the philosophy of the One, Muray looks at Joyce, who has dreamed of a victory over this illusion: "And that dream is *Finnegans Wake*" (Muray 1979, 150). Mallarmé has constantly occupied Joyce's attention, and he is often referred to in the *Wake*. In one such comment— Muray uses David Hayman's "Joyce et Mallarmé" (1956)—Joyce unambiguously and "as if by accident" claims that Mallarmé suffers from the singular but enjoys the plural: "Mutemalice, suffering unegoistically from the singular but positively enjoying on the plural" (*FW*, 488.16–17). I fail to see Mallarmé in "Mutemalice," but for Muray the simple presence of the letter "M" seems to have been enough; he refers to Mallarmé's own thoughts about that letter in "Les Mots anglais" (151). The *Wake's* first word is read as "rêver-Un" because Muray reads the book as the nightmare of the superego "whose resounding fall in the universe provokes the breakdown of its empire and especially the bitter ascent, like a colossal discharge spread over 638 [*sic*] pages, of the world of the One in a whirlpool" (151). The monistic language is attacked in its most elementary particles: all of *Finnegans Wake* becomes "an epic of this slow and difficult attempt to shake off the sleep of a rationalism that engenders the monsters of a subject, a gigantic notation of a dream as a realization of the desire of One" (155). Once again the *Wake* escapes, this time as a "Too Much" (*Trop*), opposed to a "Whole" (*Tout*).

Another Sollers epigone is Guy Scarpetta: in *L'Impureté* he shows that there is an aesthetics of impurity that manages to resist the double pressure of a return to premodernism or of the invasion by the generalized media kitsch. The framework of Scarpetta's approach coincides completely with that of Sollers in the last phase of his career and although most of Scarpetta's case studies deal with film, music, or paintings, one section discusses literature. Joyce is mentioned a couple of times: like *Ulysses* and *Finnegans Wake*, Hermann Broch's *Der Tod des Vergil* (1987) allows us "to dive, beyond a strictly literary problematic, into one of the most captivating metaphysical experiences to which we are given access, a real 'experience of the limits,' a never-ending opening toward the Infinite." The book touches "the transrationality of the mystic adventure (the access to the infinite as the only possible source to ethics, politics, and aesthetics)." In other words, Broch does with thought what Joyce had done to language in *Finnegans Wake*: "to elaborate the translinguistic 'focus' in which every individual language can be captured in the moment it is created" (Scarpetta 1985, 242). Robert Musil is transideological and a mystic; Beckett is a Gnostic and his oeuvre a work of negative theology; even autobiography as a genre is intimately linked to a Catholic experience (Saint Augustine!). Scarpetta does show in the chapter on autobiography that there is a return to the autobiographical; one example of this is the autobiography of Maria-Antonietta Macciocchi, *Deux mille ans de bonheur*, which throws a less heroic light on Sollers's central influence on the French intellectual scene of the seventies and early eighties. Macciocchi did work long enough with Sollers to borrow a reference to Joyce. When at the end of her long book she contemplates the role that time and space have played in her life, she concludes that perhaps "the key to all that may be in what Joyce said: *"Father's time, mother's species"* [in English in the text] (Macciocchi 1983, 587), a mangled version of *FW*, 600.02–03 which she may have found in Sollers's *Lois* (1972a).

Julia Kristeva, too, stays close to Sollers's thinking; as Sollers's wife she has privileged access to the writer when she analyzes his works as she does in "Polylogue" (1974b), but at the same time she belongs to an academic institution, which he has continued to oppose, and she has been quite successful, especially in the United States. Strangely enough, neither of the two partners ever talks of the other as his or her spouse, although both discuss the institution of marriage, Kristeva to explain her stay in the West, Sollers obliquely in his novels and explicitly in his theory that there is nothing more obscene than sex between two people who are married. Sollers's ambivalence about his wife's position in academia is well expressed in Macciocchi's story of the writer offering flowers to all the women seated in the front row at his wife's public defense of her dissertation (Macciocchi 1983, 418).

Kristeva has written little on Joyce, although she does refer to him as an authority all through her work, much like Pleynet or Faye. At the 1984 International James Joyce Symposium in Frankfurt, she delivered one of the main lectures, and the text was published in *L'Infini* and in the proceedings (1988). With Sollers, Muray, and Hayman, Kristeva sees Joyce as "the exemplary anti-Mallarmé," who has explored the mechanism of identification at work in the genesis of the Imaginary. Like Lacan, she stresses that Joyce seems to have had access to a knowledge "perhaps ignorant of itself as such but nonetheless assuredly at work" (1988, 168) or in other words, Joyce's work transcends his person. Transubstantiation is the center of Joyce's Catholicism ("the last religion") and an exemplary rite of identification with God's body. Joyce turns the symptom inside out and shows that now, when the Eucharist has lost its captivating power, only two paths remain open: to read literature or to attempt a reinvention of love. The proximity with psychosis (Joyce used words as if they were things) is neither due to an identification with an archaic mother, as Jung thought, nor to its opposite, Joyce as a "Saint Homme," as Lacan taught in his seminars, but it shows that he succeeded where Orpheus failed: he can look upon the feminine mystery and survive. This goes for the reader, too: through the text's signs he assimilates the real presence of a complex masculine sexuality, without any repression whatsoever.

Joyce wavers between the two definitions of love prevalent in Western civilization, the Christian *agape* of paternal transubstantiation and the Greek *eros*, which is violent and maternal, an instability in the identificatory processes that Joyce's daughter paid for with her sanity. This makes Joyce a Judaeo-Christian Orpheus who created in *Finnegans Wake* a vertiginous acceleration but in *Ulysses* places us before an Imaginary space in which a "transcorporality" disputes the place of the sacred. Kristeva has clearly adopted Sollers's Catholic perspective here, after following him first in stressing the horror in *Pouvoirs de l'horreur* (1980), then in the religious and mystical dimensions of love in *Histoires d'amour* (1983a), in which the distinction between *eros* and *agape* was first developed.

The *Tel Quel* interpretation of Joyce spans the entire history of the journal until and beyond its transformation into *L'Infini*. It moves from the *nouveau roman* references to Joyce as one of the new novel's precursors in the early sixties to a more scholarly interest in the work of Paris, Cixous, and Eco by the end of the decade. The most fanatic Maoist period sees the introduction of an antifascist and antireligious Joyce who is an important pawn in the battle between a Jungian and a Freudian psychoanalysis. In the many disagreements with Jung, with surrealism, with idealism, with the Communist party and with sexual repression, Joyce is always considered to be on *Tel Quel's* side. This remains the case after the conversion of 1976 although there is a political shift from fascism to Stalinism as the major enemy and a positive evaluation of religion. Joyce becomes a Catholic writer, but he remains an exception, a scandal in the history of literature, unanalyzable by the university. Most interesting in *Tel Quel's* many phases is the central role literature, or, more precisely, avant-garde literature, continues to play; writing such as Joyce's remains central, whatever the ideological or political perspective. In this privileging of the aesthetic, of literary discourse, and more specifically of a hermetic, difficult, and fragmentary writing, *Tel Quel* joins with Lacan, Derrida, and, behind them, with Heidegger.

FIVE

The New Joyce in England and America

In chapter 1 we saw that a number of American critics have used Joyce's works in the elaboration or presentation of their views on the theory of literature. This was first of all the case in the sixties with the introduction of a formalist structuralism in the work of the early Barthes, Roman Jakobson, and the Russian formalists. The first advocate of these ideas in the English-speaking world was Robert Scholes, whose influential *Structuralism in Literature: An Introduction* was published in 1974. In the sixties, Scholes had been one of the most active of his generations of Joyceans; he had edited the catalog of the Cornell Joyce Collection in 1961, and "The Holy Office" and "Gas from a Burner" in 1962; and he edited with Richard M. Kain *The Workshop of Daedalus* in 1965 and on his own *Dubliners* in 1967. At the same time he published a number of critical essays on various stories from *Dubliners* and on *A Portrait of the Artist as a Young Man*. His book with Robert Kellogg on *The Nature of Narrative* is the result of Scholes's interest in the theory of literature and of the novel in particular (1965). He had already edited essays by James, Frye, and Trilling in the 1961 volume *Approaches to the Novel*, and in 1965 he offered a complete survey of the history of oral and classical narratives and four chapters on meaning, character, plot, and point of view, respectively. Although formalism and structuralism are not mentioned in the book, Scholes has retrospectively claimed that the book belongs to the formalist tradition "because it attempts to treat the evolution of narrative literature primarily in terms of the working of a generic system" (1974, 209). Joyce plays an important role in *The Nature of Narrative*, and this is also true for *Structuralism in Literature*. Part of the latter book had already appeared in the *James Joyce Quarterly* in 1972 as "*Ulysses*: A Structuralist Perspective." Scholes opens the essay with the statement that the Joyce of the last chapters of *Ulysses* and of *Finnegans Wake* "was a man who had adopted an essentially structuralist view of the world" (1974, 181). A rejection of Joyce's later work may be seen as part of a larger reluctance to accept the implications of structuralism. Although Scholes supports his view of Joyce's experimentation with references to the antihumanistic tendencies in structuralism, more specifically in reference to Gregory Bateson's *Steps to an Ecology of Mind* (1972), *Structuralism in Literature* remains a part of the formalist phase of structuralism, with a clear emphasis on the works of Jakobson, Saussure, Propp, Todorov, and the early Barthes. In this, the book is an exception among structuralist introductions: Jameson's *The Prison-House of Language* (1972), for all its negative evaluation of structuralism, had already included references to poststructuralist critics such as Derrida and Lacan, who are not mentioned by Scholes. Also Jonathan Culler's *Structuralist Poetics* (1975), with its special section on *Tel Quel* and its many references to Derrida, Lacan, and Kristeva, goes beyond a purely formalist structuralism; this is a central difference between the way in which the French ideas were appropriated in the United States and their reception in other countries, where the semiotic and formalist version of structuralism had made an impact long before poststructuralism came along.

The reception of structuralism in the United Kingdom resembles that in the States in that the semiotic phase is passed over; but it also differs radically in its immediately political character. I will later discuss the apolitical poststructuralism in the United States and will present first the work of the British Joyceans who have followed French theorists in assigning a special role to Joyce in the context of a modernist discourse. For reasons that will soon become clear, this survey of British and American poststructuralist criticism will stop at the 1986 Joyce Symposium in Copenhagen.

In the case of the first British Joyce critic to turn to France, there is a distinct and immediate link with the Parisian intellectuals: Stephen Heath, who is British, published in *Tel Quel*. His involvement in French intellectual life apparently dates from as early as 1968 because his *The Nouveau Roman: A Study in the Practice of Writing* was written in 1969 and is heavily indebted to the *Tel Quel* theories of that period. In this book Heath uses Joyce as "something of a 'touchstone'" (1972a, 204n), and "Ambiviolences" (1972b, 1972c) is a development of that position. As a student of Raymond Williams and Terry Eagleton, Heath belonged to the very active New Left in Britain, and his work must be seen in this political context. The same is true for Colin MacCabe, who to a large extent followed in Heath's footsteps. From the central theme of his thesis to the authorities he quotes, all are already there in an essay on Joyce and Derrida that Heath had published in 1973. When MacCabe published his book *James Joyce and the Revolution of the Word*, based on his Cambridge doctoral dissertation (1978), it created a scandal in the British academic world that cost MacCabe his job, although he later did get the chair of English at Strathclyde University. This goes to show that the British university is far more liberal than Terry Eagleton thinks: he had predicted that the book was "not the kind of stuff to get you a chair of English" (1980, 21).

MacCabe's book is in its title and in its whole structure an attack on the traditional literary criticism as it is practiced at British universities. Its title is the same as that of an article in *Scrutiny* by F. R. Leavis, in which the father of British university criticism explicitly excluded Joyce from the modernist canon (1933). All through his book MacCabe attacks the logocentric criticism that is "central in England" (1978, 78). Along the lines of Roland Barthes's attack against the French university critics more than a decade earlier (1966a), MacCabe opposes to this traditional criticism a psychoanalytical and political interpretation of Joyce's work, which shows the lack of an authoritative voice in that oeuvre with which a reader can identify; confronted with "a surplus of meaning" readers are able "to hear the crowd of voices that composes us" (133).

MacCabe has no qualms about describing his position as French: in his preface he expresses gratitude to Stephen Heath; to Jonathan Culler; Jean-Michel Rabaté; to the École normale supérieure, where he attended a seminar on the *Wake*; and to *Screen*, a film magazine that was very influential in introducing the works of Lacan and Althusser in the United Kingdom and of whose editorial board he was a member. His bibliography lists most of Derrida's works published before 1973; most of those by Lacan, *Encore. Séminaire XX* (1975) included; various texts by Kristeva, Irigaray, Barthes, Althusser, Sollers, and almost all of the French Joyce studies: Cixous's *L'Exil* (1968)(but not her *Prénoms de personne* [1974a]), all of Heath's essays, and those by Rabaté and Sollers. MacCabe is furthermore well aware of the kind of reactions his book can expect: "It may be objected that this is 'heady stuff' or that it is impossible to 'export' such ideas across the Channel" (1978, 78).

MacCabe's brand of poststructuralism differs from the American variety. Again we can turn to the bibliography: it also lists "Lenin, V.I., *Collected Works*. 45 vols"; "Mao Tse-tung, 'On Contradiction'" and "Stalin, J. *Collected Works*, vol. 1–13 (unfinished)." With Stephen Heath, with whom MacCabe edited the series "Language, Discourse, Society" for Macmillan, he situates his work in the political context of poststructuralism before 1976, with the works of Althusser and Sollers's *Sur le matérialisme* (1971b) at the center of the discussion. In the first part of the book MacCabe does what Robert Scholes and other Joyceans had done before him: he shows how Joyce's later works seriously challenge our notions of plot, character, and language. But instead of introducing new definitions of these concepts that would accommodate the modernist forms, MacCabe avoids the formalist recuperation by stressing the unanalyzable nature of Joyce's writing from "Aeolus" and "Sirens" onward. The texts become self-referential; they deconstruct any possible author, any possible origin or end. *Finnegans Wake* is the logical outcome of this development, it is a "continuous lapsus" that subverts the cartesian subject, and it is the product of a feminine narcissistic discourse or better, of "the impact of this discourse on the phallocentric male discourse" (MacCabe 1978, 150). Again we find something in the text that transcends or escapes the control of the author, but MacCabe also goes further than the *Tel Quel* readings of the Maoist period by linking the political *effects* of the text to Joyce's real-life political opinions.

This is also the weakest point of the book; if there really is a relationship between a literary avant-garde and a political radicalism, that politics would be fascist instead of Marxist, and although it is clear that Joyce had been an anarchosyndicalist as a young man and that he never sympathized with the right-wing dictatorships, it is a rather thin claim that the apolitical stance Joyce adopted from 1916 onward is the direct result of the absence of a truly revolutionary politics in Ireland. Why should Joyce's perspective suddenly have narrowed to just the Irish political scene? MacCabe himself bases his political analysis on Joyce's reactions to the 1906 Congress of the Italian Socialist party. Surely there were enough political issues to occupy an anarcho-syndicalist on the European Continent between 1916 and 1941? It is almost perverse and at least politically very questionable when Mac-Cabe writes, "art can only participate in a revolutionary politics. If such a politics does not exist then the writer is inevitably condemned to be 'apolitical,' his or her political role reduced to a constant inter-rogation of the form of politics" (170–71). We can count ourselves lucky that so many antifascist resistance fighters did not "constantly interrogate the form of politics" and did not wait for the coming into existence of a truly revolutionary politics. But it is unfair to criticize MacCabe too harshly for this part of his analysis; after all, he does take on an additional burden of proof that the writers of *Tel Quel* simply do not even consider. And MacCabe does disagree with them about the revolutionary potential of the *Wake*: "Joyce's texts are politically ineffective because they lack any definite notion of the audience to which they are addressed" (156), whereas Sollers seems almost to suggest that copies of *Finnegans Wake* dropped over Nazi Germany would have effectively finished the National Socialist Party.

MacCabe's reading of the Joycean texts suffers from the kind of

overreading we have become accustomed to, and like his French precursors, he concentrates on self-reflexive and sexual connotations.
Emmett's last words, "When my country takes her place among the
nations of the earth, then, and not till then, let my epitaph be written," according to MacCabe, "spell out the paralysis of nationalism in
its demand that writing must be stopped until the achievement of
nationhood" (1978, 88). This is nonsense, especially in reference to a
nationalist movement that put such a great emphasis on the cultural
revival that would have to accompany the political revolution. Although I agree with MacCabe that the last sentence of "Cyclops"
combines the two "voices" of the chapter, he is wrong in stating that
no single "discourse within the text is even allowed the privilege of
physically ending it" (101): "And they beheld Him even Him, ben
Bloom Elijah, amid clouds of angels ascend to the glory of the bright-
ness at an angle of fortyfive degrees over Donohoe's in Little Green
street like a shot off a shovel" (*U*, 12.1915–18). There is a first break
between the biblical language and "at an angle of fortyfive degrees"
that may be an intrusion of the previous parodying voice (the news-
paper account of the earthquake), but the rest of the sentence is
clearly in the voice of the nameless narrator who also opened it. Later
on in his book, MacCabe discusses a passage from "Scylla and
Charybdis": "I believe, O Lord, help my unbelief. That is, help me to
believe or help me to unbelieve? Who helps to believe? *Egomen*. Who
to unbelieve? Other chap" (*U*, 9.1078-80). In order to explain these
"enigmatic words" MacCabe turns to the authority of Gifford and
Seidman's *Notes for Joyce* (1974) and he concludes that "*Egomen*" refers
to Dora Marsden's magazine, *The Egoist*, which was first called *The
Freewoman* and *The New Freewoman* but then became, on the advice of
Pound "and other men," *The Egoist*, "i.e., Ego-men" (MacCabe 1978,
118). MacCabe sees this as one of "a set of random allusions" that
point outside the text, in this case to something happening ten years
after 1904, the time of the novel's action. It does not speak for the
validity of MacCabe's point that of this whole set of random allusions
he decided to choose this particular passage. The word is not enigmatic at all: according to the *Oxford English Dictionary* an egomen is a

"monastic functionary of the Greek Church"; the reference to Latin "ego" could entail God's voice from the burning bush, which says, in the Vulgate: "Ego sum qui sum." Whether it stands for God or his priest is less important than its opposition to the devil as the "other chap" and the fact that it seems to be singular, not plural.

MacCabe's summary of what Freud was teaching at the time that Joyce was writing *Finnegans Wake*—"that the determining moment in this process is the recognition that the father is no more than a name but that this recognition is buried in an effort to control a possible riot of words" (142–43)—sounds more like a summary of what Jacques Lacan was teaching at the time MacCabe was writing *James Joyce and the Revolution of the Word*. MacCabe's remark about Joyce not being able to face the narcissistic writing of Issy and therefore scattering the text through the final version of II, 2 also does not stand up to a close scrutiny of the genesis of this chapter.

It remains ironic that the political Joyce interpretation finally appeared in printed form in England two years after it had been abandoned by the French. Although the book violates a number of the central taboos of British academic criticism, it does have one thing in common with it: the implicit and sometimes quite explicit anti-Americanism of the British and Irish critics I mentioned in chapter 1. With the French, MacCabe can presuppose the inadequacy of the Joyce industry on principle—he never even bothers to attack it openly—but his reviewers do not hesitate to draw the obvious conclusions. Eagleton reviews MacCabe's book side by side with Kenner's *Ulysses*, which is "yet another blow-by-blow bluffer's guide to *Ulysses*," written as it is by the "chief executive of the American branch of the industry" (Eagleton 1980, 21). Rabaté's review in *Critique* sees it not as a "French" book, but as a "continental" reading, opposed to "the false productions of the 'structuralist' *dumping* [in English in the text] in the U.S.A. . . . those products of the multinational daughter companies of the James Joyce Industry" (Rabaté 1980b, 434). Richard Kearney, an Irish critic who may well be the only Heideggerian to hold a chair of Metaphysics, writes of an "Anglo-Saxon" Industry, whose major achievement has been "to reduce Joyce the writer to Joyce the man." He sees MacCabe's book as an antidote to "both the cultism and psychologism of the Anglo-Saxon 'Joyce Industry'" (1980, 124). This rebuttal of the greater part of Joyce criticism comes uncomfortably close to the rejection of Joyce's later works in the United Kingdom and Ireland which those critics stress at different occasions.

MacCabe's presence at Cambridge also resulted in a series of lectures in 1980 that were published in 1982 as *James Joyce: New Perspectives* (1982a). MacCabe describes the introduction of Joyce as a special subject option in Part 2 of the Cambridge English Tripos as a significant event, because it was at Cambridge that F. R. Leavis had deliberately excluded Joyce from the modernist canon. In the book itself Patrick Parrinder describes this rejection of Joyce's work between 1914 and 1930; Rabaté writes about *Dubliners*; Heath publishes a condensed translation of "Ambiviolences"; and MacCabe includes two essays that still belong to the atmosphere of his book. The first is an introduction to *Finnegans Wake* (1982b); MacCabe shows the relevance of Bruno and Vico for the book. From Bruno, Joyce borrowed the idea of a deconstruction of identity into difference and from Vico the antihistoricist view of history as a cycle. But MacCabe stresses that Joyce only exploited these thinkers and did not necessarily believe their theories, and the rest of the essay is a rather conservative analysis of a sentence from the "Shem" chapter. "The Voice of Esau: Stephen in the Library" was part of the original Cambridge lecture on which a section of chapter 5 of MacCabe's book was based (1982c, 113).

British poststructuralism was based on an Althusserian politics that had first reformed political theory in the late sixties and early seventies and that kept in close contact with a political praxis. The impact on the criticism of film and literature comes somewhat later and, especially in the work of Terry Eagleton, continues to keep in touch with a theoretical and practical politics. It is therefore much more difficult in the United Kingdom to change your politics and keep your aesthetic tastes and critical tools intact than it is in France. This may explain MacCabe's recent silence; apparently he has joined the Social Democratic Party and is now reconciled with the democratic and reformist socialism he objected to so strongly in *James Joyce and the Revolution of the Word*.

American poststructuralism is radically different. This is the case not only because it lacks a political dimension but also because of the absence of a formalist-semiotic phase. Both exclusions have been analyzed authoritatively by Frank Lentricchia in *After the New Criticism*: he shows first how the 1966 symposium on "The Languages of Criticism and the Sciences of Man," organized by the Johns Hopkins Humanities Center, was intended to introduce structuralism into the American universities, but instead, it heralded poststructuralism, which, apart from the work of Scholes and a few other semioticians, would dominate the avant-garde wing of criticism in the next decade. The political amputation occurred, still according to Lentricchia, much later in Culler's *Structuralist Poetics* (1975), which singlehandedly managed to introduce an innocuous depoliticized version of French thinking: "Culler has made structuralism safe for us" (Lentricchia 1980, 104). It is, in any case, interesting to note that of the three introductions to structuralism, only Robert Scholes writes favorably of structuralist theory (1974): Jameson writes against structuralism for political reasons, because it is antihistorical and essentialist (1972); and Culler describes the formalist phase as superseded by the theories of Derrida and the *Tel Quel* group. In the meantime another group was establishing itself precisely on this ground, which is neatly delineated in the title of Geoffrey Hartman's collection of essays *Beyond Formalism* (1970): Harold Bloom edited *Romanticism and Consciousness* in 1970 and published *The Visionary Company* in 1971 and *The Anxiety of Influence* in 1973, and Paul de Man published *Blindness and Insight* in 1971.

But neither *Structuralist Poetics* (Culler 1975) nor the Yale critics' books seem to have had much impact on Joyceans before 1975, which may have something to do with the departmental division at North American universities. Structuralism, both in its formalist and narratological form and in its deconstructionist guise, did not immediately impose itself on specialists in twentieth-century English literature. Structuralism was the domain of French and comparative literature departments, and the Yale critics tended to concentrate on romantic poetry, so that American Joyceans could quite comfortably avoid the confrontation with the French ideas.

All this changed radically in June 1975 at the Fifth International James Joyce Symposium in Paris, which quickly turned into a regular confrontation between the French and the Americans. After having survived Lacan's opening lecture, the American Joyceans were confronted with representatives of no less than three groups, the *Change* and *Tel Quel* collectives and the critics associated with *Poétique*, who seemed to agree only on their unconditional rejection of American criticism. I was not in Paris, and my account has to rely on the testimony of Joyceans who were and on the proceedings published by Jacques Aubert and Maria Jolas. Although like all proceedings of conferences *Joyce et Paris* published only a selection of the papers and although it omitted the majority of the discussions, some of the friction does seep through. In a panel discussion on narrative in *Ulysses*, published in the second volume, Jean Paris has stressed the novel's narcissistic quality when somebody asks him to identify the speaker of a passage. Paris replies that that is not a relevant question: "It doesn't matter who is talking because language is speaking, as Lacan pointed out yesterday" (1979, 41). Somebody in the audience then asks Paris to mediate between the Americans and the French, and the speaker singles out the "irritating" statement that language speaks for itself. Does that mean that one can eliminate the hypothesis of the narrator? Paris does not agree: "It seems to me that Joyce has given up the theory of the subject so to speak, and the best man to answer your question would not be me, but Lacan. What he said yesterday." When the anonymous American replies "I understand you better than Lacan, so I would like to know the point that the Americans have missed," Paris refuses to lecture on Lacan and quickly manages to change the subject. Paris belongs to the group that is most explicitly open to American perspectives, while Sollers simply and bluntly refuses any form of communication.

Jennifer Levine has analyzed this friction as something the Americans were to blame for: she points out that the *James Joyce Quarterly*, in which she published these statements, did not react at all to what had happened:

> It seems no accident that *JJQ*'s report of the Symposium (vol.13, no. 2 [Winter 1976]) provides photographs of participants but refrains absolutely from any comment on the debate between them. The other side of silence, perhaps, is Stephen Heath's reference to "the clash of languages witnessed at that symposium." (1978–79, 26)

Levine is right about the lateness of the reception: since 1975, four years had elapsed before the *James Joyce Quarterly* published the double issue on *Structuralism/Reader Response* in which her essay appeared. The *James Joyce Quarterly*'s editor, Thomas F. Staley, writes in his introduction, "It has taken us some time to understand the various ideas and methodologies which have developed in recent years" (1978–79, 6), and the volume is supposed to remedy this lack. With its double title it certainly seems to have been the journal's purpose to kill two European birds with one stone, but the strange thing is that apart from Brook Thomas's essay, which applies some of Iser's theories to the Joycean corpus (1978–79), all of the essays refer to the formalist-narratological tradition of structuralism. Jennifer Levine briefly introduces the political interpretation of poststructuralism by *Tel Quel*, but all of the other studies, among them one by Robert Scholes on "Eveline" (1978–79), and one by Jean Ricardou himself (1978–79), are based on Brémond, Genette, Todorov, and the early Barthes of "Introduction à l'analyse structurale des récits" (1966b). This phenomenon repeated itself in 1981, when the *James Joyce Quarterly* devoted another issue to narratology, this time based on Seymour Chatman's *Story and Discourse* (1978).

But poststructuralism did not completely elude American Joyceans. One of the key figures in the reception of poststructuralist ideas in North American Joyce criticism is David Hayman, who has had, as a comparatist and at least since 1956 with his study on Joyce and Mallarmé, a continuing interest in French intellectual life. He has edited with Elliott Anderson *In the Wake of the Wake* (1977), which includes prose texts by Cixous (1977) and Sollers (1977c); and Houdebine announced in "Joyce *Tel Quel*" the publication of a book with the *Tel Quel* essays on Joyce, "to be edited by David Hayman" and a translation by Hayman of Sollers's collection of essays, *Logiques*. Neither of these books has been published yet. This interest in French thought and especially in the work of Sollers has not resulted in the adoption of a poststructuralist perspective. Hayman's own writing and especially his Joyce criticism belong completely in the North American context. The essays on Joyce he published in *Poétique* (1971, 1976) and *Tel Quel* (1977b, 1980) even tend to look at *Finnegans Wake* and *Ulysses* from the perspective of the genesis of the text, a point of view that is completely alien to the poststructuralist insistence on the reader's production of meaning and its implied acceptance of the finished form of the book.

Hayman is especially important for his interviews with Philippe Sollers in 1975 and 1978. The first interview was published in *Tel Quel*'s triple United States issue (1977b) and later included in Sollers's *Vision à New York*, a volume published by Bernard-Henri Lévy in his "Collection Figures" to accompany the publication of *Paradis* in 1981. Hayman is a good interviewer; he never imposes his own ideas and succeeds in covering a lot of ground. For Sollers these interviews are crucial; for one thing he has abandoned Maoism and joined forces with the *nouveaux philosophes* between the first and the second series of interviews which are dated October 1978, and in the latter he is able to explain his new position to an outsider. Also, Sollers is able to provide an enormous amount of autobiographical information, which is essential for an understanding of his work and especially of *Paradis*. This kind of autobiographical frankness was still exceptional at the time although it has become common practice in the recent writings of Kristeva, Derrida, Pleynet, and others. Lastly, Sollers clearly makes use of Hayman's prestige as a Joyce scholar and university professor without having to compromise with the French university: both of Hayman's functions are explicitly mentioned on the back cover of the book.

The first self-proclaimed poststructuralist American Joycean was Margot Norris, who published essays in 1974 on "The Consequences of Deconstruction" in *ELH*, on "The Function of Mythic Repetition in *Finnegans Wake*" in the *James Joyce Quarterly*, and on "The Language of Dream in *Finnegans Wake*" in *Literature and Psychology*. The three essays were incorporated two years later in *The Decentered Universe of "Finnegans Wake"* (1976), and it is in this book that Norris claims that traditional criticism has misunderstood the *Wake* by studying it as a novel and that "structuralism" (the book's subtitle is *A Structuralist Analysis*) provides a more satisfying perspective. Her new approach is based on Lévi-Strauss, Lacan, and Derrida and beyond them on Freud and Heidegger. In the final analysis, Norris considers structuralism as a unified approach to the literary text. Michael Finney has correctly observed that Norris treats structuralism as if it were "a single, homogeneous development, as if, to take a specific example, the premises and assumptions of American structural linguists were compatible with the version of semiology underlying the work of Derrida and Lacan" (1977, 100) and, one may add, as if Lacan and Derrida, or Lévi-Strauss and Derrida, are in any way reconcilable. This may be a result of the rather narrow theoretical horizon of Norris's study: she refers only to Derrida's "Structure, Sign and Play in the Discourse of the Human Sciences" which was his contribution to *The Languages of Criticism* (1970), to Lacan's "The Insistence of the Letter in the Unconscious" (1970), and Wilden's translation of the "Discours de Rome" (Lacan 1981). Although the analyses in Norris's book largely coincide with the French Joyce interpretations minus the politics, neither Norris, nor the four reviewers of her book whom I have consulted, refer to any other French Joyce study, which is surprising when we know that at least two of them had attended the Paris Symposium (Benstock 1979; O'Hehir 1978; Boyle 1977–78; Finney 1977). Instead, most of the reviewers welcome the book as opening a new avenue in Joyce studies. O'Hehir criticizes *The Decentered Universe* for its "Americanisms" and he is also the only one to give an overall negative verdict. Michael Finney points to something this book has in common with *James Joyce and the Revolution of the Word* (MacCabe 1978): like MacCabe, Norris wants to prove that Joyce was aware of the epistemological revolution that resulted in structuralism.

The "single helpful clue" that Joyce provided is found in his description of Bruno's philosophy as a dualism, which Norris compares with the binary opposition of phonemes on which structuralist linguistics is based (1976, 4–5), a rather bold juxtaposition. Both the other reviewers, Bernard Benstock and Robert Boyle, praise the book for its "tempered structuralism" and for its mediating position. Boyle writes:

> Margot Norris wants to get at some basic principles operating in *Finnegans Wake*. She uses a theory that, in some other hands, has produced perverse critical results. In hers, however, the structuralist approach, with Freudian bolstering, penetrates deep into Joyce's text. (1977–78, 615)

Benstock observes that her book "may delight nonstructuralists more than the wool-dyed partisans of the New Approach" (1979, 336).

Norris has not pursued her analysis; her first article on Joyce after *The Decentered Universe* is much more traditional although the context and the subject were perfect for a feminist-deconstructionist analysis (1982). The volume on Joyce and feminism in which Norris's essay was published also includes essays by other women who have accepted the French view of Joyce as a protofeminist (Henke and Unkeless 1982). Suzette Henke has the kind of background in phenomenology that Lentricchia has discovered in the careers of Hillis Miller and De Man. Her *Joyce's Moraculous Sindbook* grew out of her studies of phenomenological philosophy with Paul Ricoeur. In the introduction she describes her book as "an attempt to re-create *Ulysses* as an existential act of mind and a phenomenological life-world" and she associates herself with the Geneva school "represented by Georges Poulet in Europe and by J. Hillis Miller in America" (1978, 11), precisely the roots of American deconstruction Lentricchia identifies in *After the New Criticism* (1980). After the publication of her first book, Henke moved to State University of New York at Binghamton, where William Spanos, another Heideggerian who became a poststructuralist, was editing *Boundary 2* and where she came under the influence of feminist and psychoanalytical theory. The essays in *Women in Joyce* are the result of this shift in attention; in their introduction the editors,

Henke and Elaine Unkeless, stress that all the essays reveal a perspective that differs from that of traditional formalist criticism (1982, xi), and although they refer to American feminist theorists of literature such as Kate Millett, Florence Howe, Marcia Holly and Marilyn French, they also mention Julia Kristeva's *Polylogue* (1974a). In her first essay on "Stephen Dedalus and Women" Henke refers to Foucault and Freud and then to "Polylogue" in order to show how misogyny is one of the adolescent traits Stephen has to outgrow before he can become a mature artist: "Not until *Ulysses* will a new model begin to emerge—one that recognizes the need for the intellectual artist to 'make his peace' with woman and to incorporate into his work the vital, semiotic flow of female life" (Henke 1982a, 102). Her second essay, on Gerty MacDowell, is more traditionally feminist in stressing Gerty's self-definition as a romantic heroine and what this means for her own male-identified personality and for the society she lives in (1982b). None of the critics in *Women in Joyce* go even half as far as Cixous or other French feminists, and there do not seem to be any followers of Luce Irigaray's work in American or British Joyce criticism, with the possible exception of Richard Kearney, who adopts MacCabe's description of the writing of the *Wake* to conclude: "The revolution of the word has already begun with Joyce; the revolution of society to be effected by the reintegration of the female unconscious into both female *and* male thinking and behavior has yet to be achieved" (1979–80, 132).

The growing importance of the new Joyce manifested itself first in the centenary year: Colin MacCabe published his *James Joyce: New Perspectives* (1982a) and a large group of French critics attended the Eighth International Joyce Symposium in Dublin. At the conferences in Frankfurt in 1984, Philadelphia in 1985, and Copenhagen in 1986, the tentative shift had become a definite trend: almost half of the papers published in the Frankfurt proceedings are concerned with new theoretical questions, and the Philadelphia volume is even called *New Alliances in Joyce Studies* (Scott 1988a). It may be objected at this point that a volume of proceedings only publishes a selection of the work presented at a conference and close to 250 papers were read at

Frankfurt whereas only thirty were included in *The Augmented Ninth* (Benstock 1988). How representative are the proceedings of what is really going on in a scholarly community? In the case of the symposia proceedings there is a definite bias in favor of the theoretical papers and panels, and this fact alone should be of interest. The so-called new approaches are sanctioned, they receive recognition from whoever possesses the power to do so. What interest me in the American context are not so much who exactly is in control of this power and how it is used but, first, the simple fact that in the proceedings of the Dublin symposium in 1982, poststructuralism is the challenging new paradigm and that from Frankfurt in 1984 onward it very much becomes the dominating approach, and, second, that this fact is not contested by representatives of the old paradigms. The number of theoretical panels increases every year and poststructuralism, be it Derridean or Lacanian, is predominant in the work of most of the young Joyceans. That is why I will have to stop my survey of these trends with a discussion of the Copenhagen symposium in 1986: by that time poststructuralism had taken over, and it would be impossible to discuss all the work in the field.

Whereas Lacan was very much at the center of things in Frankfurt, the emphasis in Philadelphia and Copenhagen seems to have shifted toward a feminist and Derridean perspective: Frankfurt had two panels on Lacan, one French and one mostly American, but the only American critic who has pursued the Lacanian connection is Sheldon Brivic, who, inspired by Lacan and with frequent references to Derrida, has developed in his latest book a thesis that would fit the latest telquelian mold: Joyce is an active presence in his own text as a mind containing minds according to Saint Augustine's Trinitarian conception. But Brivic belongs more to the American psychoanalytical tradition; he published first a book on *Joyce Between Freud and Jung* (1980) and although in *Joyce the Creator* he frequently refers to Freud, he also mentions Jung and even Julian Jaynes's *The Origin of Consciousness in the Breakdown of the Bicameral Mind* (Brivic 1985; Jaynes 1976). But his readings of Joyce's texts suffer from the same arbitrariness that mars the critical practice of so many of the poststructuralist critics, as when he claims that the sin of Simon Magus referred to by Stephen (*P,* 159) is related to Gnosticism because Hans Jonas "quotes Simon Magus, the first major prophet of Gnosticism, as saying, 'I am God . . .'" (Brivic 1985, 159). A quick look at *Acts* 8 would have been sufficient to set him on a more orthodox track. The results of this study are in any case similar to those of the later *Tel Quel*: Joyce is a powerful presence in his own works, a presence that becomes pluralized by the end of *Ulysses* and that explodes in *Finnegans Wake.* Reference is constantly made to orthodox and mystical Christian theology and to the Kabbalah.

But the only American critic who has completely adopted the *Tel Quel* Joyce in its latest incarnation is Beryl Schlossman, who wrote a *doctorat de troisième cycle* at the Université de Paris VII under the supervision of Kristeva. The last two sections of the thesis were published in *Tel Quel* 92 (1982) and Schlossman read interim reports at the symposia in Dublin and Frankfurt. Her thesis is, according to the editors of *Tel Quel,*"simultaneously a new verification and an especially interesting continuation of the analyses presented first by Sollers in *Tel Quel*" (editorial note in Schlossman 1982, 9). Like Sollers and Houdebine, Schlossman sees Joyce's Catholicism as "an aesthetic focus and a symbolic source, inscribed in the writer's biography and imagination" (1985, ix), and she proceeds to analyze *Ulysses* and *Finnegans Wake* on the basis of these principles to conclude that "Joyce's working through language, his passage, leads him into the pentecostal multiplicity of tongues" (172). This passage, or *transitus,* or *pesah,* is also Judaic: "The *Wake* is Joyce's Torah, his fabric of proper names" (177). The simultaneous passage of Joyce into the Catholic position and his subversion of it "enters into the configuration of the spiral, the interlace," which recalls both the Celtic illuminations and the Borromean knot structures, that represent for Lacan the dimensions of subjectivity (xiii).

Joyce's Catholic Comedy of Language can be read as an elaborate set of annotations to Sollers's post-1976 theses about Joyce. It refers to the same authorities and uses the same configuration of ideas, a combination of mysticism, theology, and Lacanian psychoanalysis. The only addition seems to be a more thorough reference to Jewish thought. The footnotes refer to an enormous number of sources that include traditional Joyce criticism and poststructuralist classics by Barthes, Bataille, Houdebine, Kristeva, and Lacan. The book's origin as a French thesis is probably the reason for the presence of French quotations from Hegel, Gershom Scholem, and Sören Kierkegaard. Although Schlossman gives theology the function linguistics used to have in structuralism, she is not a trained theologian: her statements about Jewish theology come from *The Jewish Encyclopedia* and Scholem's *Zur Kabbala und ihrer Symbolik* (1960) and those on Christian theology from a *Dictionnaire de théologie catholique*, the *Dictionnaire de la Bible* and a *Histoire des dogmes*. Her use of these authorities seems to be extremely selective: a word here, a sentence there, without too much concern about context or coherence. Schlossman's text is almost compulsively punctuated by quotations, as if the reader would not be prepared to believe her when she claims, for example, that people eat eggs to celebrate Easter. That statement is followed by the footnote, "Cfr. Arnold van Gennep, *Cérémonies périodiques, cycliques, 1, Carnaval-Carême-Pâques*, vol. 1, VII in *Manuel de folklore français contemporain* (Paris, Picard, 1947), pp. 866, 1321–1322, 1335, 1339" (1985, 223). The development of the argument is less logical than associative, a technique also employed by Sollers and Derrida: although Schlossman creates the impression that she is reading Joyce's text, in reality she peppers her own discourse with quotations from Joyce or from the reminiscences of Joyce's friends. Like some of the poststructuralist critics, she does not care too much for the original context and simply fits in as much as she can: in the preface she supports her thesis about the importance of Saint Patrick for Joyce with a reference to Mercanton's *Les Heures de James Joyce* (1967). According to Jacques Mercanton, Joyce was still talking about Saint Patrick toward the end of his life. Joyce told him "that Saint Patrick's intervention was indispensable for the conclusion of his book . . . . Then with a sigh: 'Without the help of my Irish saint, I would not have been able to go *jusqu'au bout'*" (Schlossman 1985, xi–xii). If we then turn to Mercanton's book we find that the ellipsis points mark the omission of nine lines that describe the situation in which the words are spoken and from which one can conclude that the Irish saint Joyce is going to follow is Nora Joyce.

Schlossman misrepresents Joyce's text when she wants to make a point, a misrepresentation that can take different forms. The first is that of selection; the most central books in this analysis, which are most conspicuously absent in the bibliography at the end, are Hanley's (1962) and Hart's (1974) concordances to *Ulysses* and *Finnegans Wake*; Schlossman moves from theme to theme and simply looks up the words she needs in the concordances. This gives her the passages that contain words such as "easter," "pentecost" and "passover," but then these passages do not necessarily say what she wants them to say, so she uses ellipsis points or simply isolates the word she needs: "In book I, 4 [of *Finnegans Wake*], the Jewish context of the Pentecost is named as 'Yuddanfest' (82.36), i.e., *Judenfest*" (160). In the passage Schlossman quotes, Joyce gives yet another version of the meeting in the Park between the two characters, "whethertheywere Nippoluono engaging Wei-Ling-Taou or de Razzkias trying to reconnoistre the general Boukeleff, man may not say" (*FW*, 81.33–35). What this has to do with the Pentecost is beyond me, unless the whole book deals with it, which is what Schlossman is trying to establish. The feast discussed here can only be Christmas: "Billi with the Boule" says in full: "it being Yuletide or Yuddanfest" (82.36), but Christmas does not seem to suit Schlossman very much; she omits it once again six pages later:

> Hce's paschal death is announced in connection with the Pentecost in order to suggest that Joyce's languages are being crucified. His obituary is read: "after a lenty illness the roeverand Mr Easterling of pentecostitis, no followers by bequest" (130.8). His pentecostal death is prelude to the Resurrection in tongues, actualized in a thousand and one ways in the Joycean text. (Schlossman 1985, 166)

The French original was clearer in stressing that HCE dies on Pentecost (Schlossman 1982, 18), but this is simply not the case. Joyce wrote: "on Christienmas at Advent Lodge, New Yealand, after a lenty illness the roeverand Mr Easterling of pentecostitis" (FW, 130.07–09), which makes it clear that HCE dies on the unequivocally Christian Christmas Day.

Another technique is overinterpretation, when every wind or flame refers to the pentecostal experience or when the answer to the question about HCE's religion, "It was the see-you-Sunday sort. Exactly what he meant by a pederast prig? Bejacob's, just a gent who prayed his lent" (89.14–15) is interpreted like this:

> This Catholicism so lightly taken, presented in a comic manner, allows a glimpse of a more serious dimension, manifested through a visual element—"see-you-Sunday sort"—in which the three s's act as an oblique reminder of "filius et spiritu sancti": Hce's Catholicism. (Schlossman 1985, 131)

Schlossman mixes her Latin cases: "filius" is a nominative, "spiritu sancti" a genitive. If she had put everything in the nominative case, she would have had five s's, in the genitive there are only two. But that is less important than the extreme arbitrariness of her reading: if she is right, her own name would also be marked by the Trinity. It is this arbitrariness that finally defeats any validity Schlossman's central thesis may have. She explains the procedure in a footnote:

> Because of the richness and complexity of the Wake, textual quotation, paraphrasing, and explication are inevitably fragmentary. This fragmentation is perhaps compensated by the reading of heterogeneity in the text of the Wake, indicative of the plurality essential to its structural and signifying dimensions. Wherever possible, the explication attempts to illustrate both the argument and the interpretation of the text in question, without legislating the possible resonances of the latter. (194)

Is it then simply enough to stress, in a footnote, the heterogeneity of the text in order to compensate the inevitable fragmentation? I hope not, because then one could apply this same principle to a study of Finnegans Wake as a Christmas carol or of Joyce's writings as anti-Semitic and anti-Catholic tracts.

As a non-Jewish ex-Catholic, I cannot judge Schlossman's central thesis about the fundamental solidarity of Judaism and Catholicism. I can only say that history unfortunately does not seem to offer too many examples of solidarity between the two religions—on the contrary—and this is not just a minor point in the discussion. If Sollers can claim that great things will happen in New York State because there the Jews and Catholics have a majority (in Pleynet 1981a, 128), one can also feel entitled to point to the role of partly Catholic Germany and completely Catholic Poland during the World War II massacre of the Jews.

In Britain most of the critics who have adopted the poststructuralist premises have turned to Derrida: Maud Ellmann has established herself as somebody who can apply deconstructionist method to a text without having to evoke poststructuralist authorities (1981, 1982, 1986). Derek Attridge, another British academic, has moved from Jakobson to Derrida (Attridge 1983) in order to go beyond Roland Barthes in an analysis of digression in *Finnegans Wake*. As co-editor of *Post-Structuralist Joyce* (Attridge and Ferrer 1985) and contributor to deconstructionist panels at symposia, Attridge has been an essential figure in the introduction of the Derridean problematic in Joyce studies and even in English studies in general: his *Peculiar Language* constitutes an ambitious Derridean rewriting of our thinking about English literature in general (1988).

The most influential recent approach in American Joyce studies is undoubtedly the feminist reading, and it remains to be established how far Joycean feminists have been influenced by French theoretical writings. Again 1982 is the watershed: we already saw the paucity of references to French theory in *Women in Joyce* (Henke and Unkeless 1982), and papers read by Karen Lawrence and Suzette Henke at the Dublin Symposium still belong to the more traditional American "gynocritical" feminism of which Marilyn French is the most important representative. Things have radically changed at Frankfurt: Christine van Boheemen reads "Penelope" as a retroactive confirmation of the fundamental "otherness" of *Ulysses*, and she sees Molly as the one who deconstructs logocentric meaning (1988a). Between the lines of the essay, which is part of a longer discussion in *The Novel as Family Romance* (1987), there is a polemic against the "gynocritics" who attempt to escape the patriarchy by emphasizing the neglected "other" and female pole of the dichotomy instead of challenging the binary opposition itself.

The challenge to American feminism was taken up by Bonnie Kime Scott, who has written two books on Joyce and feminism. The first was published in 1984, and in its study of the historical and biographical backgrounds and the female characters in Joyce's work, it is very much a work in the American feminist tradition. In Frankfurt, Scott presented a paper on the difference between the American gynocritical approach and the deconstructive practice (1988b), and the discovery of the French continental approach, "inevitable to a Joycean of [her] generation" (1987, xvi), became the focus of her second book. In the first chapter she dates the paradigm shift for the American feminist Joyceans to 1982: "This limitation [of gynocritical research methods] was pointed out by European feminists to a predominantly American, character-oriented feminist panel at the 1982 Joyce Symposium" (1988a, 9).

A similar evolution can be observed in the work of Karen Lawrence and Suzette Henke, who read rather traditional papers on Joyce and Woolf in Dublin. Lawrence's comments on Maud Ellmann's "Polytropic Man" echo the gynocritical reservations about poststructuralism (Ellmann 1982, Lawrence 1986). Things had changed in Frankfurt: Lawrence and Ellen Carol Jones (who had already chaired the panel on deconstructive criticism) spoke about paternity with frequent references to Lacan, Derrida, and, this time without reservations, Ellmann's "Polytropic Man," whereas the panel on women in *Dubliners* was still revisionist in the American tradition (Lawrence 1988, Jones 1988). These critics had been anticipated by Jennifer Levine, who published after her introduction to *Tel Quel* Joyce an essay in *PMLA* in which she quotes Lacan, Saussure, Stephen Heath, and Margot Norris, but in which she deals with the more Derridean problematic of originality and repetition (1979). A few years later she showed how *Ulysses* is a *writable* text in Barthes's terminology. Shari Benstock, too, seems to have been slightly ahead of most Joyce critics in her explicitly Derridean readings of *Finnegans Wake* (1983, 1984,

1985), although her *Women of the Left Bank* belongs to the more traditional gynocritical interest in the women writers and publishers of Paris (1986).

In the proceedings of the Philadelphia conference, the tendency toward the new feminist approach is more pronounced. For the first time a woman, Bonnie Kime Scott, is the sole editor, and it is no accident that Scott feels the need to discuss the principle of selection of the papers: as a woman and as a young Joycean, her authority is not established. The first principle of selection is demand: "the essays included are those that people in attendance wanted most to have in print." In this way the volume "represents extensively the work of the younger generation and demonstrates to a general scholarly community how contemporary literary theory is being applied to Joyce" (Scott 1988a, 13).

The opening essay by Christine van Boheemen argues that what Derrida does in philosophy, Joyce does in his novels: both produce "pre-Oedipal" texts. Van Boheemen sees three different strategies: a first, like Ellmann's "Polytropic Man," changes the New Critical interest in ironies, paradoxes, and tensions into a focus on systems of exchange and flow. More sophisticated would be a study of the relative importance of the *functions* of "masculine" and "feminine" instead of dealing with "presences," and a third and most ambitious strategy involves a text-internal semiotics, a deconstruction of the difference between "readerly" texts such as *Dubliners* and "writerly" *Ulysses* and *Finnegans Wake*.

In the section on "Feminist Revisions" and "Joyce and Other Women Writers" echoes of Derrida and De Man are heard, and in the closing essay Marilyn Reizbaum explicitly disagrees with Gilbert's and Gubar's dismissal of Joyce as patriarchal and phallogocentric: "While Joyce does not *escape* patriarchal structures, he does valorize difference, both thematically and formally" (1988, 188).

What is surprising in this shift of paradigms in Joyce studies in general is not only the lack of opposition on the part of more traditional critics but also the absence of a serious discussion between representatives of the traditional camp and the members of the challenging paradigm. It was only at the Copenhagen conference that the two feminist camps came to some form of confrontation, and a report on the same conference occasioned the only instance of documented tension about "theory." For the *James Joyce Broadsheet*, Richard Brown collected witnesses' accounts about the conference from a number of Joyceans. Michael and Paula Gillespie noted that deconstruction and feminism have by now been domesticated by the Joyceans: "Far from disrupting any of the proceedings through demands for a reviewing of critical commonplaces regarding Joyce's works, deconstruction now seems to have been put in its place (. . .) among all other methods for deriving interpretations" (Brown 1986, 1). In the next issue of the *Broadsheet*, Alan Roughley defended deconstruction by deconstructing the Gillespies' accusation and by stressing that in the texts of Joyce and Derrida the same operation is at work: deconstruction is not just another method; it supplements these strategies by attending to the elements in Joyce's texts that cannot be understood with the traditional methods. "Deconstruction as yet one more interpretative method demands either a refusal of Derrida's writings or a disturbing readiness to ignore the important questions that they pose" (Roughley 1987, 1). The two parties in this exchange address different issues: Michael and Paula Gillespie were talking about sociological facts—they did not offer interpretations or evaluations—while Roughley reads their comments as an attack on Derrida. The implicit totalizing gesture (deconstruction is not *a* method; it is the only method) is symptomatic of most defenses of Derrida's work, and it will have to be addressed in the critique of deconstruction in my conclusion. Here we can only deplore the lack of more basic theoretical debates on deconstruction.

The English and American critics who were inspired by poststructuralist theory have been attracted to different aspects of French theory. Early English critics such as Stephen Heath and Colin MacCabe came to Joyce from an Althusserian point of view, and they emphasize in *Ulysses* and *Finnegans Wake* a political dimension that is not entirely divorced from Joyce's own political and philosophical views. After 1982 Maud Ellmann and Derek Attridge shift toward the North

American Derrida reception that stresses the feminist and philosophical potential of Joyce's work.

The American Joyceans reacted rather late to the developments in France; with Robert Scholes there is an attempt to apply the findings of a formalist structuralism and of narratology, especially in studies of Joyce's early works, but it does not gain too many adherents. The Lacanian readings date from the late seventies and precede a deconstructionist approach in the Yale school vein. Both the psychoanalytical and the philosophical poststructuralist criticism follow the lines of the American reception of Derrida described by Lentricchia: criticism is divorced from politics.

The influence of poststructuralism on feminist Joyce critics was unavoidable, given the theoretical debates between American and French feminists in the seventies. As was the case with their male colleagues, the influence was delayed by departmental divisions until the early eighties. The Dublin symposium in 1982 marked the introduction of the new paradigm, which was firmly in place by the mid-eighties. Unlike male poststructuralist criticism, feminist deconstruction continues to have a political agenda, both in the Joycean and in the larger community. But it remains ironical that by the time the North American critics have adopted the poststructuralist principles imported from France, the majority of French critics have moved on to something else.

Conclusion

Although we have been able to observe clear differences among the American, English, and French poststructuralist readings of Joyce, I will now attempt to establish the general contours of this interpretation and to offer a critique of its most basic principles.

Critics of deconstruction and poststructuralism agree that this type of criticism produces strong readings because specific texts are invariably found to do what texts by their very nature are supposed to do. The obvious results are overinterpretation of minor details of the text, on the one hand, and factual reading errors, on the other hand. Given that at least some of the French critics I have looked at are incapable of reading Joyce in the original and that Joyce's later work belongs to the most difficult in modern English literature, the total number of such errors is surprisingly small, and most mistakes occur in references to the historical context. This biographical, sociological, and political background did not of course belong to the horizon of the French poststructuralist interpretations, and it is only with the introduction of genetic studies in academic criticism that the historical context reappears; but it remains strange that such obvious errors have not been commented on before.

Other flaws are the result of faulty or partial translations of Joyce's words; precisely because most of their readers do not understand foreign languages, French critics have a great responsibility in this respect. This is clear in Derrida, whose work on Plato or German philosophy is often based on translations. His own translator, Barbara Johnson, writes that she had to adjust the English translation of the *Phaedrus* "when it seemed necessary to achieve a closer parallel to the French version with which Derrida is working" (Derrida 1981, 66). Another example can be found in *Glas* when Derrida translates Hegel: "Antigone seems to me from this point of view the most admirable (*vortrefflichste*), the most appeasing (*befriedigendste*) work of art" (Derrida 1974, 170L; Hegel 1970, 550). Since *Frieden* does mean "peace," this is an etymologically correct, but rather far-fetched translation. When he translates another Hegel passage later on, he does give the correct equivalent: "the subjectivity of satisfaction" for "die Subjektivität der Befriedigung" (1974, 195L; Hegel 1970, 552).

But the translations only intensify a problem that is not peculiar to the French interpretation of Joyce and that holds equally well for Joyce criticism in general. Even relatively short and simple texts such as *Dubliners* have given rise to completely different and even contradictory interpretations, and this is all the more true for the more complex texts such as *Ulysses* and *Finnegans Wake*. Interpreting a difficult text consists precisely in supplying a coherence the text itself seems to lack. The result is that a critic will emphasize or even overemphasize some elements and neglect others that contradict his hypothesis. The amount of pressure needed to accommodate the text to the interpretation, on the one hand, and the number of elements that are not accounted for, on the other, define the value of an interpretation. Paul Van Caspel has investigated a number of interpretations and translations of *Ulysses* and has discovered scores of factual errors in the works of respectable traditional critics (1986).

The problem is mainly rhetorical: it is always revealing to observe how sophisticated literary critics can be in identifying rhetorical devices in poems and novels and how naive they become when they are confronted with the same techniques in critical prose. When Hugh Kenner in *A Colder Eye* wants to show the importance of reincarnation as a theme in *Ulysses*, he writes that among "his first spoken words," Bloom gives an explanation of the word "metempsychosis" (1983,

101). Kenner makes this claim because it is an additional argument for his thesis, and it is an argument only because the passage comes so early in the novel. In reality, Kenner is stretching a point: Bloom talks to the cat, calls up to Molly that he is going out, greets Mr O'Rourke, wishes Dlugacz a good morning, talks to Molly about the mail, about the concert, and the funeral, and then he explains the meaning of "metempsychosis."

But even in the cases where passages are misquoted or where the text's argument is misrepresented, the English or American conventions allow the reader to refer to the critic's source and to find out for himself if the quotation is a fair representation of the original. French critical conventions are different: with the exception of the university critics, these writers do not offer bibliographical references and do not identify their sources, which makes the identification of misquotes and errors difficult, if not impossible. But the lack of bibliographical information is not a French tradition as American defenders of deconstruction have claimed: Derrida's early essays have an abundance of footnotes and references, but they have disappeared gradually. This makes a critical reading increasingly difficult and time consuming and sometimes forces the translators of these texts to supply footnotes where they are missing in the French original.

The presence or absence of footnotes has everything to do with the critic's status: if he becomes important enough like Derrida, he does not have to bother about them, but if he is only a subsidiary figure, he cannot afford to: Sollers's texts do not have footnotes, or they are supplied by Houdebine or de Haes. A weak critic can even be defined by the fact that he does little more than write footnotes to the work of strong critics.

In the case of Derrida and his followers, the next step is the disappearance of the quotation marks introducing and closing citations from primary and secondary sources until text and commentary become indistinguishable. This is accompanied by an increase in the commentary and a decrease in the length of the primary text discussed; more and more is written about less and less, until a whole paper is based on one sentence in *Ulysses* or two words in *Finnegans*

Wake. In the absence of source references and of a marked distinction between text and commentary, the names of Joyce and of writers or philosophers in general acquire a different function than they have in traditional critical discourse. A conventional Joyce critic who wants to show the importance of Hegel in Joyce's work must establish the connection by proving that Joyce read Hegel, that his thought was influenced by the German philosopher, or that it is structured similarly. A deconstructionist critic will simply refer to Jacques Aubert's book (1973), or better still, to Derrida's description of Joyce as "the most Hegelian of novelists" (1964b, 473) without having to add Derrida's qualifying "peut-être" or the source of the comment which is Jean Paris's *James Joyce par lui-même* (1957), not mentioned by Derrida. At the end of "Violence et métaphysique," the oblique mention of Joyce (the quotation is only identified in a footnote) has a specific function in the text pointing to Matthew Arnold's theory about the Hellenic and Hebraic dimensions of our culture, which Derrida had used as a motto (1964a). But the presence of a novelist in a philosophical essay may have the same effect as that of a philosopher in a literary critic's work: it shows not only that the writer is interested in areas of inquiry that are not his own but also that he is quite able to bridge the gap between the two disciplines. In this way Derrida's use of Joyce resembles the use literary critics make of Derrida's name in their discourse. This procedure has been named an "illusionisme intimidatoire" by Henri Meschonnic: the name of an authority is in itself enough to put an end to all discussion (1973). In the case of the early essays by Derrida, we are still given a page reference to *Ulysses*, although it is not clear which edition is being referred to. Without Gunn and McLeery's *The "Ulysses" Pagefinder* it would be very difficult to find out which edition Derrida is quoting (it is the Bodley Head of 1960). In later essays by Derrida or some of his followers we cannot check the author's appropriation of somebody else's words and we must simply trust him, which is not always a wise thing to do: in *La Dissémination*, Derrida includes a short comment in quotation marks about the letter "v" in *Finnegans Wake*, but he does not identify its source (1972a, 367). The information is wrong, and it is only when we happen to recognize Robert Greer Cohn's hand that we even know who is to blame (1951).

Part of this attitude is based on a general feeling of distrust of philology among literary critics and theorists. The rise of New Criticism and literary theory and their emphasis on the text and nothing but the text have resulted in a neglect of traditional philology and its emphasis on the genesis of a text and on the intentions of the author. The problem with such an attitude is that it leads, on the one hand, to a paradoxically unconditional trust in existing editions or—and on a practical level it amounts to the same thing—an equally absolute distrust and, on the other hand, to a hermeneutic such as that of Heidegger, who claimed that his text of Hölderlin's "Wie wenn am Feiertage . . ." was based on his interpretation. Although in a letter to Detlev Lüders, a young critic who had asked him about the statement, Heidegger agreed that it was nonsense and promised to have it corrected in subsequent editions, he never did (Heidegger 1981, 207), and few if any readers of Heidegger seem to worry about it.

The critics who are inspired by Heidegger all share his dismissal of philology, which, as a science, is believed to remain within metaphysics. This is probably why a Heideggerian critic such as Richard Kearney can dismiss the complete publication of Joyce's manuscripts and drafts as "the most recent and most risible example" of the Joyce industry (1980, 124). In the future both the French and the American critics will find it difficult to avoid the issue of Joyce's manuscripts. The discussions that have followed Hans Walter Gabler's edition of *Ulysses* in 1984 are sure to accompany similar attempts at establishing an error-free text of *Finnegans Wake*. Most of the French university critics have realized the importance of the manuscript material for a serious study of the *Wake*, and in a very short time Paris has become one of the few centers of work in this area. In the States only David Hayman continues the work he started with *The First-Draft Version of "Finnegans Wake"* (1963).

A second major characteristic of poststructuralist criticism is partly a result of the relationship between the critic and the primary text I have just outlined. Whether they base themselves theoretically on

Freud or on Heidegger, deconstructionist critics tend to value the fragment more than the whole, the single word more than the syntax of the sentence in which it is used, and the noun more than the adjective or the verb. In the preceding chapters I have given examples of texts quoted out of context and of the overinterpretation of single words. In extreme cases a whole analysis centers around an author's use of a single word, but usually statements are isolated from a text and analyzed in detail without reference to their original, contextual function. The result of this type of analysis, the fact that all texts are situated on the same level and that no distinction is made between different statements of an author, will be discussed later; I am here concerned only with the emphasis on the fragmentation of discourse. This type of analysis seems to have as its two immediate sources ideas in Heidegger and Freud.

The first thinker is important for his early elaboration of a theoretical basis for such a hermeneutic. Heidegger's readings of texts, especially his *Erläuterungen* about Hölderlin's poetry (1981), center around the interpretation of single words. For the French critics, Beda Allemann has concretely formulated Heidegger's possible contribution to literary criticism in his *Hölderlin et Heidegger*. In the first section of Part II, Allemann describes the specificity of Heidegger's reading of Hölderlin, an interpretation that cannot be understood apart from Heidegger's general theory about Being and about the history of metaphysics. A philosopher is not so much interested in what another philosopher has said but in what remains "unsaid by means of what is said." The interpreter does not introduce his own ideas in the text, but goes back to "a more original point of departure" (1959, 133). Since the thinking of the poetic word belongs to the surpassing of metaphysics, the rules that govern metaphysical interpretation cannot apply, and thus philology cannot possibly be of any help. Discussion or argumentation is out of the question: "In the domain of essential thinking, refutation does not make sense" (Heidegger quoted in Allemann 1959, 134). Positively, Allemann notes Heidegger's use of etymology, which remains faithful to the "more original meaning" of the words and especially his use of popular etymology and his attempt to liberate "language from its grammar and install it in a structure of more original essences" (149). The most central aspect of Heidegger's reading of Hölderlin is his "regression to the word": his attention to the word in its individuality. "Thus, in order to name the essence of being, language only has to find a single thing, the unique word" (Heidegger quoted in Allemann, 153). Whether this word is the "Andenken" or "aber" or "Natur" that structure Hölderlin's poetry or whether Heidegger reads Plato, or Kant, or Hegel, the strategy remains essentially the same.

Heidegger's rather creative use of etymology, which resembles popular etymology in its fancy and daring, and his constant recourse to homonyms and puns are adopted by almost all of the critics I have discussed here; and when Heidegger had relied heavily on his Grimm dictionaries, the French dictionary *Littré* has become one of the most important intertexts in French poststructuralist criticism. Both etymology and punning are radically unhistorical: whereas Heidegger claims to use etymology in order to identify the "original meaning" of certain words, it is clear that he is not interested in whether the authors he discusses were aware of those meanings. The practical result of the strategy is in any case that he can freely look among the numerous meanings a word may have had in the past and those it has in the present for the one that most productively suits his own purposes.

One problem is that we feel the radicalness of such a procedure more when it is applied to a language or a text we know than to one that is foreign to us: *aigle*-Hegel may shock us less than a similar pun in our own language, say Derrida, *the reader*, or Heidegger, *high digger* (for the same reason, puns tend to be wittier in somebody else's language). Another result is the untranslatability of Heidegger and Derrida's texts. Although both have found excellent translators, it is quite impossible to translate all nuances of their numerous puns and etymologies, a fact that forces their translators to introduce paraphrases, explanations, or neologisms. In Heidegger's case this is a simple consequence of his philosophy since he sincerely believes that because of its geography and its historical destiny Germany is the only country where Being can come into its own again and German the only language that can even begin to compare to Greek. Since Greece witnessed, in the pre-Socratic philosophy and in the tragedy, the presence of Being before its metaphysical identification with particular beings, the language of Heraclitus and Sophocles offers a particularly rich avenue for an existentialist inquiry. The intimate relationship between the Greek and the German tongues was not discovered by Heidegger but is part of a strong Hellenophile movement in German culture that has its roots in the romanticism and idealism of the eighteenth and nineteenth centuries (Butler 1958) and that had found its most recent expression in Stefan George's poetry and the thought it inspired. But this is not just proof of how much Heidegger's thinking fits into the general framework of a peculiarly German tradition that includes Hölderlin and Nietzsche and that would lead to much Nazi rhetoric and iconography; the philosopher remained true to these ideas until the very end of his life. In an interview with *Der Spiegel*, in many ways his testament, he mentioned the special relationship between the German language and Greek. Heidegger's German critics have strongly reacted to the implicit chauvinism inherent in his philosophy and in his reading of literary texts and to its political consequences (Heller 1976; Hühnerfeld 1959; Löwith 1953; Pöggeler 1977b; Böschenstein 1977; Farías 1989).

Also important is the fragmentary nature of Heidegger's sources: the pre-Socratic philosophers have not left us extended discussions; their thought survives only in fragments embedded in other philosophers' texts. Significantly also Hölderlin's later poetry, which Heidegger likes so much, survives only in a fragmentary form. A last dimension is the fragmentary nature of Heidegger's own discourse, which is imitated by almost all of the poststructuralist writers in their attempts to break through the traditional forms of the essay or the book, by beginning in medias res or by refusing to close a text.

Heidegger's hermeneutic has prompted at least one of his earliest critics to observe the similarities between the philosopher's reading of texts and a psychoanalytical approach (Löwith 1953, 92), and I have earlier discussed the important part Heidegger's thinking played in the formation of French psychoanalysis and in the role within Lacanian theory and practice of the "unsaid." Freud himself attempted to base his hermeneutics on the findings of historical linguistics in his "Über den Gegensinn der Urworte": "We have made the astonishing discovery that the dreamwork corresponds to a characteristic of the oldest languages we know" (Freud 1972b, 229–30). But Karl Abel's study, in which Freud found confirmation of the idea that a single word can have two opposite meanings, had been discredited even at the time when it was first published in 1884, and Émile Benvéniste has conclusively demonstrated the serious ethnocentrism of this view: a language in which a word can have contradictory meanings simply does not exist (1966, 80–83). It is only, Benvéniste adds, in myths and in some kinds of poetry that we can find similarities with the dreamwork of the unconscious: "But it is paradoxically in surrealist poetry, which Freud according to Breton did not understand, that he might have found something of what he looked for in vain in ordinary language" (83).

The interest in the fragmentary is something that poststructuralism has in common with most modern schools of criticism: the Frankfurt school stresses the "negative dialectic" of the antitotalitarian; Barthes's later writings become more and more fragmentary themselves and the same phenomenon can be found in the work of Blanchot and Derrida; Philippe Lacoue-Labarthe and Jean-Luc Nancy have even published fragments and aphorisms, a form that has its roots in the German romantics, whose texts they translated in *L'Absolu littéraire* (1978).

Although in the philosophy of the Frankfurt school the paratactic and the antisystematic elements do play an important role, Theodor Adorno's work on the fragmentary differs from that of Heidegger and the French in that he does not attempt to adapt his style and presentation to his subject matter, and he also supplies a useful distinction between different kinds of fragmentation when he describes Heidegger's pieces in *Aus der Erfahrung des Denkens* (1965) as resembling both poetry and the pre-Socratic fragment, but he also points out that the difficulty of these latter fragments is due to the fragmentariness of the tradition, not to a desire to be cryptic or obscure (Adorno 1977, 45).

The fascination with the single word and the fragment is based on a theory of language that has developed as a direct reaction to structuralism. Since Saussure, structuralist linguistics has concentrated its attention on a synchronic and formalist study of language, in the sense that it has moved away both from the study of diachronic developments and from the problem of reference. It was especially successful in phonetics and, to a lesser degree, in morphology, but it encountered growing difficulties when it attempted to tackle larger structures. This may help to explain why the structuralist analysis of literary texts concentrated on shorter forms and why it has had, with the exception of narratological ventures, little impact on the study of the novel.

Fredric Jameson has shown how Saussure's notion of contingency reminds us that the Saussurian revolution is contemporaneous with theories of "pure poetry" (1972, 10), and Frank Lentricchia adds that the ideas of French symbolism, of English aestheticism, of T. E. Hulme and so also of American New Criticism, the aestheticism of Benedetto Croce, Clive Bell, Henri Bergson and the earliest phenomenological thought of Husserl, all set forth "an ideal of disciplinary autonomy or self-sufficiency presumably guaranteed by an explicit bracketing, to cite Husserl's key term, of extrinsic conditions and causes" (Lentricchia 1980, 114). In my turn, I would want to add, first, that these ideas can also be found in Russian formalism, especially in its alliance with futurism (see Medvedev 1976, 73–77), and in surrealism and some of its offshoots such as Jolas's *révolution du mot* and, second, that all of these movements share a theory of language; all posit, next to the communicative function of language, an expressive element that is usually considered from a Platonist, romantic, or idealist perspective as more fundamental.

In its most radical expression, this view describes language as preceding and transcending man. Its sources are varied: one of them is undoubtedly historicist and romantic. Johann Georg Hamann's ideas about the origins of language in poetry and the early successes of historical linguistics and etymology contributed to it and certainly influenced Heidegger. The romantic theory of language itself is indebted to two different but related traditions: a classical one with its roots in Heraclitus and another that is biblical and Christian and that was further developed in Catholic and Jewish mysticism. Both share the concept of *Logos*, the history of which Gerard Verbeke has traced in the philosophy of Greece and Rome; in Heraclitus, *Logos* is the "immanent principle of cosmic becoming" (1980, 492), which underlies not only objective reality but also human thinking. The same parallelism can be found in Plato, but in Plato's thought *Logos* must be separated by dialogue (thinking is an interior dialogue) from nonbeing, material reality. Plato discussed the problem of reference and the origin of language in his Cratylus, and it is there that we can find the source of the central place of etymology in antiquity and the Middle Ages. Cratylus himself claims that "a power more than human gave things their first names" (see the discussion in Uitti 1969, 6–18). Aristotle, too, sees an intimate relationship between thought and language and in the work of Philo Judaeus, *Logos* stands, as the container of the Platonic ideas, between God and the world; it is both God's poetry and the interior language all humans share (Michel 1976, 24). In classical philosophy *Logos* is both the rationality of the cosmos and the structure of the human mind, and it is in most cases represented by language. This language is realistic, in the sense that words refer to ideas and that the connections between the words are less important than the link between the world and the transcendental realm. In his *Metaphysics* Aristotle even writes that substances are ontologically more fundamental than actions.

The biblical *Logos* differs from this: in the Old Testament, the expression refers to the word of God transmitted by the prophets. The New Testament adds a creation Logos, most prominently in the prologue to the fourth Gospel, which posits an eschatological dimension. Just as in the Old Testament the Judaeo-Greek *sophia* constituted the creative word, *Logos* adopts this function in the Gospels, especially of course in the fourth. Since Justin harmonized the stoic *Logos* with that of the Bible (Bühner 1980, 501), both traditions have not been clearly distinguished until recently. Christian mysticism adopted the fundamental consubstantiality of the human mind and God and posited the existence of an experience of contact between the two, made possible by what Eckhart called the *Seelenfunken*, the soul's spark (Benz 1967, 28). This idea was to become an important source for German idealism and so was Saint John's Gospel itself (Schulze 1964). The importance accorded to language as a form of mediation between God and the world has permeated Western thought from its origins in Heraclitus, and it was linked in the early Middle Ages with conceptions of the *liber naturae* (Curtius 1973, 302–47). In German idealism, the Greek and Christian sources converged again in the linguistic theories of Herder and Hamann. The doctrine can be described in the following terms: language precedes and is ontologically more important than objective reality; a study of poetry, as the most fundamental, because historically older, form of language, reveals reality in its ontologically purest form. Whether this idea is considered to be epistemological (our minds are structured like a language), or ontological (reality itself is structured like a language) is less important; the result is the same.

Neither the Christian nor the Greek traditions have room for syntax and therefore for logical connections or temporal development. The problem that faces the poststructuralist critics I have been discussing is that their interpretations of the fragmentary (or fragmented) writings of others are necessarily presented in a unifying structure and that the resulting commentary always has some kind of coherence. In other words, these critics do supply a syntax but, as I have attempted to show, not always the same as that of their primary texts. In this, literary criticism has radically parted ways with linguistics; whereas early structuralist linguistics still seemed to offer a paradigm for literary criticism, the reference to contemporary linguistics has all but disappeared from the writings on the theory of literature. The reason is obvious: at no time have the findings of linguists about the nature of language differed more radically from those of literary critics. Where structuralism failed to move beyond the level of the single word, contemporary linguistics has abandoned the concept of sentence for that of discourse and has moved on to larger structures, rejecting the word fetishism of structuralism in favor of pragmatics, semantics, speech act theory etc.

The decision of poststructuralist literary critics and theorists to ignore the findings of modern linguistics has important consequences for the theory of language poststructuralism continues to embrace, and this is equally true for its philosophy of language, which has sought, as in Hamann or Heidegger, refuge in mythico-metaphysical "original or root words and in poetic metaphors" (Apel 1974, 1385). Early in this chapter I pointed to some sources of poststructuralism's word fetishism in the romantic theories of language, in mysticism, and in the Greek and Christian philosophical traditions. Now I will look more closely at the general problem of the ontological status of language and its implications for the active exclusion of history and for the resulting doctrine that reality is a text, that there is no "hors-texte."

The critics whose work I have discussed in the preceding chapters seem to share one basic attitude with the theories of *l'art-pour-l'art*; they seem to agree that literature does not refer to anything but itself. The doctrine has two consequences, one negative and one positive: the resulting exclusion of historical reality will be discussed later; here I will simply look at the positive aspect, the self-referentiality of the kind of art advocated here. The artist focuses on the form of his art and ultimately paints the act of painting a painting or writes about writing a book. This choice has two possible results; either the artist writes mainly about himself, or he concentrates on the formal elements, ultimately writing Flaubert's book about nothing. Both kinds of writers supply the poststructuralist critics with their favorite texts: romantic, symbolist, surrealist, neosurrealist, and experimental poetry. But aestheticism also has an influence on their own approach; the poststructuralist critics have adopted the basic tenets of aestheticism, and they read literature from the same perspective, interpreting the works they are discussing either as autobiographical or as self-reflexive and programmatic. In an extreme gesture, Philippe Sollers and Jean Pierre Faye even read Joyce's works as their own autobiography.

In each of these cases the text is abstracted from the historical circumstances in which it was written or to which its words refer. Following Fredric Jameson, Frank Lentricchia has argued that Saussure's structuralism belongs in a larger context of reactions against historicism that includes French symbolism, Croce, Bergson, Husserl, and beyond them the romantic theories of organicism and even Plato (1980, 114–15). French structuralism has adopted and even reinforced this Platonic element in Saussure, not only, as Lentricchia shows, by simply ignoring the diachronic dimension, but also by widening the application to all kinds of disciplines (mythology, science, psychoanalysis) and by implying that the structures of language are similar to if not the same as those of either the universe itself (the materialist argument) or human consciousness. Fredric Jameson has pointed to a decidedly Kantian echo in the epistemological argument (1972, 109).

Although poststructuralism has criticized Saussure precisely for these idealist tendencies, it has done so by emphasizing the formal, material aspect of the sign, the *signifiant*, thereby excluding the referent even more. In their concrete interpretations of texts, poststructuralist critics avoid a discussion of the actual genesis and of the primary referents: in Joyce's case, the references to Ireland or Irish situations and to the drafts and manuscripts of his works. On the other hand, they also refrain from considering the partiality of their own approach. Bernhard Böschenstein has described the same phenomenon in Heidegger's *Erläuterungen*: "The more these interpretations seem to lack a concern for history, are even opposed to history, the more they are determined by it" (Böschenstein 1977, 86; Heidegger 1981). But structuralism and poststructuralism are not alone in this evaluation of *l'art-pour-l'art*; the same is true for hermeneutics, that other Heideggerian heir. Hans-Georg Gadamer writes that in a work of art Husserl's eidetic reduction has been fulfilled spontaneously; language is only itself in a poem and *poésie pure* is in its radicalness normative for other forms of literature (Gadamer 1977). This existentialist hermeneutic was also central in the interpretation of "aestheticist" poetry, and Bernd Witte sees a clear link with the poetics of Mallarmé (1981). Both structuralism and hermeneutics favor the poetry of symbolists and other hermetic writers. Both also adopt the bracketing of historical reality that characterizes not only the writers of *l'art-pour-l'art* as a literary movement but also phenomenological philosophies such as Husserl's and Heidegger's.

But before we can attempt to describe the exact dimensions of this type of interpretation, another consequence of the antihistorical approach needs to be mentioned. Whereas New Criticism had radically excluded any reference to the historical sources of a literary work of art, this was not the case in France, and to a large extent the discussion about the death of the author is irrelevant in French criticism. Historians see Barthes's obituary as a devastating attack against the French academic study of author and work, but what is often forgotten is that there were alternatives to that tradition in the existentialist biographies of Sartre. The representative of the university critics, Professor Picard, attacked Barthes for his undisciplined use of psychoanalysis in the study of work *and* writer, and the introduction of a mainly Lacanian psychoanalysis in literary criticism made it impossible to exclude references to the author or to his conscious and unconscious intentions. What did happen in France was that the distinction between literary and nonliterary texts became progressively vaguer until it disappeared; philosophical and nonliterary texts are now interpreted with the same critical tools as literary discourse. As in some of Sartre's more radical studies, no distinction is made between statements in letters or in novels; a writer's biography becomes one of his texts, another work. This idea is expressed by almost all of the French critics: for Cixous, Sollers, and Derrida, there seems to be no difference between an artist's work and his life; in fact Joyce's life has become a work of art. Not only is literature thus dehistoricized; history itself is: source material is simply accepted, not critically evaluated, and in the end one particular aestheticist reading of literature is applied to philosophical, to historical, and to all kinds of texts, a procedure that ends in the exclusion of all references to historical reality. The philosophical foundation of this hermeneutic consists of an idealist language theory that becomes an aesthetic ontology in Heidegger and that has roots in the writings of Herder, Hamann, and Schelling.

Heidegger's aesthetic ontology—Being manifests itself only in art—is undoubtedly an heir to what Lentricchia calls the "antihumanist strain within romanticism" (1980, 92) and to the romantic claim that the work of art transcends the artist.

The emphasis on the single word, the interest in the fragment, in etymology and in the nonreferentiality of art, the exclusion of historical reality and the ontological status of language, all contribute to what may be called the romantico-idealist nature of poststructuralism. This broader context also explains the modern critics' resistance to the Enlightenment, both as a historical movement and as the dominant contemporary discourse described by Timothy J. Reiss as "analytico-referential" (Hutcheon 1983, 33). The romantico-idealist nature of poststructuralism is evident in its theory about the production of literature, in its hermeneutic of literary texts, in its eschatological character, and finally in the poststructuralist claims about the nature of the literary message.

The problem of the production of literature has surfaced a number of times in this discussion. I have argued that whereas New Criticism excluded the producer of the literary work on principle, French critics stopped short of that conclusion and simply abolished the limits between biography and the literary work. For Maurice Blanchot the poet exists only insofar as he prefigures the time of the poem, and he is lived by a poetic destiny that ultimately destroys him (1946, 586). Jacques Derrida talks of Artaud's *aventure*, which he defines as "a totality that is anterior to the separation of life and work" (1965, 46), and Philippe Sollers's observation that Joyce, Artaud, and Hölderlin have ceased to be human also belongs in this context (1976a, 111). In all three instances, the critic assumes that the poet, in this case Hölderlin, underwent a radical experience, a kind of inspiration, which enabled him to write the way he did. The most obvious source of such an experience is Plato's concept of *mania* described in the *Phaedrus* (244a–245a) and explicitly referred to by Blanchot in "Le Tournant" (1955). In contrast to the traditional meaning of the word, which refers primarily to a divine intervention, poststructuralism has employed a secularized version. Philippe Sollers writes about an "experience of the limit" (Sollers 1966b), that can be both sexual and linguistic: the writer reaches the limits of ordinary language, of the normal use both of his body and his conscious mind and he is confronted by the Lacanian Other, Blanchot's *neutre*, Derrida's *différance*, Kristeva's semiotic, Barthes's *jouissance*.

One of the major sources of this view is undoubtedly Heideggerian; in almost everything the philosopher has written or said about Hölderlin, there is a constant movement from the active to the passive mode, for example, in his discussion of Hölderlin's poem "Der Ister": "Those that call here are those that are called," and "The opinions historical man holds about art are determined by the manner in which historical man in his turn is held and carried by the essence of art" (1984, 6, 26). *Seyn* takes possession of the poet, and what is left of its passage is the poem and, in some cases, a mad and silent poet. This concept of inspiration as a possession can be found in the literature about Hölderlin by Stefan George and his circle, and beyond it in the works of romantic contemporaries such as Bettina von Arnim and in Hölderlin's own descriptions of the movements of his soul. A similar type of concept exists in slightly different forms in the philosophies of his contemporaries, in Immanuel Fichte, in Friedrich Schelling, in Hegel, in the work of the Schlegel brothers, in Novalis. Its sources can be found in Christian mysticism (Benz 1967) and beyond that in different neo-Platonist and Platonist traditions (Vieillard-Baron 1979; Henrich 1971; Osborne 1977). The reception of Hegel in France has always stressed this personal and mystic element in Hegel, most powerfully in the secular interpretation by Kojève, which was indebted to Heidegger and which influenced philosophers as diverse as Sartre, Bataille, Hyppolite, and Levinas, but also, before Kojève, in Jean Wahl, for instance, who speaks in his introduction to *Le Malheur de la conscience dans la philosophie de Hegel* about Hegel's "mystical intuition" underlying a doctrine that is described as "a mystical philosophy" (1929, 9–11). The French reading of Hegel stresses an element in his thinking that is also prominent in Heidegger and that has a distinct relationship with the German philosopher's Greek sources. In the *Phenomenology*, Hegel sends the empiricist to the most elementary school of wisdom, the Eleusian mysteries (1971, 91), a remark that calls into mind his own poem "Eleusis," which was dedicated to Hölderlin and the latter's own elaboration of the theme in "Brod und Wine." Bernhard Böschenstein has indicated the importance of this experience when he points out that the three Hölderlin poems Heidegger has interpreted in detail all deal with a "dionysiac experience" (1977, 79).

Before I can move on to a description of the interpretation of literary texts in this light, I have to mention an alternative view of the production of literature that comes closer to Joyce's self-understanding. Whereas the inspiration theory can easily be applied to writers such as Hölderlin and Artaud, it contradicts Joyce's view of himself as a highly self-conscious demiurge, the godlike creator of an oeuvre that is a challenge to the divine creation. To a certain extent, modern French criticism shares this idea of the artist-creator, and Hélène Cixous has even claimed that a psychoanalytical approach to Joyce's work would be impossible because everything in it is conscious and there is no room for the unconscious; but on another level the materialist version of the inspiration theory seems to be more fundamental. The religious theory of inspiration is a recent development in poststructuralism: the last *Tel Quel* essays on Joyce apply the doctrine of the Trinity to Joyce's work and find that the writer himself occupies the position of the Third Person, the Christian inspirator par excellence. Beryl Schlossman's work, with its discussion of "voice" and of the pentecostal experience, is the logical outcome of such a development.

A romantic theory of interpretation opposes intuition and transparency to philology and science. Ever since Roland Barthes, French critics have expressed negative opinions about historical and philological research, and some of their English and American poststructuralist colleagues share this bias. Both groups claim that a patient study of the biographical and historical sources of Joyce's works misses their most essential insights. This reaction against philology is not restricted to poststructuralism, and it even enables us to point to a fundamental parallelism at the heart of the two opposing forces in the theoretical debates of the late sixties and early seventies: deconstruction and hermeneutics. For Gadamer, the text is the locus in which two consciousnesses meet (1977), a meeting that can result either in a complete identification with the writer (as in some of the most radical readings by Cixous, Sollers, and Faye) or in the hermeneutic of the Geneva school and of related critics such as Maurice Blanchot and Paul de Man. Frank Lentricchia has described Georges Poulet's central doctrine as a "theology of self-dispossession" that describes the complete emptying of the interpreter's self in order to receive that of the other subject and that can be defended by referring to ideas in Kant, Coleridge, Husserl, and Mallarmé (1980, 63–78). In this view it is the reader's turn to undergo a kind of mystical experience, although the primary texts these critics interpret often deal with the same kind of objectless subjectivity exemplified for most of them in the work of Jean-Jacques Rousseau. Jean Starobinski mentions Hegel's negative and Hölderlin's positive evaluation of Rousseau's "natural mysticism" (1976, 311), and Paul de Man describes the same experience in a note on Poulet: "What counts for him is the experience of an unmediated presence of the mind to itself" (1982, n.p.). De Man was among the first critics in France to apply this hermeneutic; if we want to understand his early French writings, we must refer not just to Sartre's opposition between the concepts of *en-soi* and *pour-soi* as Frank Lentricchia does but also to the direct influence of Martin Heidegger. If there are similarities with Sartre's ideas, they may equally well be due to a common source in Heidegger. In the earliest essays, De Man radicalizes Heidegger in almost Blanchotian terms and finds a similar experience of completely interiorized (objectless) subjectivity in Rousseau, Wordsworth, and Hölderlin. But in his later essays De Man adds something that was lacking before, a linguistic dimension. In "Wordsworth und Hölderlin," his inaugural lecture at the university of Geneva, and in "L'Image de Rousseau dans la poésie de Hölderlin," he stresses the mediation of language and the relationship with the interiorized consciousness: "The God in us exists in the form of language" (1966a; 1965, 165). The rhythm of poetry (the non-referential, material element) is equated with a human consciousness and opposed to the objective world. It is this change that characterized De Man and Hillis Miller's shift away from Poulet and Heidegger toward Derrida. When De Man describes Blanchot's criticism in terms of a "consciousness without subject" (1966b, 553), he is referring to the same phenomenon.

The refusal of these critics to engage in philology and source study raises an additional problem. It seems fair to say that in the Geneva school and in Heidegger, this does not imply a complete ignorance about "extrinsic" elements. On the contrary, Hillis Miller has described how Poulet's generalizations about a particular author depended on a complete and detailed study of all the available source material, and the same is to a large extent true of Heidegger's interpretations. In later French critics, and not only in the works of the poststructuralists, this preparatory research seems to be lacking more often than not. One philosophical foundation of this general attitude lies in Heidegger's rejection of science and philology as fundamentally metaphysical products, and Allemann's application of this view to the study of literature certainly had a great influence on French critics. Because it is impossible to reach *thinking* from the point of view of metaphysics, one has to risk the leap toward "the thought most worthy of thinking" (Heidegger in Allemann 1959, 245), which resembles the German idealists' "leap over Kant" Heidegger has described elsewhere. This leap is not and cannot be justified or even explained in a metaphysical language, and Heidegger's critics have time and again stressed this as a mystical dimension in his work, the philosopher donning the gown of an illuminated seer. If we accept this description, we have to question the authenticity of the experience, about which most of his critics have doubts, although David Caputo writes in his study of the problem: "I find nothing to suggest that it is a second-hand record of someone else's insight" (1978, 223), and he concludes that what Heidegger does is "an endowment, a gift of a higher order, a blessing." He concludes his book:

> In the same way Heidegger's writings must be for us not a body of texts to be subjected to a learned exegesis, but a voice which calls us to set our own reflection into motion. And whose voice is it which calls to us from these texts? Is it only the voice of Martin Heidegger of Messkirch? (263)

In the sense of a conversion this experience also resembles the Christian conversions described in the Bible and in Saint Augustine's *Confessions*. It is a momentary emptiness and a reversal of values that has affinities with Kuhn's description of a gestalt switch or with Barthes's *jouissance*. This leads us to a last aspect of this theory of reading: a practice of writing that has dictated the style not only of Heidegger himself but also of Lacan, Derrida, and Lacoue-Labarthe. All of these writers apply their theory of reading to their own writings: George Steiner is representative of scores of Heidegger followers when he discusses the difficulty of the German philosopher's writings: "Yet I can testify that much of Heidegger does 'get through,' though in ways not readily identifiable with the usual modes of understanding and 'restatability'" (1978, 18). A similar phenonomenon can be observed in the translator's note to the American edition of the *Écrits*; a glossary is provided, but "in certain cases, however, Lacan has preferred that a term be left entirely unglossed, on the grounds that any comment would prejudice its effective operation" (Lacan 1977a, vii). Inevitably, the writing of these critics and philosophers becomes more literary, and style becomes more important than content. This is certainly the case in Heidegger's later work, which is recognized by David Caputo when he answers some of Heidegger's critics by suggesting that the fact that the philosopher's works are neither philosophical nor scientific does not necessarily mean that they are mystical; one should read them as poetry and Heidegger "poetizes out of an experience of the truth of Being" (1978, 235). Steiner also compares the reading of Heidegger's texts to the "gradual comprehension or 'sufferance' of great poetry" (1978, 19); similar claims have been made for Lacan's texts and for the later essays by Barthes and Derrida; Levinas calls it "a purely literary effect, the new *frisson*, the poetry of Derrida" (1976, 82).

The third romantic element in poststructuralism lies in its eschatology, which was initially Marxist and/or secular and which has become increasingly religious over the last decade. The secular eschatology is most obvious in the revolutionary fervor of post-1968 *Tel Quel*, which claimed to model itself after the cultural revolution in China. Similar hopes can be found in the work of Kojève, and in both cases the immediate influence seems to come from Marx himself. The word *eschatology* was first used in a secular context in 1912 and it quickly became an important concept in Marxist and communist philosophy (Mahlmann 1972, 742), and in combination with Jewish messianism it becomes a central concept in the works of Walter Benjamin, Ernst Bloch, and Erich Fromm.

The religious apocalypse has two dimensions: the message itself and the way in which it is revealed; John's *Book of Revelations* is paradigmatic in its emphasis on the divine inspiration of the visions and on the distinction between those that will be saved because they interpreted the signs correctly and those who ignore or misinterpret the message and are consequently damned. It is not difficult to link the notion of divine inspiration to the mystical experience and the concept of conversion I discussed earlier, and again we find Heidegger's work at the center of an analysis of poststructuralist eschatology. First we must distinguish between two different Heidegger readings: a secular Greek interpretation and a religious Christian reading. The first group of scholars—Jean Beaufret, François Fédier, Michel Deguy, and the early Derrida—interpret Heidegger's philosophy as essentially circular: philosophy as *Seinsvergessenheit* (the forgetting of Being) starts with Plato and reaches its peak in Hegel; Heidegger's own *Denken* reaches back to pre-Socratic and tragic Greece (which Heidegger thought of as the same period). But *Denken* can only prepare the ground, it can never bring on the apocalypse itself: "Only a God can save us now" (Heidegger 1976, 209).

In this framework, history is replaced by a tragic notion of fate: man does not make history, he is determined by the movements of Being, which Heidegger has called *Geschick* or *Schickung*. But Heidegger's eschatology is Christian, too, or at least it has been an important theme in existentialist theologies. Heidegger himself has pointed to the insistence on eschatology in Overbeck's *Über die Christlichkeit unserer heutigen Theologie* (Pöggeler 1977b, 25), and he read Saint John with Rudolf Bultmann. Some critics have suggested that the eschatological dimension entered Heidegger's work only after the *Kehre* and under the influence of Schelling and there are indeed remarkable resemblances between Schelling's later work and the ideas of some of the poststructuralist critics (Dews 1987).

In France, the Judaeo-Christian apocalypse replaced Marxist messianism in 1976 in the work of *nouveaux philosophes* such as Bernard-Henri Lévy, Jean-Marie Benoist, Maurice Clavel, and Philippe Sollers. Clavel writes: "One must not 'change the world,' we must change the world by giving birth to the other world, of which this world is pregnant. . . . In one word, let us be ready for that which is coming. I want to tame the apocalypse" (Clavel and Sollers 1977, 153). Although in the later seventies he was at the center of the reaction against these new philosophers, in 1983 Jacques Derrida published a book that addresses some of their most important themes. In *D'Un Ton apocalyptique adopté naguère en philosophie*, he discusses the theoretical problems involved in an explicitly eschatological discourse. He describes the link that exists between an apocalyptic discourse and the language of initiation and inspiration (1983, 28), noting the opposition between, on the one hand, the genius and his disciples, and, on the other, the rest of humanity; between a sudden inspiration and illumination and hard work; between the cryptic language of the sect and the clear enunciation of science; between the aristocratic principles underlying the first and the democratic ones on which the second is built. In his short 1796 essay *Von einem neuerdings erhobenen vornehmen Ton in der Philosophie* (1980), Kant called the proclaimers of the death of philosophy "mystagogues," and Derrida quite correctly observes that the opposition between philosophy and its concepts, on the one hand, and the metaphors, analogies, and poetry of the mystagogues, on the other hand, remains valid today. In contrast to Kant, Derrida refuses to take sides, because, he claims, putting an end to an eschatological discourse would be eschatological itself (1983, 60).

But in the last part of the book, he does take sides: not only for his own apocalyptic writing from *Glas* (1974) onward but also for the apocalyptic tone in Blanchot and Saint John, which finds its purest expression in the word *come*. The apocalyptic structure is that of every scene of writing and it is "a transcendental condition of all discourse" (1983, 77) precisely because it lacks a sender and an addressee. *Come* becomes that which escapes all determination and thus the apocalypse of the apocalypse. But by introducing this notion (Derrida relies heavily on Saint John's *Revelations*, on Blanchot and Levinas), he moves away from the Enlightenment side of his project, and his writing becomes susceptible to the same criticism Kant formulated two centuries ago. Derrida's claim that he is not sure who is writing his texts does not take away the fact that they are published under his name and are quoted as authoritative statements about Blanchot, Plato, Joyce, and Kant. His students and disciples do in fact follow him, even when his statements become very obscure and even proto-religious. As Kant shows, the mystagogue posits the apocalypse as a means of assembling a group of dedicated and uncritical followers; the more obscure the discourse becomes, the more his disciples will depend on him for enlightenment.

It is not too difficult to identify instances of the apocalyptic tone in the essays on Joyce; the first eschatological element is the often repeated assurance that Joyce introduces a new episteme, that he has ceased to belong to metaphysics, onto-theology, phallocentrism. The second is the very real problem of the poeticization of critical discourse, which tends to become more and more literary and autobiographical. The apocalyptic meaning of Joyce's oeuvre is stressed most strongly by the *Tel Quel* critics after 1976, and Beryl Schlossman has been most candid in the alliance between Jewish and Christian sources. The problem is that Joyce's work does not really allow an apocalyptic reading: contrary to Yeats, for instance, Joyce rarely makes explicit moral or cosmological statements. The two different dimensions of the apocalyptic theme that are clearly distinguished by Derrida, the form of the revelation and its chiliastic content, are present in most of the writings by poststructuralist thinkers, but they are present in different proportions. Heidegger combines both; although he does not emphasize the messianic content, his most explicit statements on the subject have to be looked for in the interview in *Der Spiegel*.

The four characteristics of poststructuralist writing I have discussed—the freedom taken with the primary text and with the translations, the emphasis on the single word and on the fragment, the idealist doctrine that all is text and that texts are autoreferential, and, finally, the romantico-idealist theory that underlies the first three—have an important problematic in common with all idealist and religious theories; in each case, the fundamental question we must ask is: who decides and on what is this authority based?

The problem of authority is linked to that of argumentation and of critical discussion, and it is central in the three systems of thought that have contributed most to poststructuralism: Marxism, Heidegger's philosophy, and psychoanalysis. About Heidegger's philosophy, Christian Graf von Krockow wrote in 1958:

> A remarkable parallel to Marxism on the one hand and to psychoanalysis on the other can be found in the way criticism is dealt with. Just as criticism in Heidegger is a priori put aside as attempts by the "they" [das Man] to understand themselves, it is called into question in Marxism as biassed ideologies and in psychoanalysis as resistances caused by repression. (73)

The authority of Heidegger, Lacan, and Sollers has already been discussed and in each case we have observed the positing of an authority that is based primarily on the thinker's own personality, on a will to power, a narcissism that bars and actively excludes alternative perspectives and that expresses itself in a playful and eccentric style of writing that includes an important autobiographical element. In analogy with a distinction introduced by Harold Bloom in *The Anxiety of Influence* (1973), we could call Lacan, Heidegger, and others like them "strong" critics. Philippe Sollers, the later Hélène Cixous, Jacques Derrida can thus be distinguished from "weak" critics such as Jean-Louis Houdebine and Stephen Heath, who merely apply the theories or methods of strong critics. Weak critics defer their authority to that of their masters and in quite a number of cases this is made explicit: French Heideggerians such as Jean Beaufret and François Fédier repeatedly referred to personal meetings with Heidegger; Anika

Lemaire even had Lacan's *imprimatur* as an introduction to her book; William Richardson's *Heidegger: Through Phenomenology to Thought* had an introduction by Heidegger himself (1967), and Jean-Louis Houdebine incessantly refers to Sollers.

"Weak" critics have to face two kinds of problems: on the most obvious level, they are criticized by opponents of their masters for simply adopting their master's theories. On another level, they are attacked by their co-disciples for lack of originality, in short, for not being Heidegger, Lacan, or Derrida. This is most clear when they dare to employ the master's style of writing. If the disciple accepts the challenge of translating the master's style, he needs the master's explicit permission (Houdebine; Anthony Wilden; Lemaire). If his work does not have that *imprimatur*, it will be attacked by the master himself, or, more often, by his disciples, and this is what happened to most of Lacan's former collaborators, most recently to Jacques Aubert, whose Lacan-inspired notes to the *Pléiade* edition of Joyce's work were criticized by Houdebine: "J. Aubert feels authorized by the 'Lacanian' theory to advance here and there a certain number of the most curious propositions" (1983, 43). The second alternative, the adoption of the master's style, is even less enviable: David Caputo claims Heidegger's writings show a genuine insight, but this is "something one cannot say of a good deal of the Heidegger literature . . . which is often pretentious" (1978, 223) and the same claim was made about the work of most Lacanians by Cathérine Clément (1981). In this game, the disciple cannot possibly win, no matter what he does, and this fact does not need to diminish the master's power; on the contrary, as long as the disciples quarrel among themselves, they will not challenge his own authority. This has important implications for French Joyce criticism: because there is hardly any challenge of the fundamental principles underlying poststructuralist readings of literary texts in general and of Joyce's work in particular, the literary and philosophical canon of authors is fundamentally the same in *Tel Quel*, in *Change*, in *Poétique*, or in Derrida's school. Not only do these critics read the same writers, they read them in the same way; this is immediately apparent in the image of Joyce that emerges. Although there are minor variations, a unified picture of Joyce's accomplishments appears that differs considerably from that in other countries.

A master's position is diametrically opposed to that of the disciple: a strong critic cannot lose. When he does make an identifiable mistake, it is either immediately accepted as true or thought to be essentially irrelevant to the main point he is trying to make. A strong critic's playfulness and the violence he employs in his reading of a text increase as his authority grows. Derrida, Lacan, Sollers, Cixous, and Heidegger are clear examples: in their later texts bibliographical references and footnotes disappear and autobiographical elements and puns become increasingly important: a strong critic's writing tends toward the condition of literature.

When a writer's style has become so apodictic and difficult as that of Derrida in *Glas* (1974) or Lacan in *Télévision* (1974), it becomes increasingly difficult for the disciple to apply the concepts offered by the master or even simply to paraphrase their definitions. This difficulty explains the fact that the disciples will always repeat these definitions verbatim: Lacan's "the unconscious is structured like a language" and Heidegger's definition of metaphysics are good examples. Frequently the willfulness of the master is consequently masked by the use of the word "rigorous." Derrida uses it in *L'Écriture et la différence*: "If the 'destruction' of the history of metaphysics is not, in the rigorous sense in which Heidegger understands it, a simple surpassing. . . ." (1967a, 291), and Lacoue-Labarthe describes Heidegger's definition of anthropology in *Holzwege* as "rigorous" (1978, 22), where in reality it radically departs, like so many of these definitions, from the generally accepted meaning of the term.

Because any type of relativism would endanger his position, the master cannot tolerate any kind of historical perspective. This is most obvious in Heidegger, whose introduction of his own concept of history earned him quite a number of attacks, notably in Germany: Karl Löwith has pointed to the difficulties involved in deciding whether a given point in time represents a "more original" moment or is just part of the comings and goings of time (1953, 49). Christian Graf von Krockow comes to similar conclusions and finds the roots of this idea in romanticism (1958, 79–88 and 159) and so does Adorno (1977, 83–84). In direct reference to Heidegger's writings on Hölderlin, Bernhard Böschenstein claims, with Adorno but without referring to him, that these texts should be read in the contexts of the Nazi years, and he stresses the violence involved in Heidegger's attempt to abstract Hölderlin from the poet's concrete historical reality (1977, 91). The process of dehistoricization does indeed work on two levels— that of the original author and that of the critic himself—and there is a clear parallel with the concept of inspiration that is used to explain both the creation and the reception of a work of art. The process of abstraction from concrete reality finds its clearest philosophical expression in the subject-object discussions in Heidegger and De Man, where the same absolute separation of subject and object seems to result, on the one hand, in an absolutely dehumanized objectivity and, on the other, in an absolutely immaterial subjectivity. In both these processes, the problem of authority is central, and it is precisely this theme that has been analyzed in depth by Adorno and Lentricchia.

What some of the critics of poststructuralism have tended to forget is that this problem of power has already been thematized both by the deconstructionist critics themselves and by the thinkers they base their work on and that a genuinely effective critique of poststructuralism has to confront this thematization that we have already seen at work in Derrida's study of eschatology. The authority problematic can be thematized on three different levels: in the wake of Freud on a psychoanalytical level, following some themes in German idealism and its heirs on a philosophical level, and finally from a political perspective. In the discussion of Lacan's contribution to the French reading of Joyce in chapter 2, I mentioned the distinctly psychoanalytical problems of basing one's authority on the power of the unconscious and the criticism on such a procedure from Lacanians such as François Roustang: Lacan's own theory contradicts the establishment of a school or even of a method. Sigmund Freud himself has analyzed the phenomenon of group building in his "Massenpsychologie und Ich-Analyse":

Today still the mass individuals need the illusion that they are loved equally and in the same way by the leader, but the leader himself does not need to love anyone else, he must have a leader's nature, absolutely narcissistic, but self-assured and independent. (1972c, 115)

Adorno referred to this psychological portrait in an essay on Stefan George, and he found the same character traits in the personalities of Richard Wagner, Heidegger, and Bertolt Brecht (Adorno 1974b, 524); Paul Hühnerfeld comes to similar conclusions about Heidegger's creation of a unique realm:

It is a space that exists for the sole purpose of accommodating Heidegger's thinking. In the same way his thinking exists only by its own will, or better, by the will of the existence called Heidegger, who accomplishes here the greatest and most significant excess of introversion ever witnessed in German philosophy. (1959, 116)

This psychological profile is not exceptional in itself; Joyceans will recognize similar elements in Ellmann's biography, and Helm Stierlin has found the same psychological structures in the biographies of Hölderlin, Kafka, Stefan George, and Brecht (1977). What is surprising is that the masters I have been discussing are not novelists, dramatists, or poets, but critics and theoreticians.

One of the most important benefits their disciples enjoy is that the unconditional acceptance of the master's authority entails membership in an elite; negatively, Adorno speaks of a "secret society" of existentialists (1977, 67) while Friedrich Gundolf distinguishes between *Gefolgschaft* (followers) and *Jüngertum* (disciples) (in Vallentin 1967, 38–39). It is this political dimension that was attacked by critics of Stefan George and Heidegger. Paul Hühnerfeld, Adorno, Krockow, Peter Gay, and others find similar political structures in Stefan George and Heidegger's disciples as in Nazism: the same pattern of irrationalism, nationalism, and romanticism (Adorno 1977, passim; Hühnerfeld 1959, 93–95; Gay 1970, 48–86). But in France Heidegger's heirs belonged to the other side of the political spectrum and at least until the mid-seventies, poststructuralism was the domain of radically Marxist thinkers. The most prominent brand of Marxism was Maoism, which does leave room for the concept of an elite, of a cultural as well as a political avant-garde. The *Tel Quel* writers exchanged Mao for Solzhenitsyn in the mid-seventies, but their interest in the exceptional individual did not diminish: Sollers even placed de Gaulle in the same category as Mao, and the new attitude is in any case more consistent with the overall implications of an elitist ideology.

The philosophical dimensions of the authority problematic are initially linked to these political implications; a central theme in post-structuralist thinking is the heroic stance of the critic-philosopher who also ascribes it to the writers he interprets. Bataille, Artaud, Lautréamont, and Joyce are heroic figures who have ceased to be simply human and who desperately attempt to express the inexpressible. The persona we find in the writings of Heidegger, Derrida, and De Man is an existentialist hero. Frank Lentricchia has described Derrida's project as a "reenactment of the myth of Sisyphus" (1980–81, 300), and about his shattering of the certitudes and assurances of a stable ontological ground he writes: "Often this bad news is carried by an embarrassing rhetoric which portrays the avant-garde critic as an existential hero, courageous enough to face down his 'inauthentic' urges" (1980, 179).

A second philosophical thematization can be found in the post-structuralists' defense of the unique against the system. This can be observed time and again in their writings on Joyce and on other writers. The Irish author *escapes*; he is different, Other. What he escapes from may differ from critic to critic or even change within one critic's career; it could be metaphysics, religion, paganism, logocentrism, feminism, protestantism, rationalism, Jung, idealism, or materialism. A similar concern can be observed on the level of poststructuralist theory; whereas structuralism tried to identify the overall system or the deep structure of a phenomenon, poststructuralism defends its uniqueness. In Kristeva's work, for instance, it is expressed in the concept of *soma* or in the semiotic dimension: that which, by definition, is excluded from normal language. In Blanchot, it is the neuter; in Derrida, *l'écriture*, the supplement or *différance*. In Cixous and Irigaray, it is femininity; in Barthes, the zero degree of writing, *jouissance*, the unreadable. In Sollers, it is first materialism, sexuality, and perversion, then metaphysics, mysticism, and religion. Religion first belonged to the dominant culture, and psychoanalysis enabled the critic to understand its importance; after 1976 psycho-analysis had become part of the dominant ideology that could then be attacked from the perspective of theology and religion. What remains on the subversive side is the creative writing of a small number of writers: Dante, Shakespeare, Mallarmé, Lautréamont, Hölderlin, Ar-taud, Joyce.

That the theme of the unique individual also applies to the critic himself is nowhere more clear than in the case of Philippe Sollers. In a half-jocular essay about "La G.S.I." (*la Gestion des Surfaces Imprimées*, the Administration of Printed Surfaces), an organization that regu-lates the production of all written materials, he states that only two people in the world are completely unpredictable, Lacan and himself (1980b, 11), and he repeats in almost every article and even more insistently in his autobiographical novels that he is completely alone, that he alone uncovers secrets others desperately want to hide. Ro-land Barthes stresses this element in the introduction to his *Sollers écrivain*: "We accept . . . particularities but not singularities. . . . But the absolutely isolated person? He who is neither a Breton, nor a Corsican, not a woman, not gay, not mad, not an Arab, etc.? He who does *not even* belong to a minority?" (1979, 8). In the rest of the book, Barthes touches on almost all of the themes I have discussed here. He attacks the sentence and defends the single word and the fragment; he compares Sollers's texts with mystic writings, and he meditates on history and on the "eschatological dimension" of Sollers's work. In an essay devoted to *H* (Sollers 1973a), Barthes defends Sollers from the argument that his work is the sophisticated and esoteric product of a small group "which thrives triumphantly on its own exclusiveness" (1979, 72). Barthes reverses the argument: *H* is closed from the out-side; its difficulty is chosen by the reader, and a more honest critic would have to ask: "If *you* are incomprehensible, is it because I am stupid, ignorant or because I have the wrong motives? In order not to communicate, there must be at least two" (72). This leads to a call for "an affectionate criticism" that must include any knowledge the critic may have of the writer as a person (78). This evolution away from the system and toward the unique phenomenon is paralleled in Barthes's own career by the increase in the autobiographical content of his writings, starting with *Le Plaisir du texte* (1973), and culminating in *Fragments d'un discours amoureux* (1977), and *La Chambre claire* (1980), in which he even calls for a *mathesis singularis*, the impossible science of the unique being.

The third philosophical thematization once again centers on the authority of the master, more specifically on his self-justification. Most of the poststructuralist writings seem to revolve around a paradox: because language and its structures are omnipresent, the truth about language and about the world cannot be expressed in language. This explains the heroic stance of the poststructuralist who decides to express the inexpressible *anyway*. He owes his unique insight into the inexpressible to the inexpressible itself, and there seems to be a parallelism here between ontogenesis and philogenesis, which is already present in the way Wahl, Kojève, and Hyppolite stress the autobiographical nature of the *Phenomenology*. It makes the philosopher-writer into somebody who is able to incarnate the contradictions that remain hidden to the vast majority of people and who resembles the biblical prophets or the Christian mystics in that something speaks through him that transcends both his listeners and himself. A more secular version of this claim has been elaborated by Derrida in reference to Joyce: in *"Ulysse gramophone,"* the address to the ninth international Joyce symposium, he distinguishes himself from his audience in the matter of things Joycean: "I know, as you do, that I do not belong to your large, impressive family" (1988, 46). In just a few paragraphs Derrida manages to turn a confession of incompetence ("experts . . . with the lucidity and experience that a long acquaintance with Joyce confers on them, ought to know better than most to what extent, beneath the simulacrum of a few signs of complicity, of references and quotations in each of my books, Joyce remains a stranger to me" [47]) into a discussion of the structure of the community of Joyce scholars, which is already preprogrammed by Joyce himself and thus there can be no Joycean competence, in the certain and strict sense of the concept of competence, with the criteria of evaluation and legitimation that are attached to this. There can be no Joycean foundation, no Joycean family; there can be no Joycean legitimacy. (49)

This radical reversal is not untypical of Derrida's work and neither is the way it is accomplished: the structure of the Joyce Foundation is that of the *double bind* and thus the same as that of language, literature, the bible, Babel, etc. In order to effect his deconstruction of the James Joyce Foundation, Derrida resorts to the central idea behind all of his work on Joyce: that in *Ulysses* and *Finnegans Wake* there is "a hypermnesia machine" that contains the complete Western memory, "virtually all the languages in the world" and even traces of the future. And, if it is true that Derrida knows Joyce's work "only indirectly, through hearsay, through rumors, through what people say, second-hand exegeses" (47), then this insight itself is based on the work of the Joyceans whose competence does not exist.

Derrida and Lacan simply *posit* that Joyce escapes any meta-discourse because his work always already contains all the commentary that could possibly be directed at it: they cannot prove it, except by pointing to a number of Joycean coincidences in their own biographies. In a manner that cannot be accidental Derrida's performance imitates that of the *Apology* of Socrates: of all mortals Derrida is most knowledgeable about Joyce because he alone knows that he knows nothing about Joyce. In a similar movement, Lacan, in a controversial statement, wrote that the psychoanalyst "ne s'autorise que de lui-même" (quoted in Roudinesco 1986, 455), and Jean-Michel Rabaté has written the same thing about the reader of the text of Joyce.

Attractive as it may seem, this perspective overestimates Joyce and underestimates the Joyceans. The consequences of turning Joyce into a prophet or a mystic, however secular, will be discussed immediately but first we should take a closer look at the Joyceans. The kind of authority that the association of Joyce specialists, like all professional organizations of its kind, disposes of does not have to be as negative and paternal as Derrida implies. On the contrary, it could be seen as a typically liberal American organization that is much more flexible and open to change than some of its critics feared, which is obvious if we look at what has happened since the Frankfurt symposium. Like most American literature departments, it has answered the challenge of poststructuralism and feminism by adopting them, by *not* resisting theory, by co-opting women and poststructuralists as trustees of the foundation or coordinators of symposia, by organizing theory-oriented panels, and by selecting theory-oriented papers in the proceedings of these conferences. If the James Joyce Foundation is a family or a primal horde, it is, as I have argued elsewhere (1988), one of the most open and unrepressive there are.

The psychoanalytical foundation of the critic's authority has already been discussed, but there is also a philosophical basis that goes at least as far back as Heraclitus, whose concept of *Logos* not only denotes the objective structure of the world; it is also a system of argumentation: "Heraclitus is on the other hand convinced that what he says is not a purely individual statement. Through him speaks the universal Logos and this is precisely the value of that speaking" (Verbeke 1980, 492). A similar attitude can be found in the works of the German idealists through whom the Absolute Spirit expressed itself and in Heidegger's concept of *Seyn*. Where this doctrine bases the authority of the master on the structure of the intelligible universe itself, it does not leave room for criticism and a genuine critique can only radically reverse the relationship between the two and stress the arbitrary imposition of the master's will. This has been done by Régis Debray in his *Critique of Political Reason* (1983) when he distinguishes between a scientific statement, which is independent of the subject of its enunciation, and a doctrinal statement, which is not. Ernst Benz, too, interprets the doctrine of the genius in idealist philosophy as a progressive secularization of the role of the mystic "as an experience of the immersion of the I liberated completely of its own will and of all egocentrism in the pure being of God" (1967, 32). The self-justification of poststructuralist critics (as long as it is not based on the authority of another master) resembles that of mystics and of theologians writing about mysticism. Benz writes that the mystical experience itself cannot be doubted: "The history of Christian mysticism shows us that this experience is a fact, independent of all theories about the possibility and the legitimacy of that fact" (28). Jörg Splett argues similarly in *Die Rede vom Heiligen* against criticism that the formula "encounters with the holy" is sociologically elitist, by simply positing the existence of such encounters and their accessibility to only a limited number of people in order to conclude that they are exclusive by nature (1971, 266–68).

In the course of this study I have often pointed out that poststructuralist critics are self-consciously avant-garde; they ally themselves with an avant-garde literary practice and a radical left-wing politics and in some cases they even adopt a number of literary or artistic functions. Renato Poggioli, one of the theoreticians of the historical avant-garde, had already applied his findings to criticism itself when he described the relationship between New Criticism and traditional aesthetics as one of antagonism, with agonism, nihilism, and activism one of the basic characteristics of the avant-garde he has identified (1981, 33). All the critics discussed here share this antagonistic attitude; although they may disagree on every issue they discuss, they all oppose the doxa, the prevailing norms and standards. What unites them is not a common enemy; it is the antagonistic attitude itself (which should not be confused with a political radicalism), the idea that you must be right because a majority disagrees with you. Antagonism is the driving force of every avant-garde and it seems to regulate conversions or radical changes of political or theoretical positions in the careers of figures such as Breton, Lacan, and Sollers. As soon as they have assembled a certain number of followers, they *have* to dissolve the school or movement before they become part of the establishment themselves.

This dynamic closely resembles what Poggioli calls activism, and it has been thematized by both French and American poststructuralists. Sollers equates Western culture with crisis (1980a, 9), and Paul de Man writes that "all true criticism occurs in the mode of crisis" (1971, 8). The French sociologist Pierre Bourdieu has even built his theory of culture on this dynamic. On the basis of an immense amount of sociological data, some of it already analyzed in a study of museum visitors (1966), Bourdieu has articulated a theory of taste (1979), with which it has become possible to analyze the world of art, culture and taste in much the same way as society as a whole, if we adopt the concept that "symbolic goods" like economic goods divide people into classes. In an essay published eight years earlier, Bourdieu had already applied this insight to the more limited field of a study of the dynamic of the market of symbolic goods. First he diagnoses a radical break around 1830 when an antibourgeois feeling among artists resulted in the creation of a "field of restricted production," which was designed to produce cultural goods, not for the general public (catered for in the "field of greater symbolic production"), but for the producers of the symbolic goods themselves. In this way the cultural production freed itself of the demands of the public in order to obey its own logic, "that of the permanent surpassing which the dialectic of distinction engenders" (1971, 56). From that moment on, popular success entailed the exclusion from the field of restricted production (the avant-garde) and, conversely, a lack of popular success has guaranteed acceptance in the field of restricted production: "If the producers . . . never consider without suspicion . . . the works and writers who seek or receive too much popular acclaim . . ., it is mainly because the 'larger public' threatens the field's monopoly of cultural consecration" (57). The principles of differentiation are usually those that express the specificity of its practice; in the case of literature, the stylistic and technical principles. Because the dynamic entails that the larger public always in the end accepts what it first rejected, the avant-garde has to keep ahead of the general public "by quasi cumulative ruptures with earlier means of expression," which force the artists "to lock themselves up in a search for originality (with the correlative ideology of the unknown 'genius' or the 'maudit')" (60). Opposed to the avant-garde, a second force exists, the university, which is the only institution that has the power to canonize artists, and Bourdieu compares the role of the university with Max Weber's comments about the attitude of the churches toward the prophets (71–74). Boudieu furthermore applies these insights to criticism and science in general and finds that whereas criticism before 1830 (and after that in the context of the field of greater symbolic production) is essentially an instrument of appropriation, in the field of restricted production it has become "a 'creative' interpretation to be used by 'créateurs'" (56), which ensures that the public remains actively excluded from the field of restricted production. An artist's position within the small and the large field will define the limits of his ambitions and his authority, and the same rules apply to the critic. It will immediately be clear that this theory could be very helpful in a study of a form of criticism that is self-avowedly avant-garde and that it has great similarities with Kuhn's theory of scientific evolution.

In his book *Homo academicus*, Bourdieu has applied this methodology to a large-scale study of the French university at the end of the sixties and shown how the strictly hierarchical and completely centralized structure of the French academy came under attack not only from students but also from its own staff on the assistant level (1984). In just a few years the number of *assistants* and *maître-assistants* almost trebled, while the number of professorships did not follow suit (1,646 to 362 in 1965; four years later 4,171 to 492). In the period we have been discussing a number of significant shifts in French intellectual life can be observed: a movement away from the Sorbonne and Nanterre and toward the more marginal institutions, especially the École pratique des hautes études and the Collège de France; away from teaching and toward research and editorial or journalistic success; and away from the traditional disciplines such as philology and classics and toward sociology, semiotics, and other interdisciplinary approaches. These trends are obvious in the careers of the major figures in (post)structuralism. Before they became professors at the Collège de France, Claude Lévi-Strauss worked in Brazil, in the States, and at a museum; Roland Barthes taught at the École pratique, and Michel Foucault, at the University of Clermont-Ferrand. Derrida, Althusser, and Lacan taught at the École normale supérieure.

Both the École normale supérieure and the Collège de France function more as academies than as universities: new professors are elected by the whole group of their peers (120 in the former, 52 in the latter), not appointed by the government or chosen by the department or faculty. None of these "authorized heretics," as Bourdieu calls them, had any real power in the university structure itself; they also teach less, have smaller groups of students and fewer theses to supervise. At the same time they are well-known outside the university and in the media, they publish in paperback series and have often acquired "a certain social power" (1984, 140). All of them are marginal figures within the structure of the traditional French university, which is characterized by an extreme centralization (more precisely a Pariso-centrism) and by a strict hierarchy in the disciplines and within each department. Terry N. Clark has analyzed the structure of French sociology departments and come to similar conclusions: one *patron* does not only run a whole department (usually at the Sorbonne), he also runs the whole discipline, the research programs, grants and, ultimately, the very life of the researchers (Clark 1971, 1973).

Whereas in May 1968 this structure was effectively challenged, it did not simply disintegrate. The emphasis of French intellectual life may have shifted from the Sorbonne to the École normale supérieure, to the Collège de France and the École pratique des hautes études, but these schools are also based in Paris, and so are the publishing industry and the media, whose influence has become increasingly important. This is due to the presence of a third group of professional intellectuals who work as independents, as publishers, or as journalists specializing in literary and intellectual matters. The functioning of this group was studied in 1981 by two journalists, Hervé Hamon and Patrick Rotman. They discovered a self-supporting network of people who live and work in a part of Paris the size of a village and who virtually monopolize French intellectual and cultural life. There are no strict divisions among the three spheres of university, publishing, and media; most intellocrats, as Hamon and Rotman call them, combine a university position with journalistic and editorial work, publishing in magazines and newspapers, appearing regularly on television or radio shows (if they do not have their own show), and most of them also function as advisers to publishing companies or direct their own series of books. The two authors demonstrate the incestuous relationships within this group: not only do critics praise their friends' work (and receive positive reviews in return); they sometimes publish it, too, nominate it for the Prix Goncourt or Prix Médicis, and "[u]ltimately the same person is able to write a work, to publish it and to have it reviewed" (1981, 115). These friendships (or networks of loyalties) are also a result of the centralized hierarchical structure of French education; all of the intellocrats did their *khâgne* (a preparatory training for the entrance exams to the École normale supérieure) at the best Parisian *lycées*. Louis-le-Grand, Henri IV, and Janson de Sailly have as graduates Christian Bourgois, Jean-François Lyotard, Gilles Deleuze, Michel Foucault, René Girard, Emmanuel Le Roy Ladurie, Jean-Marie Benoist, Jacques Derrida, Michel Serres, and Pierre Bourdieu. Hamon and Rotman especially single out Bernard-Henri Lévy who attended Louis-le-Grand with Philippe Némo, Christian Jambet, Guy Lardreau, the authors of the *nouvelle philosophie* and of his *Collection Figures* (Grasset).

But we are not talking about just a purely symbolic production; France has a large audience interested in intellectual and literary matters and therefore a large market for books. Bernard Pivot's Friday evening television show "Apostrophes" is watched by two to four million viewers (5 to 12 percent of the public), and the appearance of an author on this show can boost his sales by up to 30 percent. Nonfiction books (essays, literary criticism, philosophy) often sell better than novels, and on the best-seller lists published by *L'Express* one regularly finds the names of Roland Barthes, Bernard-Henri Lévy, Michel Serres, Pierre Bourdieu, and Julia Kristeva. These pressures of the market, of an entire cultural industry, have made Régis Debray describe the period between 1920 and 1960 as "the editorial era" and the time from 1968 to the present as the era of the "mediacracy." The concentration of power in the mass-media has been accompanied by an atomization of the intellectuals as a class: the modern media focus on personalities and not on collectives, on the singular and not on the universal: "The 'fashion groups' [in English in the text] of the contemporary intelligentsia must do without any fixed point, any definition or logical articulation, because the truth value of their claims is less important than the 'show value' of the people who make the claims;

the content of the claims is less important than the form of the faces and the idea less than its impact" (1979, 98).

May 1968 and its philosophy, poststructuralism, have radically altered the market of symbolic goods and the structure of the academic field. The university of Paris still occupies the top of the academic pyramid, just as the Académie Française continues to group the most important writers, but the two institutions represent the conservative part of the nation's culture. Sorbonne professors and académiciens rarely leave the ivory tower, and if they do, they usually write in the more conservative journals and newspapers. Since 1968 the École normale supérieure, the École pratique des hautes études, and the Collège de France have become the unchallenged leaders in the wider intellectual field, which has been opened up to a larger public by the media and the publishing industry. Whereas the Sorbonne professors used to publish with Klinksieck or the Presses universitaires françaises, structuralists and poststructuralists reached larger audiences with general or literary publishing houses such as Seuil (Sollers, Barthes, Kristeva, Derrida, Lacan), Minuit (Derrida, Deleuze, Guattari), and Gallimard (Foucault). Since the mid-seventies a significant shift has occurred away from Seuil and toward Grasset and Denoël. By the end of the seventies poststructuralist thinkers occupied the leading positions in the academic top and subtop, at the Collège de France, the École normale and the École pratique; they also controlled the suburban campuses that represented the challenge to the Sorbonne and traditional university structures, especially the campus at Vincennes. This does not mean that the power structure itself had changed: when Lacan took over the psychoanalysis department at Vincennes, he used the most blatant *patron* manner imaginable and Sollers ran the *Tel Quel* collective as if it were a politburo. Bourdieu describes how the *nouvelle critique* controversy in the mid-sixties is paradigmatic for the growing tensions between the two fields: "the roles seem to be distributed in advance by the logic of the field" (1984, 152). The camp of the *lector* is occupied by the orthodox Sorbonne professors and the conservative journalists and that of the *auctor* by the writers who have in common that they live in one or another margin of the Parisian university system: Sartre, Gaston Bachelard, Lucien Goldmann, Georges Poulet, Jean Starobinski, and René Girard.

The third group is completely uncontaminated by the academic field, although the vast majority of free agents did go to the same *lycées* and to the same schools as their colleagues in the university. They are journalists, work for publishers, or carve out an existence as independent writers. The *Tel Quel* writers in the sixties and the *nouveaux philosophes* in the seventies existed largely outside of the academic context and even in direct opposition to it. This is not new; the Left Bank has always played a significant role in Paris, from Gide to Sartre, but the novelty is that the media have now accelerated the developments and have turned an opposition to the university into a virtue per se.

Hamon and Rotman describe day by day the release of Bernard-Henri Lévy's *l'Idéologie française* (1981), beginning with a deliberately offensive prepublication in *L'Express*, followed in the two weeks after the book publication by articles in *Le Monde, Les Nouvelles littéraires, Le Matin, L'Express* and *Le Nouvel observateur* and two appearances on television. The press, apart from Lévy's personal friends, was negative, and Lévy, grilled on "Apostrophes" by Professor Bourricaud, could not defend his most controversial theses. But the book entered the charts in *L'Express* three weeks after the publication and stayed there for ten weeks. The historical and philosophical weaknesses of the book have earned it a *succès de scandale*, which was sufficient in itself to turn it into a commercial success (Hamon and Rotman 1981, 145–48). It is this presence of a large reading public, of a centralized structure of power both inside and outside the university, and of a large number of free agents that has been conducive to the creation and the success of poststructuralism in France.

In *Homo academicus*, Pierre Bourdieu warns against the use of the "science of battles" as a weapon in the battle itself, and he especially objects to the notion that an extrascientific (extraacademic) success is necessarily bad (1984). Raymond Boudon had implied that since the French hierarchy of celebrities differs from the international one, which is scientific, it had to be extrascientific. Bourdieu refuses to accept this phenomenon as a French particularity or archaism (in equating "international" with "American" he seems to fall victim to another French particularity), but I would argue that French centralization and insularity have indeed produced a situation that is peculiar to Paris. An analysis such as Bourdieu's would be much more complicated in the United States, the United Kingdom, or other European countries, and this does not mean that these analyses do not apply outside of France, just that the structures at work are more blatantly visible in the centralized French context.

If Bourdieu attacks Raymond Boudon for becoming a participant in the field he is studying, the same holds true for his own *Homo academicus*. Pierre Bourdieu is a Parisian mandarin, and his opinions about a great variety of topics appear in newspapers and journals; he teaches at the École normale supérieure, leads research projects, edits journals, and, with apparent success, controls one section of the market he is trying to describe scientifically. Luc Ferry and Alain Renaut have rather unfairly accused Bourdieu of not having reflected sufficiently on this paradox, but it is true that an analysis of the mechanisms of the academic and intellectual market in one country should be executed by somebody who does not depend on the same market (Ferry and Renaut 1985). This seems to be true for the studies that Terry N. Clark has devoted to the *patron* system in the French sociology departments (1971, 1973), which Bourdieu does not mention at all and, I hope, for my own study. It does not follow that Clark's and my own analyses are pure and disinterested; they do play an extrascientific role, but outside the field they discuss. Bourdieu has offered different justifications for his position as participant-observer; but he is incapable of going beyond the paradox of sociology as master science. Ferry and Renaut quite rightly oppose this position with an elaboration of Kant's suggestion about the pure scientific interest along lines first proposed by Jürgen Habermas (Ferry and Renaut 1985, 227).

In the preceding pages I have offered an analysis of what I believe to be the most basic characteristics of poststructuralist criticism and theory. I have also pointed to some possible sources of the poststructuralist doctrines and practices, and I have argued that these are more often than not romantic and idealist. Although the exact genealogy of the influences is not altogether clear to me, it would be hard to maintain that the resemblances between the doctrines of deconstruction/poststructuralism and Heidegger's philosophy, French surrealism, and symbolism would be purely coincidental. The most immediate source that all these movements have in common is the reaction against the Enlightenment in German philosophy and literature, described by René Wellek in *Concepts of Criticism*:

> This new view emphasizes the totality of man's forces, not reason alone, nor sentiment alone, but rather intuition, "intellectual intuition," imagination. It is a revival of neo-Platonism, a pantheism (whatever its concessions to orthodoxy), a monism which arrived at an identification of God and the world, soul and body, subject and object. (1971, 165)

The fundamentally romantic nature of poststructuralism and its relationship with German idealism have been discussed by friends and foes. Not only do deconstructionist critics seem to have a predilection for romantic texts, but when they turn to philosophy, they always return to the German philosophers, to Kant, Hegel, Schelling, and Nietzsche.

Tzvetan Todorov has argued that the romantic ideology has been central in France since World War II: "The global context after the war, in the domain of literary and aesthetic ideas, is (remains) that of romanticism" (1979, 131). He shows how Blanchot develops Mallarmé's aesthetics and how he adopts its romantic elements:

> The poetic word is an intransitive word, which has no practical use; it does not signify, it is. The essence of poetry lies in the inquiry it conducts into its own origin. These are the romantic commonplaces that Blanchot reads in Mallarmé and that will dominate the doctrine expounded in *Le Livre à venir* and *L'Espace littéraire*. (134)

The most important romantic trait is the view that the essence of art is art itself and, consequently, that art questions its own very possibility. This results in the frequent use of the oxymoron, in the interest in unfinished works and fragments and, paradoxically, in a dislike of romantic writers, whom Blanchot distinguishes from Mallarmé, who is, according to Todorov, "the rather late French variant of the romantic doctrine" (137). It is only in *Entretien infini* (1969) that Blanchot introduces a dimension irreconcilable with the romantic doctrine of the individual identity, the *neutre*, the coexistence of opposites. Although Todorov opposes to this Otherness Blanchot's "egocentrism" and concludes that the Other is absent in Blanchot's work (1979, 140), he seems to have missed the equally romantic sources of this "heterology."

Barthes, Todorov's second example, has concentrated his critical attention on two different but equally romantic characteristics of literature: its intransitivity (autonomy) and the plurality of interpretations, which also leads him to a concept of the *neutre*, "the emptying of the 'person,' who is, if not annulled, at least rendered irretrievable" (Barthes quoted by Todorov, 145). Although Todorov is one of the few French critics to have commented on the romantic ancestry of French criticism, his diagnosis does not go far enough. I believe it would be possible to argue that the break between Barthes's formalist phase and his writings after *S/Z* (1970) resembles that between Kant and his successors. As I mentioned before, Fredric Jameson has already analyzed the Kantian premises of structuralism, and the poststructuralist interest in the escape from all structures by writers such as Hölderlin, the Schlegels, and Novalis is clear enough. In both cases we find the same reaction against a totalizing Reason and the same search for a different power (Hegel's position in this configuration remains ambivalent, but most French theorists accept Bataille's Kojèvian reading).

Both an opponent and a supporter of deconstruction agree on its idealist premises. Terry Eagleton follows Lentricchia and stresses the romantic despair underlying the deconstructionist project and the idealist doctrines that form the basis of both (Eagleton 1981), and Richard Rorty discusses some similarities between nineteenth-century idealism and what he calls "textualism," American deconstruction and French poststructuralism. What the two have in common is romanticism, "the thesis that what is most important for human life is not what propositions we believe but what vocabulary we use," an inversion of Kant's *Third Critique*:

> Kant, in saying that aesthetic judgment is noncognitive, because it cannot be brought under rules, is assigning it a second-best status—the status which the scientific culture has always assigned to the literary culture. Romanticism, on the other hand, when it says that science is *merely* cognitive, is trying to turn the tables. (1981, 158)

Where these thinkers found these ideas is less important than that they did: I believe one important genealogy goes back, via surrealism, to symbolism and especially to Mallarmé's poetics. Another and, I have attempted to show, more consistent influence is Heidegger's philosophy, in its essentially romantic reading of Hölderlin's poetry and in the antihistoricism and irrationalism of its later developments. The French critics accept the privileging of poetry and language over science and objectivity and radicalize this idealism in "textualist" terms. Maybe even more than Heidegger himself, they need witnesses who have escaped metaphysics and logocentrism, and with Heidegger they see Hölderlin as such an escapee. Against Heidegger they include a number of French symbolists and surrealist writers (Lautréamont, Mallarmé, and Artaud) and Joyce in the new canon. With Heidegger, the French critics find inspiration in different marginal systems of thought: the pre-Socratics, Gnosticism, negative theologies, mysticism. Against Heidegger, they stress the importance of Freud's psychoanalytical theory of which they stress the antirationalist, antisystematic, and romantic element.

The simple fact that quite a number of nonacademic Joyce critics whose work has been discussed in the preceding pages do not know English and know little if anything about the actual historical conditions in which Joyce lived and worked is not enough to explain their inability to offer an interpretation of a specific text of *Ulysses* or *Finnegans Wake*. Their problem is that their reading is always already established: Joyce, like Hölderlin, escapes, deconstructs, differs. The norm may be science, society, phallocentrism, or metaphysics, and the deconstruction feminist, masculinist, Marxist, or Freudian, but the a priori structure is always one of exception; in each case the attempt to describe the aberration is impossible by definition. No text could really (absolutely) escape, and if there were such a text, one could not write about it. The immense power and seductive quality of poststructuralist writing, especially Derrida's, lies in the fact that it has managed to thematize this impossibility.

The notion of escape is also present in deconstruction's understanding of its own practice: criticism should be different, original. Because of its ahistorical bias this thesis is not so difficult to defend within the deconstructive framework, but it has become one of the most important points of critique from outsiders. Lentricchia writes in his introduction:

> In fact, as I think will become clear in the pages ahead, I believe that the desire for originality, in all of its senses and variants, has seriously marred and enervated more than a few of the most brilliant critics on our contemporary scene. (1980, xi)

In the last line of his analysis of Bloom's criticism, Lentricchia identifies what is most retrograde and antiintellectual in contemporary criticism as "the desire, articulated frequently in our advanced critical journals and graduate centers of theoretical training, to be an original theorist" (346). It is this desire that can be described with the help of Pierre Bourdieu's analysis of avant-garde writing as the dynamic that powers all critical discourse in France. But the critics I have discussed only seem original; they are merely different from what English and American critics have come to expect. As I have attempted to show in the preceding pages, a historical and critical analysis can easily show the continuities, the borrowings, and the sectarian differences. It is this romantic yearning for originality in the margins of a totalizing rationality that allows fundamentally Heideggerian critics such as Derrida and Lacoue-Labarthe to borrow concepts from Benjamin and Adorno. Michael Jennings writes: "As early as the Hölderlin essay of 1915 . . . Benjamin anticipates many of the critical motifs associated with structuralist and poststructuralist criticism," and he refers to Derrida's text on Benjamin (Jennings 1983, 559; Derrida 1978c).

Maurice Blanchot had already praised Benjamin's theory of translation in 1960, and Philippe Lacoue-Labarthe discovered that Adorno's "Parataxis" deconstructs Heidegger's *Erläuterungen* (Lacoue-Labarthe quoted in Rochlitz 1984; Adorno 1974a; Heidegger 1981). In both cases it is once again the romantic, antisystematic element in the writings of the philosophers of the Frankfurt school that is appreciated.

The anti-Enlightenment critique of Adorno and Heidegger, their privileging of the aesthetic dimension and finally their concept of the nonsystematic, the negative, and the fragmentary may ultimately be based on the same neoromantic sources. In his *Theorie des kommunikativen Handelns*, Jürgen Habermas has written:

> Much as the intentions of their philosophies of history are at variance, they do resemble each other, Adorno at the end of his career, and Heidegger, in their position on the theoretical claims of an objectifying thought and of reflection: the attention for nature comes shockingly close to the Thinking-toward-Being. (1981a, 516)

He has also identified Max Weber's influence on Adorno and Horkheimer as decisive for their inability to distinguish between the process of rationalization and the oppressive forces operative in late capitalist society, on the one hand, and what he calls "communicative rationality," the real emancipatory power, on the other:

> Not just the impotent rage of a mutinous nature offers an internal logic to the resistance against the mediatization of the environment by the autodynamic of systems that have developed their own independence, but precisely this communicative rationality, which reflects itself in the self-understanding of the modern world. (1981b, 491)

Whereas Habermas had argued earlier for a "strong" variant of the "transcendental pragmatic tu-quoque argument" (it is impossible to question an argumentative rationality principle because it is presupposed not only in the question itself, but even in the basic structures of all linguistic activity [1976, 339]), other critics have decided to ignore the epistemological aspects of the antirationality argument and focus instead on its ethical aspects (Habermas's epistemological foundation is the basis for a practical philosophy or ethics). Richard Rorty rejects epistemological arguments for reasons that resemble Kuhn's and adds that the most serious objections against "textualism" are moral, not epistemological (1981, 171). E. D. Hirsch offers a similar analysis of the distinction between synthetic a priori and a posteriori positions. Neither can be refuted or confirmed, although only the second is revisable. A choice between the two positions cannot be based on philosophical grounds but must be made on the basis of an essentially political decision: "Humpty-Dumpty's question, *Who* shall be master? *Who* shall choose the cypher key? is the ultimate political question in interpretation" (1981, 239). The reader's choice for his own preferred key is an "autocratic" norm, his decision to use somebody else's is "allocratic" (240). Again the choice between the two alternatives is "ethical and political" (241), and in a footnote Hirsch gives his version of the *tu quoque*:

> I have noted before that a priorist, autocratic critics invite us to pursue an allocratic interpretation of their own writings—thus recognizing implicitly the reality of the autocratic/allocratic choice—by their actions if not by their theories. (240)

He calls the view that interpretation is always already autocratic "idealist" (*nihil in interpretatione nisi prius in schema*); the contrasting view is "realist"; followers of this theory believe that interpretation can be autocratic or allocratic or "that the truth about an historical event . . . is something that might be objectively known despite the influence of cultural schemas" (242). The choice between these two resembles Pascal's wager about the existence of God: "If you win, you win something. If you lose, you lose nothing. Do not hesitate then, gamble on the existence of objective truth" (243).

These different arguments have in common that they value revisability over rigor, communicability and consensus over authority, democracy over elitism, objectivity over subjectivity. Most of the critics I have discussed in the preceding pages have chosen the latter alternatives, and the constant references to mysticism and Gnosticism are not accidental. Some of their works even manifest an interest in the historical gnosis: although Philippe Sollers calls himself a Gnostic, most of the critics I have been discussing share an attitude that has been called Gnostic in a wider sense: the belief that the divine saving truth is contained in an esoteric revelation which is accessible only to a chosen few to whom it has been transmitted in secret and mysterious ways. It is the attitude I have earlier described as apocalyptic, mystical, esoteric; it presupposes an intuition, a religious conversion, a mystical experience, a temporary disappearance of the limits between subject and object: Philippe Sollers's *expérience des limites*, Blanchot's *neutre*, Barthes's *jouissance*, Kristeva's semiotic level, the objectless subjectivity of Poulet and Starobinski, and the subjectless objectivity of Heidegger and De Man. In the terminology of Hölderlin and his friends, it is the explicitly aesthetic intellectual intuition, which Kant had claimed was impossible in his first *Critique* and which he saw at the center of what he attacked as "mystagogy"' (Kant 1980, 386f). John Neubauer has demonstrated how this reinterpretation of Kant's term was due not only to Fichte but to a cross-fertilization of Fichte's concept with the pantheism of Spinoza and other neo-Platonist trends in the thinking of Schelling, Hölderlin, Schlegel, Novalis, and finally Schleiermacher, who added an aesthetic dimension (Neubauer 1972). Werner Beierwaltes has argued that there are fundamental similarities between Schelling's intellectual intuition and Plotinus's concept of *ecstasy* (Beierwaltes 1972), and Alfred Jäger that Heidegger during the years of the *Kehre* has identified Schelling's concept of intellectual intuition with his own "thinking of Being" (Jäger 1978, 262). Heidegger's philosophy after the *Kehre* has fundamental affinities with Schelling's intellectual intuition, with Hegel's "knowledge of the absolute," with Spinoza and with similar concepts in the work of the medieval mystics.

Stylistically this experience entails a refusal to communicate or to argue that results in a specialized vocabulary and fragmented, apodictic structures. The unwillingness to communicate (masked as an ontological inability), which these critics and philosophers have in common with the art-for-art's-sake writers since romanticism and which may have the same social and political roots, makes it difficult to accept any form of critical pluralism. As I have argued, these critics' will to power (Hirsch would say their "autocracy"), excludes the reader's own; if that is true, maybe we should, as Alexander Nehemas has argued, accept a critical monism with a postulated author as a "regulative ideal" and not the reader or the critic: "A methodological constraint on this view is that the postulated author be historically plausible; the principle is that a text does not mean what its author could not, historically, have meant by it" (1981, 145).

If one adopts a critically pluralist position, metacriticism becomes either impossible by definition or ultimately irrelevant because in the latter case different interpretations cannot possibly be compared. Paradoxically, only a critically monist position can be historical, comparative, and antidogmatic. It is this final characteristic that was central in the answer Immanuel Kant gave to the question "What is Enlightenment?" more than two hundred years ago:

Enlightenment is the breaking free of man out of a speechlessness for which he himself only can be blamed. Speechlessness is the inability to use one's own mental faculties without the help of somebody else. This speechlessness is *self-imposed,* when it is not due to a lack of intelligence, but to a lack of determination and courage to use one's own intellect without the guidance of another. Sapere aude! Be brave enough, to use your *own* intellect! is therefore the motto of the enlightenment. (Kant 1981, 53)

Bibliography

All references to Joyce's works and to Ellmann's biography follow the abbreviations suggested by the *James Joyce Quarterly*.

D	Joyce, James. 1967. *Dubliners*. Ed. Robert Scholes. New York: Viking Press.
FW	Joyce, James. 1939. *Finnegans Wake*. London: Faber and Faber.
GJ	Joyce, James. 1968. *Giacomo Joyce*. Ed. Richard Ellmann. New York: Viking Press.
JJ I	Ellmann, Richard. 1959. *James Joyce*. New York: Oxford University Press.
JJ II	Ellmann, Richard. 1982. *James Joyce*. New York: Oxford University Press.
Letters I, II, III	Joyce, James. 1966. *Letters of James Joyce*. Vol. I, ed. Stuart Gilbert. London: Faber and Faber. Vols. II and III, ed. Richard Ellmann. London: Faber and Faber.
P	Joyce, James. 1964. *A Portrait of the Artist as a Young Man*. Ed. Richard Ellmann. New York: Viking Press.
SL	Joyce, James. 1975. *Selected Letters of James Joyce*. Ed. Richard Ellmann. London: Faber and Faber.
U	Joyce, James. 1984. *Ulysses*. Ed. Hans Walter Gabler et al. New York and London: Garland Publishing.

Major French Translations of Joyce's Works

Joyce, James. 1924. *Dedalus: Portrait de l'artiste jeune par lui-même*. Trans. Ludmila Savitsky. Paris: Éditions de la Sirène.

Joyce, James. 1926. *Gens de Dublin*. Trans. Eva Fernandez, Hélène Du Pasquier, Jacques Paul Reynard. Introd. Valery Larbaud. Paris: Plon.

Joyce, James. 1929. *Ulysse*. Trans. Auguste Morel, Valery Larbaud, Stuart Gilbert, and James Joyce. Paris: La Maison des amis des livres.

Joyce, James. 1948. *Stephen le héros*. Trans. Ludmila Savitzky. Paris: Gallimard.

Joyce, James. 1950. *Les Exilés*. Trans. J. S. Bradley. Paris: Gallimard.

Joyce, James. 1950. "Poèmes." Trans. Annie Hervieu and Auguste Morel. *Mercure de France*, no. 309:5–11.

Joyce, James. 1961. *Lettres*. Ed. Stuart Gilbert. Trans. Marie Tadié. Paris: Gallimard.

Joyce, James. 1962. *Finnegans Wake*. Trans. André du Bouchet. Introd. Michel Butor. Paris: Gallimard.

Joyce, James. 1965. "Un Portrait de l'artiste." Trans. Jean Fuzier, and Hélène Berger. *Tel Quel*, no. 22:62–68.

Joyce, James. 1966. *Essais critiques*. Trans. Elisabeth Janvier. Paris: Gallimard.

Joyce, James. 1966. *Le Chat et le diable*. Trans. Jacques Borel. Paris: Gallimard.

Joyce, James. 1967. *Poèmes. Musique de chambre. Poèmes d'Api*. Trans. Jacques Borel. Paris: Gallimard.

Joyce, James. 1973. *Giacomo Joyce*. Trans. André du Bouchet and Yves Malartic. Paris: Gallimard.

Joyce, James. 1973. *Lettres*. Ed. Richard Ellmann. Trans. Marie Tadié. Paris: Gallimard.

General Bibliography

Adams, Robert M. 1966. *Surface and Symbol: The Consistency of James Joyce's "Ulysses"*. New York: Random House.

Adorno, Theodor W. 1974a. "Parataxis. Zur späten Lyrik Hölderlins." In his *Noten zur Literature. Gesammelte Schriften. Band 11*, 447–91. Frankfurt am Main: Suhrkamp.

———. 1974b. "George." In his *Noten zur Literatur. Gesammelte Schriften. Band 11*, 523–35. Frankfurt am Main: Suhrkamp.

———. 1977. *Jargon der Eigentlichkeit: Zur deutschen Ideologie*. Frankfurt am Main: Suhrkamp.

Albérès, René Marill. 1972. *Métamorphoses du roman*. Paris: Albin Michel.

Allemann, Beda. 1959. *Hölderlin et Heidegger: Recherche de la relation entre poésie et pensée*. Trans. François Fédier. Paris: Presses universitaires de France.

Althusser, Louis. 1973. *Pour Marx*. Paris: Maspero.

———. 1976. "Freud et Lacan." In his *Positions*, 9–34. Paris: Éditions sociales.

Althusser, Louis, and Étienne Balibar. 1971. *Lire le Capital*. 2 vols. Paris: Maspero.

André, Serge. 1988. "Joyce le symptôme, Hugo le fantasme." *La Part de l'oeil*, no. 4:102–25.

Apel, Karl-Otto. 1974. "Sprache." In *Handbuch philosophischer Grundbegriffe*, ed. Hermann Krings. München: Kösel.

Aragon, Louis. 1943. *Les Voyageurs de l'Impériale*. Paris: Gallimard.

Atherton, James S. 1959. *The Books at the Wake: A Study of Literary Allusions in James Joyce's "Finnegans Wake"*. London: Faber and Faber.

Attridge, Derek. 1984a. "Language as Imitation: Jakobson, Joyce, and the Art of Onomatopoeia." *MLN* 99:1116–40.

———. 1984b. "The Backbone of *Finnegans Wake*: Narrative, Digression, and Deconstruction." *Genre* 17:375–400.

———. 1988. *Peculiar Language: Literature as Difference from the Renaissance to James Joyce*. London: Methuen.

Attridge, Derek, and Daniel Ferrer, eds. 1985. *Post-Structuralist Joyce. Essays from the French*. Cambridge: Cambridge University Press.

Aubert, Jacques. 1964. "A Monument of Impropriety." *A Wake Newslitter* 1 (June): 1–4.

———. 1967. "*Finnegans Wake*: Pour en finir avec les traductions." *James Joyce Quarterly* 4:217–22.

———. 1968. "Notes on the French Element in *Finnegans Wake*." *James Joyce Quarterly* 5:110–24.

———. 1972. "riverrun." *Change*, no. 11:120–30.

———. 1973. *Introduction à l'esthétique de James Joyce*. Paris: Didier.

———. 1974. "Remarques sur quelques études critiques." In *"Ulysses" cinquante ans après*. See Bonnerot 1974, 287–97.

———. 1977. "Sur James Joyce: Galeries pour un portrait." *Ornicar? Analytica*, no. 4:3–18.

———. 1978a. "L'Épiphanie selon James Joyce: Effet de sens ou signifiance." *Bulletin du Centre de recherches sémiologiques et linguistiques* 6:189–95.

———. 1978b. "Breton Proverbs in Notebook VI.B.14." *A Wake Newslitter* 15 (December): 86–89.

———. 1982a. "Joyce, ou le malentendu." In *Études irlandaises*. See Rafroidi and Joannon 1982, 21–23.

———. 1982b. "Entretien avec Jacques Aubert." *L'Âne*, no. 6:5–7.

———. 1982c. "Introduction générale." In James Joyce, *Oeuvres I*, xi–civ. Paris: Gallimard.

———. 1983. "James Joyce et la culture celtique." *Actes du Colloque: Littérature et arts visuels en Irlande*, 21–26. Rennes: Société française d'études irlandaises.

———, ed. 1987. *Joyce avec Lacan*. Bibliothèque des Analytica. Paris: Navarin.

Aubert, Jacques, and Maria Jolas, eds. 1979. *Joyce et Paris. 1902. . . . .1920– 1940. . . . .1975: Actes du cinquième Symposium International James Joyce*. 2 vols. Paris: Éditions du CNRS.

Aubert, Jacques, and Fritz Senn, eds. 1986. *Cahiers de l'Herne No. 50: James Joyce*. Paris: Éditions de l'Herne.

Aubral, François, and Xavier Delcourt. 1977. *Contre la nouvelle philosophie*. Paris: Gallimard.

Bariou, Michel. 1982. "Le Vent paraclet: quelques aspects de l'inspiration dans *Le Portrait*." *Cahiers du centre d'études irlandaises* 7:9–19.

Barthes, Roland. 1966a. *Critique et Vérité*. Paris: Seuil.

———. 1966b. "Introduction à l'analyse structurale des récits." *Communications*, no. 8:1–27.

———. 1970. *S/Z*. Paris: Seuil.

———. 1973. *Le Plaisir du texte*. Paris: Seuil.

———. 1976. "Lettre de Roland Barthes." *Les Nouvelles Littéraires* 54, no. 2536:19.

———. 1977. *Fragments d'un discours amoureux*. Paris: Seuil.

———. 1979. *Sollers Écrivain*. Paris: Seuil.

———. 1980. *La Chambre claire. Note sur la photographie*. Paris: Gallimard/Seuil.

Bataille, Georges. 1949. *La Part maudite*. Paris: Minuit.

———. 1955. "Hegel, la mort et le sacrifice." *Deucalion* 5:21–43.

———. 1976. *Oeuvres complètes VII*. Paris: Gallimard.

———. 1988. *Oeuvres complètes XII*. Paris: Gallimard.

Bateson, Gregory. 1972. *Steps to an Ecology of Mind: Collected Essays in Anthropology, Psychiatry, Evolution and Epistemology*. Scranton, Pa.: Chandler.

Beach, Sylvia. 1950. "*Ulysses* à Paris." *Mercure de France*, no. 309:12–29.

Beaudry, Pierre. 1972. "Une écriture 'attentative'," *Change*, no. 11:70–86.

Beausang, Michael. 1976. "Vivre en marge." *Poétique*, no. 26:221–31.

———. 1985. "Repetition in *Ulysses*." In *Genèse et Métamorphoses*. See Jacquet 1985a, 97–108.

———. 1986. "'Circé': Écarts, style, communauté." In *Cahiers de l'Herne*. See Aubert and Senn 1986, 359–83.

———. 1988. "In the Name of the Law: Marital Freedom and Justice in *Exiles*." In *"Scribble" 1*. See Jacquet 1988, 39–55.

Beckett, Samuel et al. 1972. *Our Exagmination Round his Factification for Incamination of Work in Progress*. London: Faber and Faber.

Beierwaltes, Werner. 1972. *Platonismus und Idealismus*. Frankfurt am Main: Klostermann.

Beja, Morris. 1979. "Political Perspectives on Joyce's Work." In *Joyce et Paris*. See Aubert and Jolas 1972, 2:101–24.

———, ed. 1986. *James Joyce: The Centennial Symposium*. Urbana: University of Illinois Press.

Benoist, Jean-Marie. *La Révolution structuraliste*. Paris: Grasset.

———. 1980. "La Normalisation." *Tel Quel*, no. 84:48–60.

Benstock, Bernard. 1976. "The James Joyce Industry: A Reassessment." In *Yeats, Joyce, and Beckett: New Light on Three Modern Irish Writers*, ed. Kathleen McGrory and John Unterecker, 118–32. Lewisburg, Pa.: Bucknell University Press.

———. 1977. *James Joyce: The Undiscover'd Country*. New York: Barnes and Noble.

———. 1979. "Three Generations of *Finnegans Wake*." Review of *Third Census of "Finnegans Wake"* by Adaline Glasheen; *The Sigla of "Finnegans Wake"* by

Roland McHugh; *The Decentered Universe of "Finnegans Wake"* by Margot Norris. *Studies in the Novel* 9:333–38.

———, ed. 1985. *Critical Essays on James Joyce*. Boston: G. K. Hall.

———, ed. 1988. *James Joyce: The Augmented Ninth. Proceedings of the Ninth International James Joyce Symposium. Frankfurt 1984*. Syracuse: Syracuse University Press.

Benstock, Bernard, and Shari Benstock. 1980. *Who's He When He's At Home: A James Joyce Directory*. Urbana: University of Illinois Press.

Benstock, Shari. 1983. "At the Margin of Discourse: Footnotes in the Fictional Text." *PMLA* 98:204–25.

———. 1984. "The Letter of the Law: *La Carte postale* in *Finnegans Wake*." *Philological Quarterly* 63:163–85.

———. 1985. "Nightletters: Woman's Writing in the *Wake*." In *Critical Essays*. See Bernard Benstock 1985, 221–33.

———. 1986. *Women of the Left Bank*. Austin: University of Texas Press.

Benvéniste, Émile. 1966. *Problèmes de linguistique générale*. Paris: Gallimard.

Benz, Ernst. 1967. *Les Sources mystiques de la philosophie romantique allemande*. Paris: Vrin.

Berger, Hélène. 1964. "Stephen, Hamlet, Will: Joyce par delà Shakespeare." *Études anglaises* 17:571–85.

———. 1965. "L'Avant-portrait ou la bifurcation d'une vocation." *Tel Quel*, no. 22:69–76.

———. 1966. "Portrait de sa femme par l'artiste." *Lettres nouvelles* 15:41–67.

Berger, Hélène, and Jean Fuzier, trans. 1965a. "Un Portrait de l'artiste." *Tel Quel*, no. 22:62–68.

Bernard, Anne. 1980. "Joyce et l'imaginaire féminin." *Esprit* 47–48:239–44.

Blanchot, Maurice. 1946. "La Parole sacrée de Hölderlin." *Critique* 1:579–96.

———. 1955. "Le Tournant." *Nouvelle Revue Française* 5, no. 25:110–20.

———. 1959. *Le Livre à venir*. Paris: Gallimard.

———. 1960. "Reprises." *Nouvelle Revue Française* 8, no. 93:475–83.

———. 1969. *L'Entretien infini*. Paris: Gallimard.

Bloom, Harold, ed. 1970. *Romanticism and Consciousness*. New York: W. W. Norton.

———. 1971. *The Visionary Company: A Reading of English Romantic Poetry*. Ithaca: Cornell University Press.

———. 1973. *The Anxiety of Influence: A Theory of Poetry*. New York: Oxford University Press.

———, ed. 1986. *Modern Critical Views: James Joyce*. New York: Chelsea House.

Boldereff, Frances M. 1959. *Reading "Finnegans Wake"*. Woodward, Pa.: Classic Non-Fiction Library.

———. 1965. *A Blakean Translation of Joyce's "Circe"*. Woodward, Pa.: Classic Non-Fiction Library.

———. 1968. *Hermes to His Son Thoth: Being Joyce's Use of Berkeley in "Finnegans Wake"*. Woodward, Pa.: Classic Non-Fiction Library.

Bonheim, Helmut. 1967. *A Lexicon of German in "Finnegans Wake"*. Berkeley: University of California Press.

Bonnerot, Louis, ed. 1974. *"Ulysses" cinquante ans après: Témoignages franco-anglais sur le chef-d'oeuvre de James Joyce*. Paris: Didier.

Booth, Wayne C. 1978. *Critical Understanding: The Powers and Limits of Pluralism*. Chicago: University of Chicago Press.

Bosanquet, Bernard. 1892. *A History of Aesthetic*. London: Swan Sonnenschein; New York: Macmillan.

Böschenstein, Bernhard. 1977. "Die Dichtung Hölderlins: Analyse ihrer Interpretation durch Martin Heidegger." *Zeitwende* 48, no. 2:79–97.

Bouffard, Jean-Claude. 1984. "L'Artiste et ses doubles dans *Le Feu* de D'Annunzio et le *Dédalus* de Joyce." In *Le Double dans le romantisme anglo-américain*, 191–205. Clermont-Ferrand: Publications de la Faculté des lettres et sciences humaines, Université de Clermont-Ferrand II, Centre du Romantisme Anglais.

Bourdieu, Pierre. 1971. "Le Marché des biens symboliques." *L'Année Sociologique* 22:49–126.

———. 1979. *La Distinction: Critique sociale du jugement*. Paris: Minuit.

———. 1984. *Homo academicus*. Paris: Minuit.

Bourdieu, Pierre, Dominique Schnapper, and Alain Daubel. 1966. *L'Amour de l'art: Les Musées et leur public*. Paris: Minuit.

Bowen, Zack. 1974. *Musical Allusions in the Works of James Joyce: Early Works Through "Ulysses"*. Albany, N.Y.: State University of New York Press.

Boyd, Ernest. 1923. *Ireland's Literary Renaissance*. London: Grant Richards.

Boyer, Philippe. 1972. "Séries noires." *Change*, no. 11:60–69.

Boyle, Robert. 1977–78. Review of *The Sigla of "Finnegans Wake"* by Roland McHugh; *Third Census of "Finnegans Wake"* by Adaline Glasheen; *The Decentered Universe of "Finnegans Wake"* by Margot Norris. *Modern Fiction Studies* 23:614–7.

———. 1978. *James Joyce's Pauline Vision: A Catholic Exposition*. Carbondale: Southern Illinois University Press.

Brée, Germaine. 1983. *Twentieth-Century French Literature: 1920–1970*. Trans. Louise Guiney. Chicago: University of Chicago Press.

Breton, André. 1972. *Manifestes du surréalisme: Édition complète*. Paris: Jean-Jacques Pauvert.

Brion, Marcel. 1927. "L'Actualité littéraire à l'étranger: James Joyce, romancier et poète." *Les Nouvelles littéraires*, 15 October, 7.

Brivic, Sheldon R. 1980. *Joyce Between Freud and Jung*. Port Washington: Kennikat Press.

———. 1985. *Joyce the Creator*. Madison: University of Wisconsin Press.

Broch, Hermann. 1978. *Der Tod des Vergil. Kommentierte Werkausgabe. Band 4*. Frankfurt am Main: Suhrkamp.

Brochier, Jean-Jacques. 1981. "Seul contre tous . . .! Entretien avec Sollers." *Magazine littéraire*, no. 171:50–52.

Brown, John L. 1982. "*Ulysses* into French." *Library Chronicle* 20–21:29–60.

Brown, Norman O. 1973. *Closing Time*. New York: Vintage Books.

Brown, Richard. 1986. "How Copenhagen Ended." *James Joyce Broadsheet*, no. 21:1.

Budgen, Frank. 1934. *James Joyce and the Making of "Ulysses"*. London: Grayson and Grayson.

Bühner, J.-A. 1980. "Logos im Alten und Neuen Testament." *Historisches Wörterbuch der Philosophie*. Darmstadt: Wissenschaftliche Buchgesellschaft.

Burgess, Anthony. 1965. *Here Comes Everybody: An Introduction to James Joyce for the Ordinary Reader*. London: Faber and Faber.

———. 1973. *Urgent Copy: Literary Studies*. Harmondsworth: Penguin.

Butler, E. M. 1958. *The Tyranny of Greece over Germany. A Study of the Influence Exercised by Greek Art and Poetry over the Great German Writers of the 18th, 19th and 20th Centuries*. Boston: Beacon Press.

Butor, Michel. 1948. "Petite croisière préliminaire à une reconnaissance de l'archipel Joyce." *La Vie Intellectuelle* 16, no. 5:104–35.

———. 1956. *L'Emploi du temps*. Paris: Minuit.

———. 1960. *Répertoire*. Paris: Minuit.

———. 1979. "Joyce et l'aventure d'aujourd'hui." In *Joyce et Paris*. See Aubert and Jolas 1979. 1:59–94.

———. 1982. "La Langue de l'exil." *Le Monde*, 5 February, 18. Reprinted in *Répertoire 5*. Paris: Minuit.

Campbell, Joseph, and Henry Morton Robinson. 1944. *A Skeleton Key to "Finnegans Wake"*. New York: Harcourt Brace.

Caputo, David. 1978. *The Mystical Element in Heidegger's Thought*. Athens: Ohio University Press.

Cazamian, Louis. 1924. "L'Oeuvre de James Joyce." *Revue Anglo-Américaine* 2:97–113.

Céline, Louis Ferdinand. 1932. *Voyage au bout de la nuit*. Paris: Denoël et Steele.

Chamson, André. 1966. "Quand la république des Lettres fêtait le poète d'*Ulysse*." *Figaro Littéraire*, 20 January, 9–13.

Chatman, Seymour. 1978. *Story and Discourse*. Ithaca: Cornell University Press.

Chénieux-Gendron, Jacqueline. 1983. *Le Surréalisme et le roman: 1922–1950*. Lausanne: l'Age d'Homme.

Chevalier, Anne. 1981. "Les Campagnes littéraires de Valery Larbaud." In *Valery Larbaud: La Prose du monde*, ed. Jean Bressière, 55–63. Paris: Presses universitaires de France.

Christiani, Dounia Bunis. 1965. *Scandinavian Elements of "Finnegans Wake"*. Evanston, Ill.: Northwestern University Press.

Cixous, Hélène. 1967a. *Le Prénom de Dieu*. Paris: Grasset.

———. 1967b. "James Joyce et la mort de Parnell." *Langues modernes*, no. 61:142–47.

————. 1968. *L'Exil de James Joyce ou l'art du remplacement*. Paris: Grasset.

————. 1969a. *Dedans*. Paris: Grasset.

————. 1969b. Interview. *La Quinzaine littéraire*, no. 68:6–8.

————. 1970a. *Commencements*. Paris: Grasset.

————. 1970b. *Le Troisième corps*. Paris: Grasset.

————. 1970c. "Joyce, la ruse de l'écriture." *Poétique*, no. 4:419–32.

————. 1972a. *The Exile of James Joyce*. Trans. Sally A. J. Purcell. New York: David Lewis.

————. 1972b. *Le Neutre*. Paris: Grasset.

————. 1973. *Tombe*. Paris: Grasset.

————. 1974a. *Prénoms de personne*. Paris: Seuil.

————. 1974b. "D'un oeil en coin." In *"Ulysses" cinquante ans après*. See Bonnerot 1974, 161–68.

————. 1976a. *La*. Paris: Gallimard.

————. 1976b. "Fort-Sein." *Poétique*, no. 26:131.

————. 1976c. "La Missexualité: où jouis-je?" *Poétique*, no. 26:240–49.

————. 1977. "From *Partie*." Trans. Keith Cohen. In *In the Wake of the Wake*. See Hayman and Anderson 1977, 98–100.

————. 1979a. *Vivre l'orange/To Live the Orange*. Paris: Éditions des Femmes.

————. 1979b. "L'Approche de Clarice Lispector." *Poétique*, no. 40:408–19.

————. 1983. "Freincipe de plaisir; ou paradoxe perdue." *Temps de la réflexion* 4:427–33.

————. 1986. "Devant le pome." In *Cahiers de l'Herne*. See Aubert and Senn 1986, 193–202.

Clark, Terry Nichols. 1971. "Le Patron et son cercle: Clef de l'université française." *Revue Française de sociologie* 12:19–39.

————. 1973. *Prophets and Patrons: The French University and the Emergence of the Social Sciences*. Cambridge, Mass.: Harvard University Press.

Clavel, Maurice. 1975. *Ce que je crois*. Paris: Grasset.

————. 1976. *Dieu est Dieu, nom de Dieu*. Paris: Grasset.

Clavel, Maurice, and Philippe Sollers. 1977. *Délivrance? Face à face*. Paris: Seuil.

Clément, Cathérine. 1981. *Vies et Légendes de Jacques Lacan*. Paris: Grasset.

Cohn, Robert Greer. 1951. *L'Oeuvre de Mallarmé: Un Coup de Dés*. Paris: Librairie les Lettres.

Collectif "Change." 1986. "Joyce et le regards des langues: entretien odysséen." In *Cahiers de l'Herne*. See Aubert and Senn 1986, 217–41.

Condou, Claude. 1976. "Le Corps à lettre." *Poétique*, no. 26:173–79.

Conley, Verena. 1977. "Missexual Misstery." *Diacritics* 7, no. 2:70–82.

Connolly, Thomas E., ed. 1961. *Scribbledehobble: The Ur-Workbook for "Finnegans Wake"*. Evanston, Ill.: Northwestern University Press.

Corngold, Stanley. 1986. *The Fate of the Self: German Writers and French Theory*. New York: Columbia University Press.

Cortanze, Gérard de. 1984a. "Tralala lala, tralala, lalaire." *Europe* 62, no. 657–58:3–4.

———. 1984b. "Quand Joyce ira à la maternelle . . . ." *Europe* 62, no. 657–58:48–51.

Costanzo, W. V. 1971. "The French Version of *Finnegans Wake*: Translation, Adaptation, Recreation." *James Joyce Quarterly* 9:225–36.

Cote, Michel. 1969. Review of *L'Exil de James Joyce* by Hélène Cixous. *Esprit* 37:1140–43.

Crevel, René. 1926. *La Mort difficile*. Paris: Simon Kra.

Culler, Jonathan. 1975. *Structuralist Poetics: Structuralism, Linguistics and the Study of Literature*. London: Routledge and Kegan Paul.

Curtius, Ernst Robert. 1973. *European Literature and the Latin Middle Ages*. Trans. Willard R. Trask. Princeton: Princeton University Press.

Dauphiné, James. 1984. "*A Portrait of the Artist as a Young Man* et le problème de l'autobiographie." *Europe* 62, no. 657–58:83–96.

David, Alain. 1980. "Être juif?" *Exercices de la patience*, no. 1:43–50.

———. 1982. "Kant avec Joyce." *Revue des sciences humaines*, no. 185:161–74.

Davies, Stan Gébler. 1975. *James Joyce: A Portrait of the Artist*. London: Davis-Poynter.

Debray, Régis. 1979. *Le Pouvoir intellectuel en France*. Paris: Ramsay.

———. 1983. *Critique of Political Reason*. London: New Left Books.

De Haes, Frans. 1983. "*Femmes* et *Paradis*," *L'Infini*, no. 4:32–43.

———. 1985. "Philippos adamantos, homo Sollers." *L'Infini*, no. 11:98–104.

de Labriolle, Jacqueline. 1985. "Le Thème du labyrinthe chez Joyce, Michel Butor, et Alain Robbe-Grillet." In *Genèse et Métamorphoses*. See Jacquet 1985a, 229–39.

Deleuze, Gilles. 1964. *Proust et les signes*. Paris: Presses universitaires de France.

———. 1969. *Logique du sens*. Paris: Minuit.

———. 1972. "Joyce indirect," *Change*, no. 11:54–59.

Deleuze, Gilles, and Félix Guattari. 1975. *L'Anti-Oedipe: Capitalisme et schizophrénie*. Paris: Minuit.

De Man, Paul. 1955. "Les Exégèses de Hölderlin par Martin Heidegger." *Critique* 11:800–19.

———. 1965. "L'Image de Rousseau dans la poésie de Hölderlin." *Deutsche Beiträge zur geistigen Überlieferung* 5:157–83.

———. 1966a. "Wordsworth und Hölderlin." *Schweizer Monatschrift* 45:1141–55.

———. 1966b. "La Circularité de l'interprétation dans l'oeuvre critique de Maurice Blanchot." *Critique* 22:547–60.

———. 1971. *Blindness and Insight: Essays in the Rhetoric of Contemporary Criticism*. New York: Oxford University Press.

———. 1979. "Shelley Disfigured." In *Deconstruction and Criticism*, ed. Harold Bloom et al., 39–73. New York: Seabury Press.

———. 1982. "Hommage à Georges Poulet." *MLN* 97, no. 5:n.p.

Deming, Robert H. 1970. *James Joyce: The Critical Heritage. Vol. 1: 1902–1927*. London: Routledge and Kegan Paul.

Derrida, Jacques. 1962. Introduction. In Edmund Husserl, *L'Origine de la géométrie*, 3–171. Paris: Presses universitaires de France.

———. 1964a. "Violence et métaphysique: Essai sur la pensée d'Emmanuel Levinas." *Revue de métaphysique et de morale* 69:322–54.

———. 1964b. "Violence et métaphysique. Essai sur la pensée d'Emmanuel Levinas." *Revue de métaphysique et de morale* 69:425–73.

———. 1965. "La Parole soufflée." *Tel Quel*, no. 20:41–67.

———. 1967a. *L'Écriture et la différence*. Paris: Seuil.

———. 1967b. *La Voix et le phénomène: Introduction au problème du signe dans la phénoménologie de Husserl*. Paris: Presses universitaires de France.

———. 1967c. *De la grammatologie*. Paris: Minuit.

———. 1967d. "De l'économie restreinte à l'économie générale: un hégélianisme sans réserve." *L'Arc*, no. 32:24–45. Reprinted in *L'Écriture et différence*. See Derrida 1967a, 369–406.

———. 1968a. "La Pharmacie de Platon 1." *Tel Quel*, no. 32:3–48.

———. 1968b. "La Pharmacie de Platon 2." *Tel Quel*, no. 33:18–59.

———. 1969. "La Dissémination." *Critique* 25:99–139, 215–49.

———. 1970. "Structure, Sign, and Play in the Discourse of the Human Sciences." In *The Languages of Criticism and the Sciences of Man: The Structuralist Controversy*, ed. R. Macksey and E. Donato, 247–72. Baltimore: Johns Hopkins University Press.

———. 1972a. *La Dissémination*. Paris: Seuil.

———. 1972b. *Positions: Entretiens avec Henri Ronse, Julia Kristeva, Jean-Louis Houdebine et Guy Scarpetta*. Paris: Minuit.

———. 1972c. "Les Fins de l'homme." In his *Marges de la philosophie*, 131–64. Paris: Minuit.

———. 1973. *Speech and Other Phenomena. And Other Essays on Husserl's Theory of Signs*. Trans. David Allison. Evanston, Ill.: Northwestern University Press.

———. 1974. *Glas*. Paris: Galilée.

———. 1975. "Le Facteur de la vérité." *Poétique*, no. 21:96–147.

———. 1976. *Of Grammatology*. Trans. Gayatri Chakravorti Spivak. Baltimore: Johns Hopkins University Press.

———. 1977a. "Scribble (pouvoir/écrire)." Introduction. In William Walburton, *Essai sur les hiéroglyphes des égyptiens*. Trans. Léonard des Malpeines, 5–43. Paris: Aubier Flammarion.

———. 1977b. "Signature Event Context." *Glyph*, no. 1:172–97.

———. 1978a. *Éperons: Les Styles de Nietzsche*. Paris: Flammarion.

———. 1978b. *Writing and Difference*. Trans. Alan Bass. Chicago: University of Chicago Press.

———. 1987c. "Ein Porträt Benjamins." In *"Links hatte noch alles sich zu enträtseln . . ."*: *Walter Benjamin in Kontext*, ed. Burkhardt Lindner. 171–79. Frankfurt am Main: Syndikat.

———. 1979. "Scribble (Writing-Power)." *Yale French Studies*, no. 58:117–47.

————. 1980. *La Carte postale de Socrate à Freud et au-delà*. Paris: Flammarion.

————. 1981. *Dissemination*. Trans. Barbara Johnson. Chicago: University of Chicago Press.

————. 1983. *D'Un Ton apocalyptique adopté naguère en philosophie*. Paris: Galilée.

————. 1985a. "*Ulysse* gramophone: l'oui-dire de Joyce." In *Genèse de Babel*. See Jacquet 1985b, 227–64.

————. 1985b. "Two Words for Joyce." In *Post-Structuralist Joyce*. See Attridge and Ferrer 1985, 145–59.

————. 1986. "Deux mots pour Joyce." In *Cahiers de l'Herne*. See Aubert and Senn 1986, 203–16.

————. 1987. *Ulysse gramophone; Deux mots pour Joyce*. Paris: Galilée.

————. 1988. "Hear say yes in Joyce." In *The Augmented Ninth*. See Benstock 1988, 27–75.

Desanti, Jean-Toussaint. 1976. "Les Malheurs de philosophie." Interview with Jean-Paul Dollé. *Les Nouvelles Littéraires* 54, no. 2536:18.

Descombes, Vincent. 1979. *Le Même et l'Autre: Quarante-cinq ans de philosophie française (1933–1978)*. Paris: Minuit.

Des Forêts, Louis-René. 1943. *Les Mendiants*. Paris: Gallimard.

Dews, Peter. 1987. *Logics of Disintegration: Post-Structuralist Thought and the Claims of Critical Theory*. London: Verso.

Di Pietro, Robert J. 1972. "Sur quelques types de phrases joyciennes." *Change*, no. 11:34–46.

Dollé, Jean-Paul. 1976. *Haine de la pensée*. Paris: Hallier.

Dolto, Françoise, and Gérard Séverin. 1977. *L'Évangile au risque de la psychanalyse*. Paris: Delarge.

Driver, Clive, ed. 1975. "*Ulysses*": *The Manuscript and First Printings Compared*. New York: Octagon / Farrar, Straus, and Giroux; Philadelphia: The Philip H. and A. S. W. Rosenbach Foundation.

Dujardin, Edouard. 1924. *Les Lauriers sont coupés*. Paris: Messein.

————. 1931. *Le Monologue intérieur: Son apparition. Ses origines. Sa place dans l'oeuvre de James Joyce*. Paris: Messein.

Dumay, Manuela. 1984. "'Es-tu bien irlandais, oui ou non?'" *Europe* 62, no. 657–58:14–19.

Duplaix, Georges. 1925. "Joyce à la *Revue des deux mondes*." *La Revue Nouvelle*, no. 10–11:23–29.

Eagleton, Terry. 1980. "Molly's Piano." *New Statesman* 100 (19 September):21.

————. 1981. "The Idealism of American Criticism." *New Left Review*, no. 127:53–65.

————. 1983. *Literary Theory: An Introduction*. London: Basil Blackwell.

Eco, Umberto. 1962a. *Opera aperta*. Milan: Bompiani.

————. 1962b. "Le Moyen-âge de James Joyce." *Tel Quel*, no. 11:39–52.

————. 1963. "Le Moyen-âge de James Joyce." *Tel Quel*, no. 12:83–92.

————. 1965. *L'Oeuvre ouverte*. Paris: Seuil.

———. 1968. *La struttura assente: Introduzione alla ricerca semiologica*. Milan: Bompiani.

———. 1971. *Le forme del contenuto*. Milan: Bompiani.

———. 1974. "Sémantique de la métaphore." *Tel Quel*, no. 55:25–46.

Eisenstein, S. M. 1972. "Sur Joyce." *Change*, no. 11:48–53.

Ellmann, Maud. 1981. "Disremembering Dedalus: *A Portrait of the Artist as a Young Man*." In *Untying the Text: A Post-Structuralist Reader*, ed. Robert Young, 189–206. London: Routledge and Kegan Paul.

———. 1982. "Polytropic Man: Paternity, Identity and Naming." In *New Perspectives*. See MacCabe 1982a, 73–104.

———. 1986. "To Sign or to Sing." In *The Centennial Symposium*. See Beja 1986, 66–69.

Erman, Adolphe. 1934. *Die Religion der Ägypter: Ihr Werden und Vergehen in Vier Jahrtausenden*. Berlin and Leipzig: Walter de Gruyter.

Farías, Victor. 1989. *Heidegger und der National sozialismus*. Frankfurt am Main: Fischer.

Faye, Jean Pierre. 1961. *La Cassure*. Paris: Seuil.

———. 1962. *Battement*. Paris: Seuil.

———. 1964a. *Analogues: Récit autocritique*. Paris: Seuil.

———. 1964b. *L'Écluse*. Paris: Seuil.

———. 1966. "Ça Ira." *Tel Quel*, no. 25:87–90.

———. 1967. "Post-scriptum: Shem trouvé." *Tel Quel*, no. 30:56–7.

———. 1970. *Les Troyens: Hexagramme ou Roman*. Paris: Seuil.

———. 1974. *Migrations du récit sur le peuple juif*. Paris: Belfond.

———. 1975. *Inferno Versions*. Paris: Seghers/Laffont.

———. 1976. Interview. In *French Novelists Speak Out*, ed. Bettina Knapp, 73–92. Troy, N.Y.: Whitston.

———. 1979. "La Dispersion et la carte: Du cauchemar de l'histoire à l'enfer des versions." In *Joyce et Paris*. See Aubert and Jolas 1979, 1:21–28.

———. 1980. *Commencement d'une figure en mouvement*. Paris: Stock.

Faye, Jean Pierre, and Jacques Roubaud. 1975. *Changement de forme, Révolution, Langage*. Paris: Union générale d'éditions.

Felman, Shoshana. 1977. "Turning the Screw of Interpretation." *Yale French Studies*, no. 55–56:94–207.

———. 1980–1981. "The Originality of Jacques Lacan." *Poetics Today* 2, no. 1b:45–57.

Ferrer, Daniel. 1976. "Hissheory ou le plaisir en trop." *Poétique*, no. 26:232–39.

———. 1984. "Miroirs aux sirènes." *Europe* 62, no. 657–58:99–106.

———. 1985a. "Hemingway aux sources de la Liffey." In *Genèse et Métamorphoses*. See Jacquet 1985a, 223–28.

———. 1985b. "The Freudful Couchmare of ∧ d: Joyce's Notes on Freud and the Composition of Chapter XVI of *Finnegans Wake*." *James Joyce Quarterly* 22:367–82.

————. 1985c. "La Scène primitive de l'écriture: Une Lecture joycienne de Freud." In *Genèse de Babel*. See Jacquet 1985b, 15–36.

————. 1985d. "Circe, Regret and Regression." In *Post-Structuralist Joyce*. See Attridge and Ferrer 1985, 127–44.

————. 1986a. "Circe: ou les regrès éternels." In *Cahiers de l'Herne*. See Aubert and Senn 1986, 341–58.

————. 1986b. "Le Texte sur sa réserve: D'Un usage inouï de la citation chez Joyce." In *L'Ente et la Chimère: Aspects de la citation dans la littérature anglaise*, ed. Lucien Le Bouille, 121–30. Caen: Centre de Littérature, Civilisation et Linguistique des Pays de Langue Anglaise.

————. 1988. "Archéologie du regard dans les avant-textes de 'Circe'." In *"Scribble"* 1. See Jacquet 1988, 95–106.

Ferry, Luc, and Alain Renaut. 1985. *La Pensée 68: Essai sur l'anti-humanisme contemporaire*. Paris: Gallimard.

Feshbach, Sidney, and William Herman. 1984. "The History of Joyce Criticism and Scholarship." In *A Companion to Joyce Studies*, ed. Zack Bowen and James F. Carens, 727–80. Westport, Conn.: Greenwood Press.

Fierobe, Claude. n.d. "Consonantia: harmonie et ésthétique dans *A Portrait of the Artist as a Young Man*." In *Visages de l'harmonie dans la littérature anglo-américaine*, 113–25. Reims: Publications du Centre de recherches sur l'imaginaire dans les littératures de langue anglaise.

Finel-Honigman, Irene. 1981. "American Misconceptions of French Feminism." *Contemporary French Civilization* 5:317–26.

Finney, Michael. 1977. Review of *The Decentered Universe of "Finnegans Wake"* by Margot Norris. *James Joyce Quarterly* 15:98–101.

Fischer, Michael. 1985. *Does Deconstruction Make Any Difference? Poststructuralism and the Defense of Poetry in Modern Criticism*. Bloomington: Indiana University Press.

Forrester, Viviane. 1975. "Les Relectures d'Hélène Cixous." Review of *Prénoms de personne* by Hélène Cixous. *Quinzaine littéraire*, no. 202:6.

Foucault, Michel. 1963. "Le Langage à l'infini." *Tel Quel*, no. 15:44–53.

————. 1966. *Les Mots et les choses: une archéologie des sciences humaines*. Paris: Gallimard.

Foucault, Michel et al. 1968. *Théorie d'ensemble*. Paris: Seuil.

Frank, Manfred. 1984. *Was ist Neostrukturalismus?* Frankfurt am Main: Suhrkamp.

Frank, Nino. 1949. "Souvenirs sur James Joyce." *La Table ronde*, no. 23:1671–93.

————. 1967. "L'Ombre qui avait perdue son homme." *Mémoire brisée*, 27–64. Paris: Calmann-Lévy.

Freud, Sigmund. 1972a. "Der Witz und seine Beziehung zum Unbewussten." In his *Psychologische Schriften. Studienausgabe. Band IV*, 9–219. Frankfurt am Main: Fischer.

——. 1972b. "Über den Gegensinn der Urworte." In his *Psychologische Schriften. Studienausgabe. Band IV*, 227–34.

——. 1972c. *Fragen der Gesellschaft. Ursprünge der Religion. Studienausgabe. Band IX.* Frankfurt am Main: Fischer.

Freund, Gisèle. 1966. "En rouge et en noir." *Figaro Littéraire*, 20 January, 8.

Frye, Northrop. 1957. "Quest and Cycle in *Finnegans Wake*." *James Joyce Review* 1, no. 1:39–47. Reprinted in his *Fables of Identity*, 256–64. New York: Harcourt, Brace and World, 1963.

Gadamer, Hans-Georg. 1977. "Poesie und Philosophie." In *Geist und Zeichen: Festschrift für Arthur Henkel zu seinem sechzigster Geburtstag dargebracht von Freunden und Schülern*. Ed. Anton Herbert, Bernhard Gajek, and Peter Pfaff, 121–26. Heidelberg: Winter.

Garvin, John. 1976. *Joyce's Disunited Kingdom and the Irish Dimension*. London: Gill and Macmillan.

Gay, Peter. 1970. *Weimar Culture: The Outsider as Insider*. New York: Harper and Row.

Genet, Jacqueline. 1981. "Le Mythe de Dédale et d'Icare dans *A Portrait of the Artist as a Young Man*." *Gaéliana*, no. 3:149–64.

Gensbourger, Nelly. 1976. "La Confabulation ou *La Nuit de rêve* du Rabuliste." In *De Shakespeare à T.S.Eliot: Mélanges offerts à Henri Fluchère*, 253–62. Paris: Didier.

George, François. 1979. *L'Effet 'Yau-de Poêle' de Lacan et des lacaniens*. Paris: Hachette.

Gheerbrant, Bernard. 1949. *James Joyce: Sa Vie, Son Oeuvre, Son Rayonnement*. Paris: La Hune.

Gifford, Don, and Robert J. Seidman. 1974. *Notes for Joyce: An Annotation of Joyce's "Ulysses"*. New York: Dutton.

Gilbert, Stuart. 1930. *James Joyce's "Ulysses": A Study*. London: Faber and Faber.

——. 1950. "Souvenirs de voyage." *Mercure de France*, no. 309:38–44.

——. 1966. "On comprendra *Finnegans Wake* dans cent ans!" *Figaro Littéraire*, 20 January, 9.

Gillet, Guillaume. 1966. "Un diner en ville." *Figaro Littéraire*, 20 January, 9.

Gillet, Louis. 1925. "Du Côté de chez Joyce." *Revue des deux mondes* 28:686–97.

——. 1941. *Stèle pour James Joyce*. Marseille: Sagittaire.

Glasheen, Adaline. 1956. *A Census of "Finnegans Wake"*. Urbana: University of Illinois Press.

——. 1963. *A Second Census of "Finnegans Wake"*. Urbana: University of Illinois Press.

——. 1977. *A Third Census of "Finnegans Wake"*. Berkeley: University of California Press.

Glob, P. V. 1969. *The Bog People*. London: Faber and Faber.

Glucksmann, André. 1975. *La Cuisinière et le mangeur d'hommes: Essai sur les rapports entre l'état, le marxisme et les camps de concentration*. Paris: Seuil.

———. 1975. "Réponses." *Tel Quel*, no. 64:67–73.

———. 1977. *Les Maîtres penseurs*. Paris: Grasset.

Goldman, Arnold. 1966. *The Joyce Paradox*. Evanston, Ill.: Northwestern University Press.

Goldberg, S. L. 1961. *The Classical Temper*. New York: Barnes and Noble.

Godin, Jean-Guy. 1987. "Du symptôme à son épure: le sinthome." In *Joyce avec Lacan*. See Aubert 1987, 159–211.

———. 1988. "Sur le Sinthome." In *The Augmented Ninth*. See Benstock 1988, 210–14.

Gorman, Herbert. 1924. *James Joyce: His First Forty Years*. New York: B. W. Huebsch.

———. 1939. *James Joyce*. New York: Farar and Rinehart.

Graff, Gerald. 1987. *Professing Literature: An Institutional History*. Chicago: University of Chicago Press.

Greene, Robert W. 1977. "Poetry, Metapoetry and Revolution: Stages on Marcelin Pleynet's Way." *Romanic Review* 68:128–40.

Guiguet, Jean. 1974. "Virginia Woolf et James Joyce: un problème de dates et de tempéraments." In *"Ulysses" cinquante ans après*. See Bonnerot 1974, 23–32.

Gunn, Ian, and Alistair McCleery. 1988. *The "Ulysses" Pagefinder*. Edinburgh: Split Pea.

Habermas, Jürgen. 1976. *Zur Rekonstruktion des historischen Materialismus*. Frankfurt am Main: Suhrkamp.

———. 1981a. *Theorie des kommunikativen Handelns: Band 1: Handlungsrationalität und gesellschaftliche Rationalisierung*. Frankfurt am Main: Suhrkamp.

———. 1981b. *Theorie des kommunikativen Handelns: Band 2: Zur Kritik der funktionalistischen Vernunft*. Frankfurt am Main: Suhrkamp.

Hallier, Jean-Edern. 1962. "Descendance hölderlinienne." *Tel Quel*, no. 10:73–75.

———. 1973. *La Cause des peuples*. Paris: Seuil.

Hamacher, Werner. 1978. "pleroma—zu Genesis und Struktur einer dialektischen Hermeneutik bei Hegel." In Georg Wilhelm Friedrich Hegel, *Der Geist des Christentums: Schriften 1796–1800*. Ed. Werner Hamacher, 7–333. Frankfurt am Main: Ullstein.

Hamon, Hervé, and Patrick Rotman. 1981. *Les Intellocrates: Expédition en haute intelligentsia*. Bruxelles: Complexe.

Handler, Philip Leonard. 1961. *Joyce in France: 1920–1959*. Ph.D. diss., Columbia University.

Hanley, Miles L. 1962. *Word Index to James Joyce's "Ulysses"*. Madison: University of Wisconsin Press.

Hart, Clive. 1962. *Structure and Motif in "Finnegans Wake"*. Evanston, Ill.: Northwestern University Press.

———. 1974. *A Concordance to "Finnegans Wake"*. Mamaroneck, N.Y.: Paul P. Apple.

Hart, Clive, and Leo Knuth. 1976. *A Topographical Guide to James Joyce's "Ulysses"*. Colchester, England: A Wake Newslitter Press.

Hartman, Geoffrey. 1970. *Beyond Formalism: Literary Essays, 1958–1970*. New Haven: Yale University Press.

———. 1981. *Saving the Text: Littérature/Derrida/Philosophy*. Baltimore: Johns Hopkins University Press.

Hayman, David. 1956. *Joyce et Mallarmé*. 2 vols. Paris: Les Lettres modernes.

———. 1963. *A First-Draft Version of "Finnegans Wake"*. Austin: University of Texas Press.

———. 1971. "Clowns et Farce chez Joyce." *Poétique*, no. 6:173–99.

———. 1976. "Réseaux infra-structurels dans *Finnegans Wake*." *Poétique*, no. 26:207–20.

———. 1977a. "Stephen on the Rocks." *James Joyce Quarterly* 15:5–17.

———. 1977b. "Entretien avec Philippe Sollers." *Tel Quel*, no. 71–73:20–36.

———. 1980. "Stephen on the Rocks." *Tel Quel*, no. 83:89–102.

———. 1987. "Some French Connections." *James Joyce Quarterly* 25:133–43.

Hayman, David, and Elliott Anderson, eds. 1977. *In the Wake of the Wake*. Special publication of *TriQuarterly*, no. 38.

Heath, Stephen. 1972a. *The Nouveau Roman: A Study in the Practice of Writing*. London: Elek.

———. 1972b. "Ambiviolences: Notes pour la lecture de Joyce." *Tel Quel*, no. 50:22–43.

———. 1972c. "Ambiviolences–2." *Tel Quel*, no. 51:64–76.

———. 1973a. "L'Écriture spiralée (la socialité comme drame)." *Discours sociale*, no. 3–4:9–21.

———. 1973b. "Trames de lecture (A propos de la dernière section de *Finnegans Wake*)." *Tel Quel*, no. 54:4–15.

———. 1974a. *Vertige du déplacement: Lecture de Barthes*. Paris: Fayard.

———. 1974b. "La Déversée." *Tel Quel*, no. 57:117–26.

———. 1982. "Joyce in Language." In *New Perspectives*. See MacCabe 1982a, 129–48.

Hegel, G. W. F. 1970. *Vorlesungen über die Ästhetik III*. Frankfurt am Main: Suhrkamp.

———. 1971. *Phänomenologie des Geistes*. Frankfurt am Main: Suhrkamp.

Heidegger, Martin. 1962a. *Chemins qui ne mènent nulle part*. Trans. Wolfgang Brokmeier. Ed. François Fédier. Paris: Gallimard.

———. 1962b. *Approche de Hölderlin*. Trans. Henri Corbier, Michel Deguy, François Fédier, and Jean Launay. Paris: Gallimard.

———. 1965. *Aus der Erfahrung des Denkens*. Pfullingen: Neske.

———. 1976. "Nur noch ein Gott kann uns retten." *Der Spiegel* 30, no. 23 (31 May): 193–219.

———. 1981. *Erläuterungen zu Hölderlins Dichtung. Gesamtausgabe Band 4*. Frankfurt am Main: Klostermann.

————. 1984. *Hölderlins Hymne 'Der Ister.' Gesamtausgabe Band 53.* Frankfurt am Main: Klostermann.

Heller, Erich. 1976. "Thinking about Poetry, Hölderlin and Heidegger." In *Herkommen und Erneuerung: Essays für Oskar Seidlin*, ed. Gerald Gillespie and Edgar Lohner, 168–84. Tübingen: Niemeyer.

Hemingway, Ernest. 1925. *In Our Time.* New York: Boni and Liveright.

Henke, Suzette A. 1978. *Joyce's Moraculous Sindbook: A Study of Ulysses.* Columbus: Ohio State University Press.

————. 1980. "Feminist Perspectives on James Joyce." *Canadian Journal of Historical Studies* 6, no. 1:14–22.

————. 1982a. "Stephen Dedalus and Women: A Portrait of the Artist as a Young Misogynist." In *Women in Joyce.* See Henke and Unkeless 1982, 82–107.

————. 1982b. "Gerty MacDowell: Joyce's Sentimental Heroine." In *Women in Joyce.* See Henke and Unkeless 1982, 132–49.

————. 1986. "Virginia Woolf Reads James Joyce: The *Ulysses* Notebook." In *The Centennial Symposium.* See Beja 1986, 39–42.

————. 1988. "Speculum of the Other Molly: A Feminist/Psychoanalytical Inquiry into James Joyce's Politics of Desire." *Mosaic* 21:149–64.

Henke, Suzette, and Elaine Unkeless, ed. 1982. *Women in Joyce.* Urbana: University of Illinois Press.

Henrich, Dieter. 1971. *Hegel im Kontext.* Frankfurt am Main: Suhrkamp.

Herring, Phillip. 1972. *Joyce's "Ulysses" Notesheets in the British Museum.* Charlottesville: University Press of Virginia.

Higginson, Fred H., ed. 1960. *Anna Livia Plurabelle: The Making of a Chapter.* Minneapolis: University of Minnesota Press.

Hillis Miller, J. 1982. "From Narrative Theory to Joyce; From Joyce to Narrative Theory." In *The Seventh of Joyce*, ed. Bernard Benstock, 3–4. Bloomington: Indiana University Press.

Hirsch, E. D. Jr. 1981. "The Politics of Theories of Interpretation." *Critical Inquiry* 9:235–47.

Hodgart, Matthew J. C., and Mabel P. Worthington. 1959. *Song in the Works of James Joyce.* New York: Columbia University Press.

Hölderlin, Friedrich. 1943. In *Grosse Stuttgarter Ausgabe.* Ed. Friedrich Beissner, vol. 2:1. Stuttgart: Kohlhammer.

Houdebine, Jean-Louis. 1971a. "Position politique et idéologique du néo-surréalisme." *Tel Quel*, no. 46:35–40.

————. 1971b. "Méconnaissance de la psychanalyse dans le discours sur-réaliste." *Tel Quel*, no. 46:67–82.

————. 1972. "L'Ennemi du dedans (Bataille et le surréalisme: éléments, prises de parti)." *Tel Quel*, no. 52:49–73.

————. 1973a. "La Cause des peuples? D'extrême gauche en apparence, d'ex-trême droite en réalité." *Tel Quel*, no. 53:102–4.

———. 1973b. "Littérature et révolution: Vérité de l'avant- garde. Entretien réalisé par J.-L. Houdebine." *Promesse*, no. 34–35:5–38.

———. 1973c. "Response." Letter from J.-L. Houdebine to J. Derrida (1-7-71). *Diacritics* 3:57.

———. 1974. "Le Chant (ou sens vivant) des langues." *Tel Quel*, no. 57:85–116.

———. 1975a. "Biographies du stalinisme." *Tel Quel*, no. 63:44–45.

———. 1975b. "Aux couleurs de la France." *Tel Quel*, no. 63:52–65.

———. 1976a. "Les Vérités de la palice ou les erreurs de la police." *Tel Quel*, no. 67:87–97.

———. 1976b. "Friedrich Hölderlin: Fragments inédits: Traduits par J.-L. Houdebine." *Tel Quel*, no. 68:35–36.

———. 1976c. "L'Impasse du langage dans le marxisme." *Tel Quel*, no. 68:81–96.

———. 1977a. *Langage et marxisme*. Paris: Klincksieck.

———. 1977b. "Idanov ou Joyce." *Tel Quel*, no. 69:29–50.

———. 1977c. "L'Impasse du langage dans le marxisme (II)." *Tel Quel*, no. 69:74–96.

———. 1979a. "Du simple au double." *Tel Quel*, no. 79:51–61.

———. 1979b. "La Signature de Joyce." *Tel Quel*, no. 81:52–62.

———. 1979c. "Jung et Joyce." *Tel Quel*, no. 81:63–65.

———. 1980. "James Joyce: Obscénité et Théologie." *Tel Quel*, no. 83:23–24.

———. 1981a. "De nouveau sur Joyce: 'Littérature' et 'Religion'." *Tel Quel*, no. 89:41–73.

———. 1981b. "Jung et Picasso: le déni de l'exception." *Tel Quel*, no. 90:45–55.

———. 1983. "Joyce *Tel Quel*." *Tel Quel*, no. 94:35–44.

———. 1984. *Excès de langages (Hölderlin, Joyce, Duns Scot, Hopkins, Cantor, Sollers)*. Paris: Denoël.

Houdebine, Jean-Louis, and Philippe Sollers. 1980a. "La Trinité de Joyce I." *Tel Quel*, no. 83:36–62.

———. 1980b. "La Trinité de Joyce II." *Tel Quel*, no. 83:63–88.

Hühnerfeld, Paul. 1959. *In Sachen Heidegger: Versuch über ein deutsches Genie*. Hamburg: Hoffman und Campe.

Hutcheon, Linda. 1983. Review of *The Discourse of Modernism* by Timothy Reiss. *Diacritics* 13, no. 4:33–42.

IJsseling, Samuel. 1969. "Filosofie en Psychoanalyse: Enige Opmerkingen over het Denken van M. Heidegger en J. Lacan." *Tijdschrift voor Filosofie* 31:261–89.

Ionescu, Cornel Mihai. 1983. "Heidegger 'traduit' par Lacan." *Cahiers roumains d'études littéraires* 1:93–110.

Irigaray, Luce. 1974. *Speculum de l'autre femme*. Paris: Minuit.

———. 1977. *Ce Sexe qui n'en est pas un*. Paris: Minuit.

Iser, Wolfgang. 1976. *Der Akt des Lesens: Theorie ästhetischer Wirkung*. München: Wilhelm Fink.

Jacquet, Claude. 1972. *Joyce et Rabelais: Aspects de la création verbale dans "Finnegans Wake".* Paris: Didier.

———. 1974. "Les Plans de Joyce pour 'Ulysse'." In *"Ulysses" cinquante ans après.* See Bonnerot 1974, 45–82.

———. 1977. "La Création verbale dans *Finnegans Wake.*" *Littérature et Politique. Société des anglicistes de l'enseignement supérieur. Actes du Congrès de Nantes. Études anglaises,* no. 66:317–33. Paris: Didier.

———. 1978. "Fonctions du langage dans *Finnegans Wake*: Néologismes et Glossolalies." *Autour de l'idée de nature, histoire des idées et civilisation, pédagogie, et divers. Études anglaises,* no. 67:253–66. Paris: Didier.

———. 1979a. "Aspects de la genèse d'Ulysse: de Télémaque à Calypso." *Rhétorique et Communication. Société des anglicistes de l'enseignement supérieur. Actes du congrès de Rouen, 1976. Études anglaises,* no. 75:397–409. Paris: Didier.

———. 1979b. "L'Eau et les Rêves dans 'Anna Livia Plurabelle'." In *Joyce et Paris.* See Aubert and Jolas 1979, 2:154–58.

———. 1980. "Anna Livia Plurabelle et les lavandières de la nuit." *Gaéliana,* no. 2:63–75.

———. 1981a. "Joyce." *L'Herne,* no. 40:412–24.

———. 1981b. "James Joyce: Les 'Épiphanies' et le Portrait." *Gaéliana,* no. 3:129–47.

———. 1982. "Bisquebasque: le basque dans le carnet VI.B.46 et dans *Finnegans Wake.*" *Études anglaises,* no. 35:311–16.

———. 1983. "L'Artiste et ses doubles: Conscience de soi et création dans l'oeuvre de James Joyce." In *Genèse de la conscience moderne: Études sur le développement de la conscience de soi dans les littératures du monde occidental,* ed. Robert Ellrodt, 386–402. Paris: Presses universitaires de France.

———, ed. 1985a. *Genèse et Métamorphoses du texte joycien.* Paris: Publications de la Sorbonne.

———, ed. 1985b. *Genèse de Babel: Joyce et la création.* Paris: Éditions du CNRS.

———. 1985c. "Aspects de la genèse de *Finnegans Wake*: ALP ou les métamorphoses du texte." In *Genèse et Métamorphoses.* See Jacquet 1985a, 93–154.

———. 1985d. "Valises ou Chimères: Du langage universel dans les manuscrits de *Finnegans Wake.*" In *Leçons d'écriture: Ce que disent les manuscrits: En hommage à Louis Hay,* ed. Almuth Grésillon and Michael Werner, 129–39. Paris: Lettres Modernes-Minard.

———. 1986. "Métamorphoses de 'Circé': l'élaboration d'un chapitre d'*Ulysse.*" In *Cahiers de l'Herne.* See Aubert and Senn 1986, 384–99.

———, ed. 1988. *"Scribble" 1: Genèse des textes: James Joyce, 1.* Revue des lettres modernes, no. 834–39. Paris: Minard.

Jäger, Alfred. 1978. *Gott: Nochmals Martin Heidegger.* Tübingen: J. C. B. Mohr (Paul Siebeck).

Jakobson, Roman, and Claude Lévi-Strauss. 1962. "'Les chats' de Charles Baudelaire." *L'Homme* 2, no. 1: 5–21.

Jambet, Christian, and Guy Lardreau. 1976. *L'Ange: pour une cynégétique du semblant.* Paris: Grasset.

Jameson, Fredric. 1972. *The Prison-House of Language: A Critical Account of Structuralism and Russian Formalism.* Princeton: Princeton University Press.

Jamme, Christoph. 1984. "'Dem Dichten Vor-denken': Aspekte von Heideggers 'Zwiesprache' mit Hölderlin im Kontext Seiner Kunstphilosophie." *Zeitschrift für philosophische Forschung* 38:191–218.

Jaynes, Julian. 1976. *The Origin of Consciousness in the Breakdown of the Bicameral Mind.* Boston: Houghton Mifflin.

Jennings, Michael W. 1983. "Benjamin as a Reader of Hölderlin: The Origins of Benjamin's Theory of Literary Criticism." *German Quarterly* 66:544–62.

Joannon, Pierre. 1982. "La France qui a découvert James Joyce est-elle en train de l'oublier?" *Historia*, no. 433:150–55.

Jolas, Eugène. 1932. "Homage to James Joyce." *transition*, no. 21:250–53.

———. 1933. "Marginalia to James Joyce's *Work in Progress.*" *transition*, no. 22:101–5.

———. 1938. "Homage to the mythmaker." *transition*, no. 27:169–75.

Jolas, Maria. 1950. "Joyce en 1939–1940." *Mercure de France*, no. 309:45–58.

———. 1966. "Joyce et ses amis." *Figaro Littéraire*, 20 January, 13.

Jones, Ellen Carol. 1988. "'Writing the Mystery of Himself': Paternity in *Ulysses.*" In *The Augmented Ninth.* See Benstock 1988, 226–32.

Jouve, Nicole Ward. 1977. "Tentative de greffe d'une colonne vertebrale sur Molly Bloom." In her *Le Spectre du gris*, 185–221. Paris: Des Femmes.

Joyce, Stanislaus. 1966. *Le Gardien de mon frère.* Trans. A. Grieve. Paris: Gallimard.

———. 1976. *Le Journal de Dublin.* Trans. Marie Tadié. Paris: Gallimard.

Kain, Richard M., and Marvin Magalaner. 1956. *Joyce: The Man, the Work, the Reputation.* New York: New York University Press.

Kant, Immanuel. 1980. *Schriften zur Metaphysik und Logik 2.* Frankfurt am Main: Suhrkamp.

———. 1981. "Beantwortung der Frage: Was ist Aufklärung?" *Schriften zur Anthropologie, Geschichtsphilosophie, Politik and Pädagogik 1,* 51–61. Frankfurt am Main: Suhrkamp.

Kearney, Richard. 1980. "Joyce on Language, Women and Politics." *Screen* 20, no. 3–4:124–34.

Kenner, Hugh. 1956. *Dublin's Joyce.* Bloomington: Indiana University Press.

———. 1980. *"Ulysses".* London: Allen and Unwin.

———. 1983. *A Colder Eye: The Modern Irish Writers.* New York: Alfred A. Knopf.

Kojève, Alexandre. 1979. *Introduction à la lecture de Hegel.* Ed. Raymond Queneau. Paris: Gallimard.

Kristeva, Julia. 1967. "Pour une sémiologie des paragrammes." *Tel Quel*, no. 29:53–75.

——. 1969. *Sémeiotikè: Recherches pour une sémanalyse*. Paris: Seuil.

——. 1972. "Le Sujet en procès." *Tel Quel*, no. 52:12–30.

——. 1973. "Le Sujet en procès (suite)." *Tel Quel*, no. 53:17–38.

——. 1974a. *La Révolution du langage poétique: l'avant-garde à la fin du dix-neuvième siècle, Lautréamont et Mallarmé*. Paris: Seuil.

——. 1974b. "Polylogue." *Tel Quel*, no. 57:19–55.

——. 1974c. "Sujet dans le langage et pratique politique." *Tel Quel*, no. 58:22–27.

——. 1975. "D'une identité l'autre (Le Sujet du langage poétique)." *Tel Quel*, no. 62:10–27.

——. 1980. *Pouvoirs de l'horreur. Essai sur l'abjection*. Paris: Seuil.

——. 1983a. *Histoires d'amour*. Paris: Denoël.

——. 1983b. "Mémoire." *L'Infini*, no. 1:39–54.

——. 1984. "Joyce, le retour d'Orphée." *L'Infini*, no. 8:3–12.

——. 1988. "Joyce 'The Gracehoper' or the Return of Orpheus." In *The Augmented Ninth*. See Benstock 1988, 167–80.

Kristeva, Julia, Marcelin Pleynet, and Philippe Sollers. 1977. "Pourquoi les États-Unis." *Tel Quel*, no. 71–73:3–19.

Krockow, Christian Graf von. 1958. *Die Entscheidung: Eine Untersuchung über Ernst Jünger, Carl Schmitt, Martin Heidegger*. Stuttgart: Ferdinand Enke.

Kuhn, Thomas S. 1970. *The Structure of Scientific Revolutions*. Chicago: University of Chicago Press.

Kuntz, Monique, ed. 1978. *Valery Larbaud: 1881-1957*. Brussels: Bibliothèque Royale Albert 1ier.

Lacan, Jacques. 1956. Trans. of "Logos," by Martin Heidegger. *La Psychanalyse*, no. 1:57–79.

——. 1966. *Écrits*. Paris: Seuil.

——. 1970. "The Insistence of the Letter in the Unconscious," trans. Jan Miel. In *Structuralism*, ed. Jacques Ehrmann, 101–37. New York: Doubleday.

——. 1971. "Lituraterre." *Littérature* 1, no. 3:3–10.

——. 1973. *Les Quatre Concepts fondamentaux de la psychanalyse*. *Séminaire XI*. Paris: Seuil.

——. 1974. *Télévision*. Paris: Seuil.

——. 1975. *Encore*. *Séminaire XX*. Paris: Seuil.

——. 1976a. "Le Sinthome: Le Séminaire du 18 novembre 1975." *Ornicar?* no. 6:3–11.

——. 1976b. "Le Sinthome: Le Séminaire du 9 décembre 1975." *Ornicar?* no. 6:12–20.

——. 1976c. "Le Sinthome: Le Séminaire du 16 décembre 1975." *Ornicar?* no. 7:3–9.

——. 1976d. "Le Sinthome: Le Séminaire du 13 janvier 1976." *Ornicar?* no. 7:9–17.

——. 1976e. "Le Sinthome: Le Séminaire du 20 janvier 1976." *Ornicar?* no. 7:17–18.

——. 1976–1977a. "Le Sinthome: Le Séminaire du 10 février 1976." *Ornicar?* no. 8:6–13.

——. 1976–1977b. "Le Sinthome: Le Séminaire du 17 février 1976." *Ornicar?* no. 8:13–20.

——. 1977a. *Écrits: A Selection*. Trans. Alan Sheridan. New York: Norton.

——. 1977b. "Le Sinthome: Le Séminaire du 16 mars 1976." *Ornicar?* no. 9:32–40.

——. 1977c. "Le Sinthome: Le Séminaire du 13 avril 1976." *Ornicar?* no. 10:5–12.

——. 1977d. "Le Sinthome: Le Séminaire du 11 mai 1976. L'Égo de Joyce." *Ornicar?* no. 11:21–29.

——. 1979. "Joyce le symptôme." In *Joyce et Paris*. See Aubert and Jolas 1979, 1:13–17.

——. 1981. *Speech and Language in Psychoanalysis*. Trans. and ed. Anthony Wilden. Baltimore and London: Johns Hopkins University Press.

——. 1982. "Joyce le Symptôme." *L'Âne*, no. 6:3–5.

——. 1987a. "Le Sinthome: Séminaire du 18 novembre 1975." In *Joyce avec Lacan*. See Aubert 1987, 37–48.

——. 1987b. "Le Sinthome: Séminaire du 20 janvier 1976." In *Joyce avec Lacan*. See Aubert 1987, 49–67.

Lacoue-Labarthe, Philippe. 1978a. "La Césure du spéculatif." In his *Hölderlin: L'Antigone de Sophocle*, 187–223. Paris: Bourgois.

——. 1978b. "Mimesis and Truth." *Diacritics* 8, no. 1:10–23.

Lacoue-Labarthe, Philippe, and Jean-Luc Nancy. 1978. *L'Absolu Littéraire: Théorie de la littérature du romantisme allemand*. Paris: Seuil.

Lang, H. 1977. "Zum Verhältnis von Strukturalismus, Philosophie und Psychoanalyse—Konkretisiert am Phänomen der Subjektivität." *Tijdschrift voor Filosofie* 38:559–73.

Larbaud, Valery. 1923. *Amants, Heureux Amants*. Paris: Nouvelle Revue Française.

——. 1922. "James Joyce." *Nouvelle Revue Française* 18:385–404.

——. 1925. "A Propos de James Joyce et de *Ulysses*: Réponse à M. Ernest Boyd." *Nouvelle Revue Française* 24:5–17.

Lavergne, Philippe, trans. 1967. "Shem." *Tel Quel*, no. 30:67–87.

Lawrence, Karen. 1986. "Gender and Narrative Voice in *Jacob's Room* and *A Portrait of the Artist as a Young Man*." In *The Centennial Symposium*. See Beja 1986, 31–38.

——. 1988. "Paternity as Legal Fiction in *Ulysses*." In *The Augmented Ninth*. Benstock 1988, 233–43.

Leavis, F. R. 1933. "Joyce and 'The Revolution of the Word'." *Scrutiny* 2:193–201.

Lemaire, Anika. 1970. *Jacques Lacan.* Brussels: Dessart.

Lemaire, Georges. 1984. "La Bataille du *Finnegans Wake.*" *Europe* 62, no. 657–58:120–26.

Lentricchia, Frank. 1980. *After the New Criticism.* Chicago: University of Chicago Press.

———. 1980–81. "Derrida, History and Intellectuals." *Salmagundi,* no. 50–51:284–301.

Léon, Paul. 1942. "In Memory of Joyce." *Poésie,* no. 5:35.

Lernout, Geert. 1984. "James Joyce and Friedrich Hölderlin in Contemporary French Criticism." Ph.D. diss, University of Toronto.

———. 1988. "Joyce or Lacan." In *The Augmented Ninth.* See Benstock 1988, 195–203.

Lévi-Strauss, Claude. 1976. "Le Philosophe et le savant." Interview with Jean-Marie Benoist. *Les Nouvelles Littéraires* 54, no. 2536:20.

Levin, Harry. 1941. *James Joyce: A Critical Introduction.* Norfolk, Conn.: New Directions.

Levinas, Emmanuel. 1976. *Noms propres.* Montpellier: Fata Morgana.

Levine, Jennifer. 1978–1979. "Rejoycings in *Tel Quel.*" *James Joyce Quarterly* 16:17–26.

———. 1979. "Originality and Repetition in *Finnegans Wake* and *Ulysses.*" *PMLA* 94:106–20.

———. 1983. "Reading *Ulysses.*" In *Centre and Labyrinth: Essays in Honour of Northrop Frye,* ed. Eleanor Cook et al., 264–83. Toronto: University of Toronto Press.

Lévy, Bernard-Henri, ed. 1976. "Dossier: les nouveaux philosophes." *Les Nouvelles Littéraires* 54, no. 2536:15–22.

———. 1978. "La Preuve du pudding." *Tel Quel,* no. 77:25–35.

Lévy, Françoise. 1976. *Karl Marx: Histoire d'un bourgeois allemand.* Paris: Grasset.

Litz, A. Walton. 1961. *The Art of James Joyce: Method and Design in "Ulysses" and "Finnegans Wake".* New York: Oxford University Press.

Loehrich, Rolf R. 1953. *The Secret of "Ulysses": An Analysis of James Joyce's "Ulysses".* McHenry, Ill.: Compass Press.

Lojkine-Morelec, Monique. 1985. "Aspects de l'intertextualité dans les manuscripts de *The Waste Land* et *Ulysses,* 'Dirge' et 'Death by Water'." In *Genèse et Métamorphoses.* See Jacquet 1985a, 211–22.

Loubère, J. A. E. 1975. *The Novels of Claude Simon.* Ithaca: Cornell University Press.

Löwith, Karl. 1953. *Denker in dürftiger Zeit.* Frankfurt am Main: Fischer.

Luccioni, Jean-Michel. 1984. "Joyce chez Sally." In *Études sur les Oeuvres Complètes de Sally Mara,* ed. Evert van der Starre, 22–34. Groningen: Instituut voor Romaanse Talen.

Lyotard, Jean-François. 1980. *La Condition Postmoderne: Rapport sur le savoir*. Paris: Minuit.

MacCabe, Colin. 1978. *James Joyce and the Revolution of the Word*. London: Macmillan.

———, ed. 1982a. *James Joyce: New Perspectives*. Brighton: Harvester Press.

———. 1982b. "An Introduction to *Finnegans Wake*." In *New Perspectives*. See MacCabe 1982a, 29–41.

———. 1982c. "The Voice of Esau: Stephen in the Library." In *New Perspectives*. See MacCabe 1982a, 111–128.

Macciocchi, Maria-Antonietta. 1971. *De la Chine*. Paris: Seuil.

———. 1975. "Marx, la cuisinière et le cannibale." *Tel Quel*, no. 64:61–66.

———. 1983. *Deux mille ans de bonheur*. Trans. Jean-Noël Schifano. Paris: Grasset.

Magalaner, Marvin. 1959. *Time of Apprenticeship*. New York: Abelard-Schuman.

Mahlmann, Th. 1972. "Eschatologie." *Historisches Wörterbuch der Philosophie*. Darmstadt: Wissenschaftliche Buchgesellschaft.

Majault, Joseph. 1963. *Joyce*. Paris: Éditions Universitaires.

———. 1971. *James Joyce*. Trans. Jean Stewart. London: Merlin Press; Redwood City, Calif., and Toronto: Pendragon House.

Makward, Christiane. 1976. "Interview with Hélène Cixous." *Sub-stance* 13:19–37.

Martin, Jacky. 1982. "Pessimisme et fonctionnements textuels dans *Dubliners* de James Joyce." *Cahiers victoriens et édouardiens*, no. 15:87–90.

Martin, Jean-Paul. 1976. "La Condensation." *Poétique*, no. 26:180–206.

Mauriac, Claude. 1958. "*L'Alittérature contemporaine*. Paris: Albin Michel.

———. 1961. *La Marquise sortit à cinque heures*. Paris: Albin Michel.

———. 1963. *Agrandissement*. Paris: Albin Michel.

Maurois, André. 1966. "Un des saints patrons de la jeune littérature." *Figaro Littéraire*, 20 January, 8.

Mauss, Marcel. 1966. "Essai sur le don: Forme et raison de l'échange dans les sociétés archaïques." In his *Sociologie et Anthropologie*, 143–279. Paris: Presses universitaires de France.

Mayoux, Jean-Jacques. 1965. *James Joyce*. Paris: Gallimard.

———. 1974. "Du Côté de chez Circé." In *"Ulysses" cinquante ans après*. See Bonnerot 1974, 189–96.

McHugh, Roland. 1976. *The Sigla of "Finnegans Wake"*. Austin: University of Texas Press.

———. 1980. *Annotations to "Finnegans Wake"*. Baltimore: Johns Hopkins University Press.

———. 1981. *The "Finnegans Wake" Experience*. Dublin: Irish Academic Press.

McLuhan, Marshall. 1969. *The Interior Landscape: The Literary Criticism of Marshall McLuhan: 1943–1962*. Ed. Eugene McNamara. New York: McGraw-Hill.

McMillan, Dougald. 1975. *Transition: The History of a Literary Era. 1927–1938.* London: Calder and Boyars.

Medvedev, Pavel. 1976. *Die formale Methode in der Literaturwissenschaft.* Ed. Helmut Glück. Stuttgart: Metzler.

Mercanton, Jacques. 1967. *Les Heures de James Joyce.* Lausanne: L'Age d'Homme.

Mercier, Vivian. 1965. "Bibliographical Note: Some French Joyceana." *James Joyce Quarterly* 3:63–64.

———. 1971. *The New Novel: From Queneau to Pinget.* New York: Farrar, Straus and Giroux.

———. 1974. "James Joyce and French Literature." In *Cahiers Irlandais: France-Ireland: Literary Relations,* ed. Patrick Rafroidi et al., 215–27. Paris: Éditions Universitaires.

Meschonnic, Henri. 1973. "La poétique parmi les pratiques actuelles de lecture et d'écriture." *Pour la Poétique II,* 71–144. Paris: Gallimard.

Meylan, Jean Pierre. 1969. *La Revue de Genève: Miroir des lettres européennes: 1920–1930,* 390–95. Genève: Librairie Droz.

Micha, René. 1966. *Sarraute: Classiques du XXe Siècle.* Paris: Éditions universitaires.

Michel, Alain. 1976. *In Hymnis et canticis: Culture et Beauté, dans l'hymnique chrétienne latine.* Louvain: Publications universitaires; Paris: VanderOyez.

Milesi, Laurent. 1985. "L'Idiome babélien de *Finnegans Wake*: Recherches thématiques dans une perspective génétique." In *Genèse de Babel.* See Jacquet 1985b, 155–215.

———. 1988. "Vico . . . Jousse. Joyce . . . Langue." In *"Scribble" 1.* See Jacquet 1988, 143–62.

Millington, James. n.d. *English as She is Spoke.* London: Field and Tuer.

Millot, Catherine. 1987. "Épiphanies." In *Joyce avec Lacan.* See Aubert 1987, 87–95.

———. 1988. "On Epiphanies." In *Joyce avec Lacan.* See Benstock 1988, 207–9.

Minière, Claude. 1984. "La Musique des îles." *Europe* 62, no. 657–58:140–41.

Mink, Louis O. 1980. *A "Finnegans Wake" Gazetteer.* Bloomington: Indiana University Press.

Monnier, Adrienne. 1950. "La Traduction d'*Ulysses*." *Mecure de France,* no. 309:30–37.

Monod, Sylvère. 1985. "Lecture d'Eveline." In *Genèse et Métamorphoses.* See Jacquet 1985a, 27–43.

Moreau, Jean A. 1975. "Question de per sonne." Review of *Prénoms de personne* by Hélène Cixous. *Critique* 31:297–306.

Morenz, Siegfried. 1962. *La Religion égyptienne: Essai d'interprétation.* Paris: Payot.

Muray, Philippe. 1979. *L'Opium des lettres.* Paris: Christian Bourgois.

Nadeau, Maurice. 1964. *Histoire du surréalisme. Suivie de Documents surréalistes.* Paris: Seuil.

Nehemas, Alexander. 1981. "The Postulated Author: Critical Monism as a Regulative Ideal." *Critical Inquiry* 8:133–49.

Némo, Philippe. 1977a. "Job et le mal radical." *Tel Quel*, no. 70:76–88.

———. 1977b. "Job et le mal radical II." *Tel Quel*, no. 71–73:271–93.

Neubauer, John. 1972. "Intellektuelle, intellektuale und ästhetische Anschauung: Zur Entstehung der romantischen Kunstauffassung." *Deutsche Vierteljahrschrift für Literaturwissenschaft und Geistesgeschichte* 46:294–319.

Noel, Jean. 1985. "De quelques épiphanies de James Joyce dans le contexte du manuscrit 'Cornell 17'." In *Genèse et Métamorphoses*. See Jacquet 1985a, 3–24.

Norris, Margot. 1974a. "The Function of Mythic Repetition in *Finnegans Wake*." *James Joyce Quarterly* 11:343–54.

———. 1974b. "The Consequence of Deconstruction: A Technical Perspective of Joyce's *Finnegans Wake*." *ELH: A Journal of English Literary History* 41:130–48.

———. 1974c. "The Language of Dream in *Finnegans Wake*." *Literature and Psychology* 24:4–11.

———. 1976. *The Decentered Universe of "Finnegans Wake." A Structuralist Analysis*. Baltimore: Johns Hopkins University Press.

———. 1982. "Anna Livia Plurabelle: The Dream Woman." In *Women in Joyce*. See Suzette Henke and Elaine Unkeless 1982, 197–213.

———. 1987a. "Narration under a Blindfold: Reading Joyce's 'Clay,'" *PMLA* 102:206–15.

———. 1987b. "The Last Chapter of *Finnegans Wake*: Stephen Finds His Mother." *James Joyce Quarterly* 25:11–30.

O'Brien, Darcy. 1968. *The Conscience of James Joyce*. Princeton: Princeton University Press.

O'Hehir, Brendan. 1967. *A Gaelic Lexicon for "Finnegans Wake"*. Berkeley: University of California Press.

———. 1978. "Sigla, 'Structure,' Census." Review of *The Sigla of "Finnegans Wake"* by Roland McHugh; *The Decentered Universe of "Finnegans Wake"* by Margot Norris; and *Third Census of "Finnegans Wake"* by Adaline Glasheen. *Novel* 12:78–85.

O'Hehir, Brendan, and John Dillon. 1977. *A Classical Lexicon for "Finnegans Wake"*. Berkeley: University of California Press.

Olteanu, Tudor. 1974. "James Joyce vu par *Tel Quel*." *Cahiers roumains d'études littéraires*, no. 2:150–52.

Osborne, Harold. 1977. "Inspiration." *British Journal of Aesthetics* 17:242–53.

Paris, Jean. 1957. *Joyce par lui-même*. Paris: Seuil.

———. 1962. "Joyce au bordel." *Cahiers de la Compagnie Madeleine Renaud–Jean-Louis Barrault*, no. 37:32–36.

———. 1966. "Hamlet et ses frères." *Cahiers Renaud-Barrault*, no. 57:63–89.

———. 1967. "Finnegans, Wake!" *Tel Quel*, no. 30:58–66.

———. 1972. "L'Agonie du signe." *Change*, no. 11:133–72.

———. 1975a. "Hamlet et ses frères." *Univers parallèles 1: Théâtre*, 43–69. Paris: Seuil.

———. 1975b. "Finnegans, Wake!" *Univers parallèles 2: le point aveugle: Poésie, roman*, 223–35. Paris: Seuil.

———. 1984. "Du monologue et de ses précurseurs." *Europe* 62, no. 657–58:52–64.

Parrinder, Patrick. 1982. "The Strange Necessity: James Joyce's Rejection in England (1914–30)." In *New Perspectives*. See MacCabe 1982a, 151–67.

Pestureau, Gilbert. 1983. "Les techniques anglo-saxonnes et l'art romanesque de Raymond Queneau." *Europe* 62, no. 650–51:110–15.

Phipps, Frances. 1987. *Let Me Be Los: Codebook for "Finnegans Wake"*. Barrytown, N.Y.: Station Hill Press.

Pichette, Henri. 1952. *Les Épiphanies*. L'Arche.

Pinard-Legry, Jean-Luc. 1981. "Alexandre Kojève: Zur französischen Hegel-Rezeption." In *Vermittler*, ed. Jürgen Siess, 105–18. Frankfurt am Main: Syndikat.

Plato. 1978. *The Collected Dialogues*. Ed. Edith Hamilton and Huntington Cairns. Princeton: Princeton University Press.

Pleynet, Marcelin. 1973. *Stanze: Incantation dit au bandeau d'or I-IV*. Paris: Seuil.

———. 1977a. *Art et littérature*. Paris: Seuil.

———. 1977b. *Transculture: Entretiens, essais et conférences*. Paris: Union générale d'éditions.

———. 1981a. *Spirito Peregrino. Chroniques du journal ordinaire: 1979*. Paris: Hachette.

———. 1981b. "Lettre." *Courrier du centre international d'études poétiques*, no. 139–40:15–18.

———. 1984a. *Les Trois Livres: Provisoires amants des nègres. Paysages en deux, suivi de Les Lignes de la prose. Comme*. Paris: Seuil.

———. 1984b. *Fragments du choeur: vers et proses*. Paris: Denoël.

Pöggeler, Otto. 1977a. "Es fehlen heilige Namen. Das Denken Martin Heideggers in seinem Bezug auf Hölderlin." *Zeitwende* 48, no. 2:65–79.

———. 1977b. "Heideggers Begegnung mit Hölderlin." *Man and World* 10:13–61.

Poggioli, Renato. 1981. *The Theory of the Avant-Garde*. Cambridge, Mass.: Harvard University Press.

Praz, Mario. 1978. *The Romantic Agony*. Trans. Angus Davidson. London: Oxford University Press.

Queneau, Raymond. 1933. *Le Chiendent*. Paris: Gallimard.

———. 1948. *Saint Glinglin*. Paris: Gallimard.

———. 1950a. *Petite cosmogonie portative*. Paris: Gallimard.

———. 1950b. "Une traduction en joycien." in *Batons, Chiffres et Lettres*, 239–42. Paris: Gallimard.

———. 1962. *Les Oeuvres Complètes de Sally Mara*. Paris: Gallimard.

Rabaté, Jean-Michel. 1974. "La 'missa parodia' de *Finnegans Wake*." *Poétique*, no. 17:75–95.

———. 1976. "Lapsus ex machina." *Poétique*, no. 26:152–72.

———. 1980a. "Les enjeux d'*Ulysse*." *Magazine littéraire*, no. 161:26–29.

———. 1980b. Review of *The Revolution of the Word* by Colin MacCabe. *Critique* 36:433-35.

———. 1981a. "A Clown's Inquest into Paternity: Fathers, Dead or Alive, in *Ulysses* and *Finnegans Wake*." In *The Fictional Father: Lacanian Readings of the Text*, ed. Robert Con Davis, 73–114. Amherst: University of Massachusetts Press.

———. 1981b. "La Mort-Vigile." *Exercices de la Patience*, no. 2:189–96.

———. 1981c. "Le Silence dans *Dubliners*." *Cahiers victoriens et édouardiens* 14:13–27.

———. 1982a. "De la hauteur à laquelle l'autorité se noue (Joyce, Hegel et la Philosophie)." *Revue des sciences humaines*, no. 185:51–75.

———. 1982b. "Bogland: Quelques Tours de Tourbe, de James Joyce à Seamus Heaney." *Critique* 38:512–36.

———. 1982c. "Joyce and Broch: Or, Who Was the Crocodile?" *Comparative Literature Studies* 19, no. 2:121–33.

———. 1982d. "Alimentaire et Vestimentaire dans *Finnegans Wake*." *Études anglaises*, no. 35:268–79.

———. 1982e. "Vers une approche de l'idiolecte de *Finnegans Wake*." In *Études irlandaises*. See Rafroidi and Joannon 1982, 111–24.

———. 1982f. "Silence in *Dubliners*." In *New Perspectives*. See MacCabe 1982a, 45–72.

———. 1983a. "La seconde patrie de l'exil: Joyce à Trieste." *Critique* 39:691–716.

———. 1983b. "Ce qu'aurait montré le silence des Sirènes." *Fabula*, no. 2:49–64.

———. 1984a. *James Joyce: Portrait de l'auteur en autre lecteur*. Petit-Roeuls: Cistre.

———. 1984b. "Qu'il faut—La Chute: chutes, lapsus et parachutes dans *Finnegans Wake*." *Europe* 62, no. 657–58:133–39.

———. 1985b. "Broch et Joyce." In *Genèse et Métamorphoses*. See Jacquet 1985a, 189–210.

———. 1985c. "Pour une cryptogénétique de l'idiolecte joycien." In *Genèse de Babel*. See Jacquet 1985b, 49–91.

———. 1985d. "Joyce: les lèvres circoncises." In *Leçons d'écriture: Ce que disent les manuscrits: En hommage à Louis Hay*, ed. Almuth Grésillon and Michael Werner, 107–28. Paris: Lettres modernes–Minard.

———. 1986a. "*Finnegans Wake*: La bi-sexualité, états d'un vestiaire." In *Cahiers de l'Herne*. See Aubert and Senn 1986, 453–82.

———. 1986b. "'Alphybettyformed Verbage': The Shape of Sounds and Letters in *Finnegans Wake*." *Word and Image* 2:237–43.

———. 1987a. "Berkeley entre Joyce et Beckett." In *Berkeley et l'Irlande: Études irlandaises*, ed. Patrick Rafroidi, n.s., 11:57–76.

———. 1987b. "Note sur les ex-ils." In *Joyce avec Lacan*. See Aubert 1987, 97–106.

Rafroidi, Patrick, and Pierre Joannon, eds. 1982. *Études irlandaises: James Joyce Centenary Issue*. Lille: Université de Lille III.

Raimond, Michel. 1966. "Le monologue intérieur." In *La crise du roman: Des lendemains du naturalisme aux années vingt*, 257–98. Paris: José Corti.

Raval, Suresh. 1981. *Metacriticism*. Athens: University of Georgia Press.

Reizbaum, Marilyn. 1988. "A 'Modernism of Marginality': The Link between James Joyce and Djuna Barnes." In *New Alliances*. See Scott 1988a, 179–89.

Ricardou, Jean. 1978–1979. "Time of the Narration, Time of the Fiction." *James Joyce Quarterly* 16:81–93.

Ricardou, Jean, and Françoise Van Rossum-Guyon, eds. 1974. *Nouveau Roman: Hier, Aujourd'hui I: Problèmes généraux*. Paris: Union générale d'éditions.

Richardson, William, J. 1967. *Heidegger: Through Phenomenology to Thought*. The Hague: Nijhoff.

———. 1980. "Phenomenology and Psychoanalysis." In *Nachdenken über Heidegger: Eine Bestandsaufnahme*, ed. Ute Guzzoni, 232–52. Hildesheim: Gerstenberg.

Risset, Jacqueline. 1974. "Joyce traduit par Joyce." *Tel Quel*, no. 55:47–58.

———. 1982a. *Tel Quel*. Roma: Bulzoni; Paris: Nizet.

———. 1982b. *Dante écrivain ou l'intelletto d'amore*. Paris: Seuil.

Robbe-Grillet, Alain. 1975. *Pour un nouveau roman*. Paris: Minuit.

Rochlitz, Rainer. 1984. "Adorno entre Lyotard et Habermas." *La Quinzaine littéraire*, no. 417:19–20.

Romains, Jules. 1966. "'Aussi peu Anglais que possible." *Figaro Littéraire*, 20 January, 9.

Ronat, Mitsou. 1972. "l'Hypotexticale." *Change*, no. 11:26–33.

———. 1975. "l'Hypotexticale." *La Langue manifeste: Littérature et théories du langage*, 89–100. Paris: Action poétique.

———. 1979. "Joyce l'a-syntaxe." In *Joyce et Paris*. See Aubert and Jolas 1979, 1:29–35.

———. 1980. *Faye*. Cahiers CISTRE. Lausanne: L'Âge d'homme.

Ronse, Henri. 1968. "Retour à Joyce." *L'Arc*, no. 36:1–3.

Rorty, Richard. 1981. "Nineteenth-Century Idealism and Twentieth-Century Textualism." *The Monist* 64:155–74.

Rose, Danis. 1978. *James Joyce's Index Manuscript: "Finnegans Wake" Holograph Workbook VI.B.46*. Colchester: A Wake Newslitter Press.

Rose, Danis, and John O'Hanlon. 1982. *Understanding "Finnegans Wake": A Guide to the Narrative of James Joyce's Masterpiece*. New York: Garland Publishing.

————, eds. 1989. *The Lost Notebook: New Evidence on the Genesis of "Ulysses".* Edinburgh: Split Pea.

Rose, Thomasine. 1982. *Verbi-Voco-Visual: The Presence of Bishop Berkeley in "Finnegans Wake".* Lubbock, Tex.: Thoth-Maatian Press.

Rossman, Charles. 1973. Review of *The Exile of James Joyce* by Hélène Cixous. *James Joyce Quarterly* 10:360–64.

Roudinesco, Elisabeth. 1986. *La Bataille de cent ans: Histoire de la psychanalyse en France 2. 1925–1985.* Paris: Seuil.

Roughley, Alan. 1987. "Defending Deconstruction." *James Joyce Broadsheet,* no. 21:1.

Roustang, François. 1976. *Un Destin si funeste.* Paris: Minuit.

Saint John Perse. 1942. *Exils.* Marseille: Cahiers du Sud.

————. 1946. *Vents.* Paris: Gallimard.

Sallenave, Danièle. 1972. "A Propos du 'monologue intérieur': lecture d'une théorie." *Littérature,* no. 5:69–87.

Sarraute, Nathalie. 1964. *L'Ère du soupçon.* Paris: Gallimard.

Sartre, Jean Paul. 1947. *Baudelaire.* Paris: Gallimard.

————. 1949a. *La Nausée.* Paris: Gallimard.

————. 1949b. *Le Sursis.* Paris: Gallimard.

————. 1949c. *La Mort dans l'âme.* Paris: Gallimard.

————. 1952. *Saint Genet.* Paris: Gallimard.

————. 1971–1972. *L'Idiot de la famille.* 3 vols. Paris: Gallimard.

Saurat, Denis. 1924. "Proust et Joyce." *Marges* 31 (15 December): 244–46.

Scarpetta, Guy. 1985. *L'Impureté.* Paris: Grasset.

Schlegel, August Wilhelm, and Friedrich Schlegel, eds. 1970. *Athenaeum. Eine Zeitschrift. Erster Band. Zweites Stück.* Darmstadt: Wissenschaftliche Buchgesellschaft.

Schlossman, Beryl. 1982. "Joyce et le don des langues." *Tel Quel,* no. 92:9–30.

————. 1985. *Joyce's Catholic Comedy of Language.* Madison: University of Wisconsin Press.

————. 1986a. "L'écriture joycienne: Juive ou Catholique?" In *Cahiers de l'Herne.* See Aubert and Senn 1986, 318–33.

————. 1986b. "*Finnegans Wake*: The Passage toward Pentecost." In *The Centennial Symposium.* See Beja, 123–31.

Schneiderman, Stuart. 1980. "Lacan et la littérature." *Tel Quel,* no. 84:39–47.

————. 1983. *Jacques Lacan: The Death of an Intellectual Hero.* Cambridge, Mass.: Harvard University Press.

Scholem, Gershom. 1960. *Zur Kabbala und ihrer Symbolik.* Zürich: Rhein-Verlag.

Scholes, Robert, ed. 1961. *Approaches to the Novel: Materials for a Poetics.* Scranton, Pa.: Chandler.

————. 1965. "James Joyce, Irish Poet." *James Joyce Quarterly* 2:255–70.

————. 1972. "*Ulysses*: A Structuralist Perspective." *James Joyce Quarterly* 10:161–71.

———. 1973. "In Search of James Joyce." *James Joyce Quarterly* 11:5–16.

———. 1974. *Structuralism in Literature: An Introduction.* New Haven: Yale University Press.

———. 1978–1979. "Semiotic Approaches to a Fictional Text: Joyce's 'Eveline'." *James Joyce Quarterly* 16:65–80.

Scholes, Robert, and Richard M. Kain, eds. 1965. *The Workshop of Daedalus: James Joyce and the Raw Materials for "A Portrait of the Artist as a Young Man".* Evanston, Ill.: Northwestern University Press.

Scholes, Robert, and Robert Kellogg. 1965. *The Nature of Narrative.* New York: Oxford University Press.

Schulze, Wilhelm A. 1964. "Das Johannesevangelium im deutschen Idealismus." *Zeitschrift für philosophische Forschung* 18:85–118.

Schutte, William M. 1957. *Joyce and Shakespeare: A Study in the Meaning of "Ulysses".* New Haven: Yale University Press.

Scott, Bonnie Kime. 1984. *Joyce and Feminism.* Bloomington: Indiana University Press.

———. 1987. *James Joyce.* Brighton: Harvester Press.

———, ed. 1988a. *New Alliances in Joyce Studies: When it's aped to foul a delfian.* Newark: University of Delaware Press.

———. 1988b. "Character, Joyce, and Feminist Critical Approaches." In *The Augmented Ninth.* See Benstock, 158–64.

Serres, Michel. 1976. "Le philosophe et la guerre." Interview with Françoise Lévy. *Les Nouvelles Littéraires* 54, no. 2536:21.

Sollers, Philippe. 1960. "Sept propositions sur Alain Robbe-Grillet." *Tel Quel,* no. 2:49–53.

———. 1963. "Logique de la fiction." *Tel Quel,* no. 15:3–29.

———. 1964. Review of *Proust et les signes* by Gilles Deleuze. *Tel Quel,* no. 19:94–95.

———. 1965. "Dante et la traversée de l'écriture." *Tel Quel,* no. 23:12–33.

———. 1966a. "Une Oeuvre extraordinairement réfléchie." *Figaro Littéraire* 20 January, 9.

———. 1966b. "Le Roman et l'Expérience des limites." *Tel Quel,* no. 25:20–34.

———. 1967. "Programme." *Tel Quel,* no. 31:3–7.

———. 1968a. *Nombres.* Paris: Seuil.

———. 1968b. *Logiques.* Paris: Seuil.

———. 1969. "Écriture et révolution." *Tel Quel,* no. 37:95–103.

———. 1971a. *L'Écriture et l'expérience des limites.* Paris: Seuil.

———. 1971b. *Sur le matérialisme.* Paris: Seuil.

———. 1972a. *Lois.* Paris: Seuil.

———. 1972b. "Das Augenlicht." *Tel Quel,* no. 51:3–30.

———. 1973a. *H.* Paris: Seuil.

———. 1973b. "Argument." *Tel Quel,* no. 54:17–18.

———. 1973c. "A propos de l'avant-garde." *Peinture: Cahiers théoriques,* no. 6–7:7–22.

———. 1974. "Critiques." *Tel Quel*, no. 57:127–37.

———. 1975a. "Joyce and Co." *Tel Quel*, no. 64:3–14.

———. 1975b. "La main de Freud." *Tel Quel*, no. 64:25–30.

———. 1976a. "La renommée." *Tel Quel*, no. 65:99–101.

———. 1976b. "Vers la notion de 'paradis'." *Tel Quel*, no. 68:102–3.

———. 1977a. "Deux interventions aux États-Unis." *Tel Quel*, no. 69:6–10.

———. 1977b. "'Folie', mère-écran." *Tel Quel*, no. 69:97–102.

———. 1977c. "From *Paradis*," trans. Carl Lovitt. In *In the Wake of the Wake*. See Hayman and Anderson 1977, 101–6.

———. 1978a. "Le marxisme sodomisé par la psychanalyse elle-même violée par on ne sait quoi." *Tel Quel*, no. 75:56–60.

———. 1978b. "Le sexe des anges." *Tel Quel*, no. 75:87–91.

———. 1978c. "Vers la notion de 'paradis' (2)." *Tel Quel*, no. 75:92–99.

———. 1979a. "L'Auguste Comte." *Tel Quel*, no. 79:40–50.

———. 1979b. "Pourquoi je suis si peu religieux." *Tel Quel*, no. 81:7–25.

———. 1980a. "On n'a encore rien vu." *Tel Quel*, no. 85:9–31.

———. 1980b. "Le G.S.I." *Tel Quel*, no. 86:10–16.

———. 1981a. *Paradis*. Paris: Seuil.

———. 1981b. *Vision à New York*. Paris: Grasset.

———. 1981c. "Gloria (Journal de Paradis)." *Tel Quel*, no. 87:13–14.

———. 1982a. "Portrait de l'artiste en voyageur humain." In *Trois jours avec Joyce*, ed. Gisèle Freund, 9–17. Paris: Denoël.

———. 1982b. "Comme si le vieil Homère." *Le Nouvel Observateur*, 6 February, 73–74.

———. 1983a. *Femmes*. Paris: Gallimard.

———. 1983b. "Éditorial." *L'Infini*, no. 1:3–6.

———. 1983c. "Paradis." *L'Infini*, no. 1:7–10.

———. 1983d. "Aragon." *L'Infini*, no. 1:121–22.

———. 1983e. "L'Analyse infinie." *L'Infini*, no. 2:16–25.

———. 1983f. "*Femmes* et *Paradis*." *L'Infini*, no. 4:32–43.

———. 1984. *Portrait du joueur*. Paris: Gallimard.

———. 1985. "Monnaie de singe." *L'Infini*, no. 11:89–97.

———. 1986a. *Théorie des exceptions*. Paris: Gallimard.

———. 1986b. *Paradis II*. Paris: Gallimard.

———. 1987. *Le Coeur absolu*. Paris: Gallimard.

Solzhenitsyn, Aleksandr. 1974. *The Gulag Archipelago, 1918–1956: An Experiment in Literary Investigation*. New York: Harper and Row.

Sorrentino, Gilbert. 1979. *Mulligan Stew*. New York: Grove Press.

Soupault, Philippe. 1945. *Souvenirs de James Joyce*. Paris: Charlot.

———. 1963. "James Joyce." In his *Profils perdus*, 47–70. Paris: Mercure de France.

———. 1980. *Vingt mille et un jours: Entretiens avec Serge Faucherau*. Paris: Belfond.

Spivak, Gayatri Chakravorty. 1981. "French Feminism in an International Frame." *Yale French Studies*, no. 62:154–84.

Splett, Jörg. 1971. *Die Rede vom Heiligen: Über ein religions philosophisches Grundwort*. Freiburg, München: Alber.

Staley, Thomas, F. 1976. "James Joyce." In *Anglo-Irish Literature: A Review of Research*, ed. Richard J. Finneran, 366–435. New York: Modern Language Association.

———. 1978–1979. "Introduction." *James Joyce Quarterly* 16:5–6.

Starobinski, Jean. 1976. *Jean-Jacques Rousseau: La Transparence et l'Obstacle. Suivi de sept essais sur Rousseau*. Paris: Gallimard.

Steiner, George. 1978. *Martin Heidegger*. London: Fontana/Collins.

Stéphane, Nelly. 1984. "L'Homme-fiction." *Europe* 62, no. 657–58, 5–13.

Stierlin, Helm. 1977. "Warum Künstler mit ihrem Leben nicht fertig werden (Hölderlin, Kafka, George)." *Psychologie heute* 4, no. 7:28–35.

Susong, Gilles. 1977. "Sur l'apologie de Platon." *Tel Quel*, no. 71–73:301–4.

Tanner, Stephen L. 1984. "Joyce and Modern Critical Theory." *Arizona Quarterly* 40 (Autumn):269–79.

Tardits, Annie. 1985. "Joyce en Babylonie." *Le manque à lire: Cahiers de lectures freudiennes*, no. 7–8:93–110.

———. 1987. "L'Appensée, le renard et l'hérésie." In *Joyce avec Lacan*. See Aubert 1987, 107–58.

Thoma-Herterich, Christa. 1976. *Zur Kritik der Psychokritik: Eine literaturwissenschaftliche Auseinandersetzung am Beispiel französischer Arbeiten*. Frankfurt am Main: Peter Lang.

Thomas, Brooke. 1978–1979. "Not a Reading *of*, but the Act of Reading *Ulysses*." *James Joyce Quarterly* 16:81–93.

Thorburn, David. 1973. "Portraits of the Artist." Review of *The Exile of James Joyce* by Hélène Cixous. *Partisan Review* 40:306–9.

Tindall, William York. 1950. *James Joyce: His Way of Interpreting the Modern World*. New York: Scribner's.

———. 1959. *A Reader's Guide to James Joyce*. New York: Octagon Books.

———. 1969. *A Reader's Guide to "Finnegans Wake"*. New York: Farrar, Straus, and Giroux.

Todorov, Tzvetan. 1979. "La Réflexion sur la littérature dans la France contemporaine." *Poétique*, no. 38:131–48.

Topia, André. 1976a. "La Cassure et le flux." *Poétique*, no. 26:132–51.

———. 1976b. "Contrepoints joyciens." *Poétique*, no. 27:351–71.

———. 1982. "James Joyce: quelle Irlande?" Review of *James Joyce: the Undiscover'd Country* by Bernard Benstock, and *Ulysses* by Hugh Kenner. *Critique* 38:499–511.

———. 1983. "James Joyce: Le roman introuvable." *Fabula*, no. 1:71–92.

———. 1985a. "L'écriture hallucinée dans 'Circé': du visuel au phonique." In *Genèse et Métamorphoses*. See Jacquet 1985a, 73–84.

———. 1985b. "The Matrix and the Echo: Intertextuality in *Ulysses*." In *Post-Structuralist Joyce*. See Attridge and Ferrer 1985, 103–25.

———. 1986. "'Ithaque' et Robbe-Grillet: Une analogie trompeuse." In *Cahiers de l'Herne*. See Aubert and Senn 1986, 400–41.

———. 1988. "'Sirènes': l'expressivité nomade." In *"Scribble" 1*. See Jacquet 1988, 69–93.

Trilling, Jacques. 1973. "James Joyce, ou l'écriture matricide." *Études freudiennes*, no. 7–8:7–70.

Turkle, Sherry. 1978. *Psychoanalytic Politics: Freud's French Revolution*. New York: Basic Books.

Uitti, Karl D. 1969. *Linguistics and Literary Theory*. New York: Norton.

Vallentin, Berthold. 1967. *Gespräche mit Stefan George: 1902–1931*. Amsterdam: Castrum Peregrini.

Van Boheemen, Christine. 1987. *The Novel as Family Romance: Language, Gender, and Authority from Fielding to Joyce*. Ithaca: Cornell University Press.

———. 1988a. "Joyce, Derrida and the Discourse of 'the Other'." In *The Augmented Ninth*. See Benstock 1988, 88–102.

———. 1988b. "Deconstruction after Joyce." In *New Alliances*. See Scott 1988a, 29–36.

Van Caspel, Paul P.J. 1986. *Bloomers on the Liffey: Eisegetical Readings of James Joyce's "Ulysses"*. Baltimore: Johns Hopkins University Press.

Van Laere, François. 1970. Review of *L'Exil de James Joyce* by Hélène Cixous. *James Joyce Quarterly* 7:259–66.

Verbeke, Gerard. 1980. "Der Logos-Begriff in der antiken Philosophie." *Historisches Wörterbuch der Philosophie*. Darmstadt: Wissenschaftliche Buchgesellschaft.

Vieillard-Baron, Jean-Louis. 1979. *Platon et l'idéalisme allemand (1770–1830)*. Paris: Beauchesne.

Villelaur, Anne. 1969. Review of *L'Exil de James Joyce* by Hélène Cixous. *Lettres françaises*, 12 February, 10.

Vitoux, Pierre. 1974. "Joyce et Landor dans 'The Oxen of the Sun'." In *"Ulysses" cinquante ans après*. See Bonnerot 1974, 203–8.

Wahl, Jean. 1929. *Le Malheur de la conscience dans la philosophie de Hegel*. Paris: Rieder.

———. 1955. "L'Introduction à Hegel de A. Kojève." *Deucalion*, no. 5:77–99.

Wehle, Winfried. 1972. *Französischer Roman der Gegenwart: Erzählstruktur und Wirklichkeit im Nouveau Roman*. Berlin: Erich Schmidt.

Weldon, Thornton. 1968. *Allusions in "Ulysses": An Annotated List*. Chapel Hill: University of North Carolina.

Wellek, René. 1971. *Concepts of Criticism*. New Haven: Yale University Press.

Wellmer, Albrecht. 1985. *Zur Dialektik von Moderne und Postmoderne: Vernunftkritik nach Adorno*. Frankfurt am Main: Suhrkamp.

Wilden, Anthony, trans. and introd. 1981. "Lacan and the Discourse of the Other." In *Speech and Language in Psychoanalysis*. See Lacan 1981, 157–311. Baltimore: Johns Hopkins University Press.

Willet-Shoptaw, John. 1983. Review of *James Joyce and the Revolution of the Word* by Colin MacCabe, and *Women in Joyce*, ed. Suzette Henke and Elaine Unkeless. *Studies in the Novel* 15:162–65.

Wilson, Edmund. 1932. *Axel's Castle: A Study in the Imaginative Litterature of 1870–1930*. New York: Scribner's.

Witte, Bernd. 1981. "Zu einer Theorie der hermetischen Lyrik: Am Beispiel Paul Celans." *Poetica* 13:133–48.

Index